50

WORLD-CHANGING EVENTS IN CHRISTIAN HISTORY

Church history is too often confined to the college or seminary classroom. This is a tragedy because church history is the story of God's providential workings from the days of the New Testament to the day before yesterday. Pastor Earl Blackburn has done a great service to the body of Christ by making church history accessible to everyday Christians. *Fifty World-Changing Events in Christian History* is a helpful overview of church history written from an evangelical and reformed perspective. I hope it will help many believers understand how their own lives and local churches fit into the ongoing story of God's new covenant people from every tribe, language, and nation.

NATHAN A. FINN,
Associate Professor of Historical Theology and Baptist Studies,,
Southeastern Baptist Theological Seminary, Wake Forest, North Carolina

Pastors, have you ever wondered how to give your people some knowledge of the historical roots of their faith? Brother or sister in Christ, would you like to know more about your Savior's work among His people after the age of the Apostles? Here is the book for you. Pastor Earl Blackburn's *Fifty World-Changing Events in Christian History* has provided us with a very useful survey of many of the important events in the history of the Christian church. As a professor of Church History, one of the most frequent questions I am asked is for a recommendation of a simple survey of the life of the church over the last 2,000 years. Now I have the answer to that question. This book is great for personal study and especially useful for pastors and churches. Fifty short chapters provide fifty lessons – almost exactly what is needed for a wonderful year of learning of the power of Christ in His church. Actually, with the conclusion, entitled 'What's Next?' a total of fifty-two lessons are provided. Take this book and use it. Learn the lessons, good and bad, from the history of the church. And thank God that He has blessed His people with faithful servants in every century.

JAMES M. RENIHAN,
Dean and Professor of Historical Theology,,
Institute of Reformed Baptist Studies, Escondido, California

50

WORLD-CHANGING EVENTS IN CHRISTIAN HISTORY

EARL M. BLACKBURN

CHRISTIAN
FOCUS

Copyright © Earl M. Blackburn 2016

hardback ISBN 978-1-78191-749-7
epub ISBN 978-1-78191-870-8
mobi ISBN 978-1-78191-871-5

Published in 2016
by
Christian Focus Publications Ltd,
Geanies House, Fearn, Ross-shire,
IV20 1TW, Great Britain.
www.christianfocus.com

Cover design by Pete Barnsley

Printed and bound by Bell & Bain, Glasgow

MIX
Paper from
responsible sources
FSC® C007785

Contents

Foreword

Of what service is the knowledge of history to the church? As Paul gave instruction to the church at Corinth about some vital aspects of Christian living, he referred to the history of Israel, and, after making pertinent application, said, 'But they were written down for our instruction, on whom the end of the ages has come' (1 Cor. 10:11). The past held vital instruction for the present. Even in that state of incomplete revelation and reduced operations of the Spirit of God, the lives of those that God had singled out for a covenant relationship with Him held instructive value. But now, since the coming of the new covenant and the pouring out of the Spirit as a manifestation of the adoptive grace of God, as did Paul, we should view that coming of Christ as the culmination of the ages. God's purpose of redemption, prophesied in the ages before Christ, came to perfect fulfillment in the person of the Lord Jesus Christ and His work of redemption. Subsequent to Christ's ascension, everything that was contained in that work has been unloading into the gathering years, centuries, and now millennia.

First, Christ's work in saving sinners, His effectual determination in bringing all those to salvation given Him by the Father prompted Peter to write, 'Count the patience of our Lord as salvation' (2 Pet. 3:15). As long as the world endures, the church will be adding to its body those redeemed by the Son, for 'he (God the Father) put all things under his feet and gave him as head over all things to the church, which is his body, the fullness of him who fills all in all' (Eph. 1:22-23).

Second, and at the same time, in each generation, God is dividing those that have true faith from the world and from false professors. Paul told the Philippians not to be frightened by their opponents, for their opposition was a 'clear sign to them of their destruction, but of your salvation, and that from God' (Phil. 1:28). When he was told of division in the church at Corinth, he said, 'I believe it in part, for there must be factions among you in order that those who are genuine among you may be recognized' (1 Cor. 11:18-19). Peter wrote, 'The Lord knows how to rescue the godly from trials, and to keep the unrighteous under punishment until the day of judgment' (2 Pet. 2:9).

A third important development in the constant flow of years since Christ's ascension is the greater understanding of the revelation given to the church so that we might 'understand the things freely given us by God' (1 Cor. 2:12) and might also 'contend for the faith that was once for all delivered to the saints' (Jude 3). Paul taught that 'some will depart from the faith by devoting themselves to deceitful spirits,' and Peter warned that 'there will be false teachers among you, who will secretly bring in destructive heresies' (1 Tim. 4:1; 2 Pet. 2:1).

Church history is the arena is which we can investigate the work of God in accomplishing each of these goals. The

10

advancement of the church through conversion, the chastening of the church through controversy and division, and the clarifying of the church's truth through conflict with false or erroneous teachers, through both heresy and heterodoxy, constitute the narrative of the church's history. We have no inspired interpretation of the way these three aspects of Christ's work have been adjudicated and executed through history; we need, therefore, a reliable, honest, and discerning historical guide to come to grips with these important witnesses to the faithfulness of God to His purpose in the gospel. The study of church history provides the source for this most pleasing and edifying observation. For well-trained and discerning church members, the investigation of church history should accompany the study of the Bible and Christian theology.

This compact volume on the history of the Christian church provides a vital link for tasting the work of God from the New Testament era to the present. It also provides a pleasant and well-attested link between the academy and the church. Earl Blackburn, a seasoned and pastorally sensitive veteran of the pulpit, gives an overview of fifty of the strategically important events in the history of the church. Blackburn's savvy approach and comments show that he has been a contributing participant in the theological dynamics that have defined modern conservative Christianity. From the rarified theological air of monothelitism to the rigorously pragmatic practice of the 'anxious bench,' the author engages idea after idea that continues to give shape to the Christian faith in the twenty-first century. While the author works with great success at accuracy, and looks for the positive elements of witness in virtually all of the events upon which he reports, he also gives helpful critique and even warning about dangerous tendencies within some of these events. He shows why even those that are mainly negative should nevertheless be seen as momentously important.

Throughout these chapters, Blackburn explains why he considers each of the chosen events as a part of necessary knowledge for today's Christian. He shows why the issue developed, what is positive about the event or movement, what dangers exist, and what kind of contemporary significance it has. He gives us sketches of true godliness in which grace often grew to heroic proportions. He gives terse and accurate insights into church councils and the theological impact that has emerged from them. He shows why confessions have developed, how they embody vital elements of gospel witness, the vibrancy that can be manifest in confessional Christianity, and the deadness and nominalism that comes from a Christianity that is merely confessional. When we read with care, we find how the church-state complex developed and trace out some of the great difficulties that have attended that unscriptural union. We encounter a discussion of the development of orthodoxy and how necessary it is for faithful proclamation of Christian truth. We see the power of the development of evangelical truth in the Reformation as opposed to the sacramentalism of the Middle Ages. We find the significance of different views of the order and constitution of the church. We look at the importance of the church's engagement of moral issues and see the legitimate complementary relation between these issues and the task of evangelism; we also catch a glimpse of what happens when moral and social issues eat up the church's energy and replace the commission of conversion work through gospel preaching.

Time well-spent in a church's life would include classes using this book as a guide to understanding many vital aspects of Christian truth. Broken into very readable portions and written with engagingly clear diction, *Fifty World-Changing Events* neither intimidates the novice nor insults the initiated. This treatment of historical high points in the church will help arm the entire spectrum of believers against the ever-overflowing pool of religious error. Such study will increase Christian faithfulness and serve as an encouraging witness to God's faithfulness.

Tom J. Nettles,
Professor of Historical Theology,
The Southern Baptist Theological Seminary, Louisville, Kentucky.

Preface

Sir Winston Churchill once said that 'writing a book is an adventure.' For me, that is an understatement. Yes, writing this book has indeed been an enriching adventure; nevertheless, it has also been an arduous task. When originally asked to write this, the publisher specified that the discussion of each event be approximately twelve to thirteen hundred words, more or less. Concise writing is always difficult, but in this case, especially so. To illustrate, a colleague phoned one day while I was writing and asked what I was doing. I told him and he said, 'Oh, that should be easy.' I then asked him that if he were asked to write on the subject of the Council of Nicaea, would he choose 1,200, 12,000, or 40,000 words. He replied, 'You know the answer.' I said, 'Yes, but I want to hear you say it.' He responded, 'Forty thousand.' I agreed. To describe thoroughly yet concisely a history-shaping and world-changing event in twelve to thirteen hundred words or so, without being simplistic and omitting vital details, has been almost Herculean – at least for me.

World history in general, and Christian history in particular, have been great loves of my life. Some would think me boring, because one of my favorite pastimes is reading a book of history. In light of this habit, this book has been decades in the writing, though it has taken me only eighteen months or so to put it into pen and ink. I have read so much over the years from numerous authors; many times in reading, I would scribble observations, and at other times hastily copy and paste thoughts or quotes for possible usage, usually without attribution (for which there is no excuse), without realizing that one day I would be writing an entry-level book on church history. Over the years, I have not always precisely noted from whom I gleaned much of my knowledge: who said what and when. Thus, in addition to those I cite below, I am profoundly indebted to a number of historians, secular and Christian, in writing this book, for they have shaped my thinking over the years. I have profited from the writings of David Bebbington, Harry R. Boer, Earle Cairns, Kenneth Curtis, Leo Donald Davis, Will and Ariel Durant, Everett Ferguson, Justo Gonzales, Jesse Lyman Hulbert, Frank A. James III, Paul Johnson, J. N. D. Kelly, Kenneth Scott Latourette, N.R. Needham, Mark Noll, Roger Olsen, Philip Schaff, Williston Walker, and John D. Woodbridge. Also of great benefit have been primary sources of the early church fathers and the Protestant Reformers, along with countless historical articles in magazines and historical lectures too numerous to remember. I especially profited from the lectures of Dr John R. W. deWitt. Oftentimes in writing, I would ask myself if these were my own words, did they belong to an un-recollected source whose nugget I tugged out of my distant memory, or were they simply the ebb and flow of accumulated and intermingled data? Readers familiar with the above-mentioned works will recognize their formative imprint on my writing. If anywhere I have not given proper credit or credit at all, please forgive the unintentional oversight. Much gratitude is owed to several people. Many thanks to Deanna Boshoven, Courtney Brown, Tom Wells, and especially Holly Nicholls for all their invaluable insights and suggestions to help make this book more readable to the lay person. In addition, Ashley Adams conducted some detailed research for me. Special thanks is due to Drs Nathan Finn, Tom Nettles, and James Renihan for taking the time to read and check the manuscript for historical accuracy, though any inaccuracies discovered are completely my own. Moreover, their kind commendations are humbly appreciated. Particular thanks to Dr Nettles, who in the midst of his busy teaching schedule wrote a gracious Foreword. My deep gratitude also goes to Heritage Baptist Church in Shreveport, who generously gave me writing sabbaticals from my pastoral labors and who lovingly encouraged and prayed for me each step along the way. It is a pleasure to be your pastor! Deserving of particular gratitude is my son Caleb Andrew, who, in the midst of my 'oft' physical infirmities and pastoral toils, was a research assistant *par excellence*. Last but not least is my darling wife Debby. She brought me breakfast, lunch, and, oftentimes, supper as I was secluded in my study hammering away at this book. They would say here in the Deep South, 'She spoiled me rotten.' I certainly will not argue about that. Apart from my salvation, she is the greatest gift of Christ to me, and my best friend.

And so it is with a weighty sense of indebtedness of having received more than I have given, that I present this work to the public. As you read of His 'mighty acts' in redemptive history (Ps. 150:2 ASV), may your appetite be whetted to further study and may the triune God alone be praised.

EARL M. BLACKBURN
Bossier City, Louisiana.
July 29, 2015
(The 427th anniversary of Sir Francis Drake's defeat of the Spanish Armada)

Introduction

History is exciting and wonderfully informative – at least, some people think so. It is filled with heroes and villains, saints and sinners, along with adventure stories that even the most creative Hollywood screenwriter could not imagine. But mostly, history is about ordinary people, sometimes even dull people, who did extraordinary things. This is especially true concerning Christian history. Christianity has enriched the world in ways the majority does not realize.

When publically polled or personally asked, the average believer in the pew or workplace is sadly ignorant of the Christian history that has formed and shaped his or her past, the past where God worked excitingly and wonderfully! This history, throughout which the Lord performed His mighty acts, contains stories that bear repeating to our children's children. In his *History of Christianity*, noted British historian and biographer Paul Johnson states, 'Christianity has, perhaps, proved more influential in shaping human destiny than any other institutional philosophy.' If he is correct, then Christians, more than any others, should know their long and storied legacy. Johnson continues, 'Christianity is essentially an historical religion. It bases its claims on the historical facts it asserts. If these are demolished it is nothing.'

When encountering names such as Polycarp, Ignatius, Tertullian, Cyprian, Athanasius, Monica, Augustine, Anselm, Aquinas, Huss, Katherine von Bora, Zwingli, Calvin, Owen, Whitefield, Carey, Judson, or Bonhoeffer, the average believer will respond with a puzzled look and say, 'Huh?' It is easy to dwell in our own small-world mentality, focusing on a little corner of a photograph without seeing the 'big picture.' This book is for laypeople, and it is all about the big picture of *His* story. The events described in this book are short, pithy, summary narratives of situations that literally impacted and shaped the world, though most of the individuals involved in the events at the time did not realize their significance. The discussions are not exhaustive, only introductory. From the pages of these chapters, it is hoped that readers will know and understand their distant (spiritual) relatives and family memoirs, and come to prize and take joy in them with a never-before-experienced exuberance. Especially, it is hoped that the reader will be stimulated to research and study further each event.

Those who suppose history is boring and without any relevance should consider the very nature of history. Several views of history are held by respective schools of thought, with one view being more prominent than the others at any given time in history.

One particular view is that history is spiraling downward. In other words, everything is getting worse and worse. A second view is that history is spiraling upward, just the opposite of the downward spiral, and everything is getting better and better: utopia is on the horizon. Another view is that historical events are not connected. Each culture developed in its own distinctive, closed-in systems, and there is no correlation among the various civilizations, past or present. The subtle thought behind this view is that not only are cultural histories separate from each other; they are also separate from God the Creator. A fourth, and perhaps the most common view, is that history is cyclical or that it continually repeats itself.

Almost everyone has heard the oft-repeated expression, 'History repeats itself.' Even Christians sometimes fall into this mode of thinking. What must be understood is that while this view is popular, it is thoroughly secular; no biblical or Christian foundation supports it. While there are many aspects of distant ages and past cultures that are repetitions of recurring themes and actions, history is not repeating itself. For example, from 1861 to 1865, the United States was engaged in what Abraham Lincoln called 'a great Civil War.' While there may one day be another civil war in the United States (God forbid), it will not be like the first one. There may be some similarities between the two, but they will never be the same. If there are civil wars in other nations and in various eras, history is not repeating itself. It simply means there is a common thread of evil that runs throughout all humanity throughout the centuries.

In addition to the four views named above, one final option must be considered, and it is this view that forms and flows through the events of this book. It is the conviction that history is linear or moving in a straight line. This has always been the Judeo-Christian belief and tradition. From creation in

Genesis 1 to the new heavens and earth in Revelation 22, history is moving forward toward a pre-appointed end. However, that does not mean it is moving in a straight line without direction or purpose. Yes, history is filled with repeated, common experiences such as war, natural disasters, oppressive governments and violent overthrows of the same. Evil actions do recur and not only break upon the shores of time, but dot the worldwide landscape of the past. Comparable and similar wicked events shall continue.

Yet, a time is coming when the world as it is now known shall come to an end. Jesus the Christ shall return; He *alone* shall judge the world in righteousness (see Acts 17:31); the new world of Christ's kingdom will come and eternity shall begin. All Christians shall then be with God in heaven, the end that God intended all along. It should be remembered that no single thing happens by luck, chance, or accident, according to the Bible (see Eph. 1:11). This view should be especially thrilling for Christians, because it lets them view God's almighty hand at work in every period of time, behind each event in history, and encourages them to be strong and do exploits (see Dan. 11:32) for their Savior and Lord in their own historical time-frame.

Additionally, allow me to say a word about the system of dating events. This is a book of history, so, naturally, it will have dates, and plenty of them. First of all, 'circa' (c.) is used when the *exact* date is not known. It means the approximate time. Secondly, for centuries, it has been traditional to use B.C. *after* a date, denoting *before* the birth of Christ, and A.D. (Latin – *anno domini* – in *the year of the Lord*) *before* a date of an event *after* the birth of Christ. The following are examples:

Rome founded................................. 753 B.C.

Babylonian Captivity begins .... 606 B.C.

John Chrysostom born.................... A.D. 349

Byzantine Empire fell.................... A.D. 1453

Some postmodern historians and writers dislike the historical usage of B.C. and A.D. and have switched to using B.C.E. (Before the Common Era) and C.E. (Common Era) to designate dates before or after the birth of Christ. As a biblical, orthodox Christian, I have encountered no substantial reason to switch from a Christian heritage that has literally shaped the world to non-religious, postmodern designations that appear innovative, yet reject Christ. Therefore, any dates given in this book that occurred before Christ's birth will have B.C. after the date, and, where it is needed, A.D. is written before the date when it occurred after Christ's birth. If there is no designation, the date of the event is always after the birth of Christ. It is not that I am unable to adjust and learn a new method; rather, it is that I refuse to yield to a classification that must grudgingly acknowledge the greatest world-changing event – the incarnation, birth, and coming of Jesus Christ into our world.

Finally, a few things about the selection of events covered in this book. First, the inclusion of an event does not necessarily mean the author theologically or ethically approves of the event. It simply denotes that the author believes the event (whether good or bad) is so history-shaping and world-changing that it must be studied and cannot be ignored. Second, why fifty? Why not 100 or 200, which would allow for five or ten events to be covered in every century of Christianity? These are good questions. Secular and church historians have discussed and debated for years the crucial, world-changing, and future-shaping events of Christian history. Fifty was thought to be a good general introduction. Third, admittedly, there are gaps in these fifty covering approximately 2,000 years. Many events from each century could be included, and each is not without its own significance. Yet, to cover every single event would require a multi-volume set of books, which would defeat the purpose of this introductory volume. The fifty chosen are vignettes, or little pictures, that have been deemed radically impacting and formative, not only of Christianity, but of our present world. Hopefully, most will agree on those chosen, and for those who thoughtfully disagree, their opinions are respected.

1

The Destruction of Jerusalem – 70

*A*FTER the crucifixion, resurrection, and ascension of Christ, a looming obstacle fought the progress of Christianity: the religion of the Jews. Christianity was birthed in Jerusalem, the center of Judaism and 'the joy of the whole earth' (Ps. 48:2 NIV). The first opponents to this new faith were the Jews themselves. The hub of the Jewish religion, with all its priesthood, sacrifices, feast days, and rituals, was the Temple. The first Temple was built by Solomon and destroyed by the Babylonians around 606 B.C. The second Temple, the one during Jesus' life and ministry, was rebuilt by Zerubbabel after the seventy-year 'Babylonian Captivity,' c. 516 B.C.

Christians could not go anywhere in the city of Jerusalem without seeing the Temple. The ancient and well-established faith of Abraham, Isaac, Jacob, Moses, and David defiantly stared into the face of this new belief in great David's greater

Son, Jesus of Nazareth, the Messiah. Remember, all the first converts to Christ came from the Jewish religion. What were these new believers to do about the Law, the priesthood, and the sacrifices, which had shaped their lives since infancy and held their focus on Jerusalem and the Temple? Were they to go to the Temple functions on Saturday and then attend their house churches for worship on Sunday? If a new Christian sinned, was he to ask his Savior for forgiveness and then confess to the priest at the Temple and offer the required sacrifice for that sin? To further complicate matters, the message of Christ was carried outside of Jerusalem into Judea and Samaria, and Gentiles began converting to 'the faith' of this Jewish Messiah.

Christians understood from apostolic teaching (see Rom. 11) that God temporarily cut off the natural olive branch (Israel) and grafted in the wild olive branch (Gentiles – the Church). What God had promised to Abraham and proclaimed through the prophets, especially Isaiah – that heathen lands and Gentile peoples from all parts of the earth would come in and become part of God's covenant people – was now taking place on a grand scale. The unheard of, at least to the Jewish mind, was happening. Rather than re-studying their Old Testament Scriptures and understanding God's intended purposes all along, Jewish leaders began persecuting the humble followers of this 'sect' (see Acts 3 and 4). Persecution became more intense under Saul of Tarsus, who vehemently killed and imprisoned Christians, until his conversion to Christ (Acts 9). Saul later became Paul the Apostle, but the Jewish persecutions continued.

Thus, Judaism was in conflict with God's eternal purpose and was an affront to Christ, the only-begotten of the Father, and the gospel (see 1 Thess. 2:14-16). Would God allow His Son or those who loved His Son to be diminished and destroyed by an antagonistic religion? Something had to be done, and something was. What is ironic is that it was the Jews themselves who brought about their own undoing.

Decades before the birth of Christ, Palestine (as Israel was then known) came under the control of the Roman province of Syria. The Roman legates, rather than directly governing the several sections of the province, preferred to govern indirectly through regional leaders, who were supportive of Roman rule. The Herodian line of rulers or kings were one such group. Within Judaism were two primary parties: the Sadducees, the wealthy, aristocratic priests who had no problem collaborating with Rome, and the Pharisees, who were strict and devout regarding the Law and tradition, and less certain about working too closely with Rome. Both are mentioned in the Gospels, and both fiercely opposed Jesus.

There arose a third party within Judaism, whose rank-and-file members represented every stream of Jewish society. They were called the Zealots. (Simon, one of the Twelve Apostles, was converted to Christ from their number – see Luke 6:15.) Though more closely aligned with the Pharisees in their theology, the Zealots were radical and seditious in their politics. Visions of David and Solomon's ancient glory danced in their minds and filled their ideology. Their claim: only the God of David could rule over Israel, and the Romans and all foreign powers must be expelled. For decades, the Zealots had been a thorn in the Romans' side, continually skirmishing with their legions over occupation and taxation. Eventually, they fanned the flame that became the fire of the Jewish War (Revolt), lasting from A.D. 66 to 73. A Jewish historian named Josephus

Flavius gives a detailed account of the war in his *Antiquities*. Josephus was originally in favor of and fought in the revolt. He was captured and held prisoner by Vespasian. The Roman general liked the brilliant Jew, and Josephus eventually adopted the general's family name of Flavius.

According to Josephus, in 66, the Roman emperor Nero dispatched two legions (the 10th and 5th), under the leadership of General Vespasian, to subdue the Jewish uprisings. Vespasian was joined by his son Titus, who arrived from Alexandria, Egypt, commanding another legion (15th). Nero committed suicide in June of 68, thereby ensuring chaos for the next eighteen months as Galba, Marcus Salvius Otho, and Aulus Vitellius respectively acceded to power. After the successive deaths of these leaders, Vespasian (Titus' father) became emperor. Vespasian returned to Rome and ordered Titus to continue subduing the Jews. Titus laid siege to Jerusalem, cutting off all escape. The death toll from starvation and disease, not to mention the fighting, was atrocious. Josephus says in his *The Jewish War* that 1.1 million Jews died or were killed, and 97,000 were sold into slavery. These numbers are likely exaggerated, but they do make obvious the horrors of war. Finally, on September 2, 70, Jerusalem was conquered and destroyed, along with the Temple and all its records of priestly lines. Jesus had predicted the Temple's destruction in Luke 21:5–6! In 73, the entire city complex was razed, and the few remaining inhabitants were scattered to the ends of the earth, an event known as the *diaspora*. The only part of Jerusalem that remained was what is known today as the 'Wailing Wall,' the lower part of the western wall of the Temple.

What is the significance of Jerusalem's destruction and its mention as the first key event? The Jewish religion, *as divinely revealed in the Old Testament,* was primarily and indi‹ based upon several things: a central place of worshi was originally the Tabernacle and later replaced by the Temple in Jerusalem, a set of five ritual animal sacrifices (see Lev. 1–6), a priesthood taken exclusively from the tribe of Levi, and a high priest that was chosen exclusively from the sons of Aaron (the brother of Moses and also from the tribe of Levi). With the destruction of the Temple, the Jewish religion (*according to the Old Testament*) was completely destroyed. Once before, the Temple (Solomon's) had been destroyed, but the Jewish religion continued because the sacrifices and priesthood continued. However, with the destruction of this second Temple (Zerubbabel's), the God-ordained animal sacrifices ended, the priesthood ceased to exist, and all priesthood records were annihilated so that the priesthood could never be re-established.

The Jewish religion, *in the biblical sense of the definition,* was no more. The Jewish religion, as it is known today, is little more than the cultural traditions of the Talmud and the rabbis. It bears very little or no resemblance to the divinely established religion of the Old Testament. Furthermore, the *diaspora* did as much to spread Christians across the empire as it did to disperse the Jews. Using the revolt of the Jews and the retaliation of the Romans, God removed the immediate obstacle to gospel progress and softened the defiant stare of Judaism upon Christianity.

2

The Publication of *The Didache* – 100

MOST Christians have little or no doubt that the Bible is the inspired Word of God and was given to the world through the prophets and apostles of Christ or their associates. Most evangelical Christians have little or no doubt about its inerrancy (that it is without error). But what about those writings of the early Christian church that were not included in the canon of Scripture? Do any of these writings give intricate detail about the early Christian practices and inner workings of the churches? If so, are they of any value to Christianity?

The answer to these questions is: yes, there are several, and yes, they are of value to the church. They may not be Scripture, but they can provide insight nevertheless.

The first and most important written work that supplements Scripture is the *Didache* (Greek for 'teaching'). It is not a letter, but a manual. Formally known as *The Lord's Teachings through the Twelve Apostles to the Nations*, it is the first major non-inspired writing of the Christian church.

Discovered in an old monastery within Constantinople in 1883, this short work continues to be one of the most studied and disputed documents of early Christian history. The dispute is not over its authenticity, but over its age. Some scholars think it possibly emerged as early as 70, and others around 150. The exact date is not known. However, there is no doubt about its authenticity, and the new consensus among scholars is that it was written around 100 and thus is a legitimate representative of the teaching of the early church (for further discussion of this matter, see *The Oxford Dictionary of the Christian Church*).

What does this work teach us? The *Didache* is a summary of basic instruction about the Christian life to be taught to *catechumens*, or those who were preparing for baptism and church membership. These catechumens went through a rigorous program of study or *catechesis* that often lasted for up to two years. They were *catechized* (*taught and initiated*) into the Christian faith before they were baptized and brought into the church.

The period of *catechesis* was a time when young believers learned the nature of the Christian life and what was expected after baptism. The early church was concerned about how Christians lived in a pagan society and in the church. This special time of instruction gave the church time to evaluate potential converts and gave potential converts time, and appropriate teaching, to understand what faith in Christ was all about.

The *Didache* is a summary of the kind of teaching a *catechumen* might have heard as he or she was preparing to enter the church.

Immense insight into early and post-apostolic church life is given in the sixteen chapters of this work. The following is based on M. B. Riddle's excellent translation, published in the *Ante-Nicene Fathers* series.

Chapter 1 begins by explaining that there are 'two ways' a person can go. The difference between these two ways is simple but stark: one leads to life, and the other leads to death. The *Didache* says that the difference between them is 'great.' It explains the way of life by referencing the 'first commandment,' that is 'to love God who made you,' and the second, 'to love your neighbor as yourself.' These encapsulate the Ten Commandments and are also the commandments named by Jesus in Matthew 22. The rest of the chapter is a summary of Jesus' *Sermon on the Mount* (see Matt. 5–7).

Chapter 2 provides a list of several forbidden activities such as stealing, lying, committing adultery, and coveting. Many of these mirror the prohibitions on the second tablet of the Ten Commandments.

Chapter 3 continues the tone and focus of chapter 2, but especially mentions murmuring and being self-willed, which can lead to blasphemy. It condemns soothsayers, astrologers, and other pseudo-religious practices that were common in that day. A biblical grasp of God's sovereign providence is implied by the writer(s), as young believers are taught to 'accept whatever happens to you as good, knowing that apart from God nothing comes to pass.'

Chapter 4 begins with an exhortation to honor the one who ministers the Word of God – 'honor him as you do the Lord.' Here, a high view of the Scriptures and the gospel ministry is seen: 'For wherever the lordly rule is uttered, there is the Lord.' A plea for unity is given, along with other ethical imperatives, closing with 'In the church you shall acknowledge your transgressions, and you shall not come near [the church] for your prayer with an evil conscience. This is the way of life.' Rather than communicating a lax or disrespectful attitude toward church, the *Didache* shows a holy esteem for the gathering of God's people.

Chapter 5 turns from the way of life to the way of death. It offers a litany of sins, named one after the other, and closes with, 'Be delivered, children, from all these.'

Chapter 6 warns 'against false teachers' and 'food offered to idols.' It cautions that anyone who teaches another way is in error.

Chapter 7 deals with baptism. It states, 'And concerning baptism, baptize this way: After reviewing all of this teaching, baptize in the Name of the Father, Son, and Holy Spirit, in living water. But if you have no living water, then baptize into other water; and if you cannot do so in cold water, do so in warm.'

Note there are several things that are clear in this statement: 1) baptism (Gk. *baptizein*) in the early church was originally by immersion; and 2) it was to be done in 'the name of the Father, and of the Son, and of the Holy Spirit.' This negates baptism in 'Jesus' name' alone or 'in the name of the Lord,' a practice common among certain sects today. 3) Baptism was to be performed in 'living' [running] water, meaning in a river or stream; 4) allowances were made for pools and those desert dwellers who had no access to either rivers or pools; and 5) the chapter goes on to say that if immersion was not possible, pouring (effusion) was allowed, but it was to be done three times on the person's head in the triune name. The person to be baptized was also to fast 'one or two days before.' This is one of the more detailed instructions concerning baptism that survives from the early church.

Chapter 8 deals with fasting and the Lord's Prayer. Fasting is not to be done like the hypocrites, but on 'the Preparation Friday.' Also, prayer is not to be 'like the hypocrites', 'but rather as the Lord commanded in his Gospel.' The Lord's Prayer (found in Matt. 6:9-12) is then quoted verbatim. The Christians are to pray this prayer three times a day.

Chapter 9 spells out the way to partake of the Eucharist (Communion or the Lord's Supper). Warning is given not to eat of the bread or drink of the wine unless the person has been baptized, 'lest that which is holy is given unto dogs.'

Chapter 10 gives a specific prayer of 'Thanksgiving' that was to be offered to God after Communion. A warm Christ-centeredness exudes from the prayer.

Chapter 11 instructs concerning itinerant 'Teachers, Apostles, and Prophets.' The way to distinguish between the true and false is simple: if either teaches anything contrary to *The Didache*, asks for money, or stays longer than three days in the church, he is false.

Chapter 12 explains hospitality and rebukes those who are idle and will not work.

Chapter 13 describes the Old Testament example of how prophets are to be supported.

Chapter 14 addresses the matter of 'Christian Assembly on the Lord's Day.' The break with Saturday as the Jewish Sabbath is clear, and Sunday is established as the Lord's Day, the day of Christian worship and rest.

Chapter 15 commands the church to appoint qualified 'bishops and deacons' [in the churches], who shall 'render to you the service of prophets and teachers.'

Chapter 16, the final chapter, exhorts watchfulness for the [second] coming of the Lord. It warns that false prophets, wolves in sheep's clothing, and all sorts of 'corrupters' will multiply. Love will decrease and 'lawlessness' will increase. Christians shall be hated and persecuted, and 'the world-deceiver as Son of God' shall appear and do 'iniquitous things which have never yet come to pass since the beginning.' Then shall 'the creation of men come into the fire of trial' and 'only those who endure in their faith shall be saved.' Three final things shall happen: 1) 'the sign of an outspreading in heaven,' 2) the 'sound of the trumpet,' and 3) 'the resurrection from the dead.'

This delightful little book concludes with these words: 'Then shall the world see the Lord coming upon the clouds of heaven.' What a marvelous faith in a world of skepticism! The *Didache* was a manual, fleshed out from Old and New Testament writings, that molded the shape of the churches for centuries to come.

3

Justin Martyr Writes an Early Defense of Christianity *(Apology)* – c. 150

*T*HE *First Apology of Justin* was influential during the early decades of Christianity in ways that are still experienced today. The word 'apology' (Gk. *apologia*) in this title does not equate to its definition in modern thought; the work does not ask for forgiveness or admit wrongdoing. Instead, an 'apology' in antiquity was a defense of something, an explanation of its worth. In this case, Justin's subject was a defense of the Christian faith.

Why was such a defense needed? At first, Rome left Christians alone, thinking they were nothing more than a schismatic fraction of Judaism. But by 100, Christianity, as a distinct and separate group from Judaism, had spread all over the Roman Empire. The beliefs the 'followers of the Way' propagated and the radically different lifestyles they lived were so diametrically opposed to existing philosophies and practices of the time that attention swirled around Christians. The Christians referred to all of these other religions, with the exception of Judaism, as 'pagan.'

Through the preaching of the gospel over time, in some geographical locations entire towns and cities were converted or, at least, came under the influence of Christianity.

The authorities soon felt they had a major problem on their hands. Just when persecution from the Jews died down, persecution from Rome resurrected. In 64, a fire was started, and three-quarters of the city of Rome burned to the ground. Wildly insane, the Emperor Nero probably set the fire, and to cover his nefarious deed, he blamed the city's destruction on the Christians. Government authorities all over the Empire began stridently persecuting Christians. Pagan philosophers and intellectuals proved to be formidable opponents. They began to slander and bring outrageous accusations against the humble followers of Christ, who gave little resistance. For the next eighty years, varying levels of persecution would arise in sundry parts of the Empire, and many Christians would die for their faith.

Scholarly figures from a few churches began to write intelligent and reasoned responses to pagan charges and slanders. These responses took the form of treatises, and those who wrote them, contending for their faith, later became known as the 'Apologists.' Justin Martyr, as he was named after his martyrdom, was the one of the first of these noble apologists. He was followed by Irenaeus (c. 130–200), Tertullian (c. 160–220), Clement of Alexandria (c. 155–220), and Origen (c. 185–254).

Justin was born to rich, pagan parents in present-day Nablus. He studied several pagan philosophies, and like many before and after him, found them to be empty and vain. Justin at last found peace when he came to faith in Christ and embraced orthodox Christianity (c. 130). He devoted his life to teaching the gospel and the Christian faith, first in Ephesus and then in Rome. This noble contender for the faith was martyred under the order of Emperor Marcus Aurelius in 165.

Justin's *First Apology* was written to Emperor Antoninus Pius, his (adopted) sons Marcus Aurelius and Lucius Verus, and the 'sacred Senate.' His literary style was simple, yet intelligent and fiercely bold. Without apology (pun intended), he penned his *First Apology*. His main purpose for writing was to make a reasonable appeal to the 'powers that be' and furnish a positive exposition of the Christian faith – to contend that Christians are not 'atheists' but true worshipers of God. In so doing, Justin also dispelled false charges against Christians and their churches.

Immediately after his respectful introduction, Justin de-clared, 'You can kill us. But you cannot hurt us.' (Here and below, quotations from the *First Apology* are taken from the Ante-Nicene Fathers series.) By that he did not mean that Christians cannot suffer pain, but that the killings would not diminish or annihilate the Christian faith; it would continue to grow. He then demanded that 'the charges against the Christians be investigated.' If the government officials did not do so, they would be 'governing affairs by emotions rather than intelligence.' His defense continued by bravely charging the imperial leaders with unjustly punishing Christians for allegedly being wicked and immoral. He turns the table on them by citing the duplicity of their own actions. By alluding to 'defiled women and corrupted boys,' Justin brought to mind what most Romans knew – that many of their consuls, emperors, and imperial magistrates were rapists, adulterers, and pedophiles.

The *First Apology* admits that in the Roman sense, Christians *are* atheists, in that they do not worship the mythological gods (so-called) of Greece and Rome. However, he insisted, Christians are not atheists, because they worship the true and living God. Justin's arguments against Rome's false charges mounted. Christ's kingdom is different. It is not a human kingdom, but a heavenly one. Thus, Christians do not follow all geographical customs, but truth in which there is mystery and holiness. Justin explains that 'our teacher' Jesus Christ is the Son of the true God, was crucified under Pontius Pilate, was buried, rose again, ascended into heaven, and is worshiped. Worship in the Christian assemblies is simply set forth:

> On the day called Sunday, all who live in cities or in the country gather together to one place, and the memoirs of the apostles, called Gospels, or the writings of the prophets are read, as long as time permits; then, when the reader has ceased, the president [minister/pastor] verbally instructs, and exhorts to the imitation of these good things. Then we all rise together and pray, and, as we before said, when our prayer is ended, bread and wine ... are brought, and the president in like manner offers prayers and thanksgivings, according to his ability, and the people assent, saying *Amen*; and there is a distribution to each, and a participation of that over which thanks have been given, and to those who are absent a portion is sent by the deacons.
>
> An offering is collected and deposited to the church leader, who distributes to the needs that abound.

Justin then gave a biblical and theological reason why Christians worship on Sunday:

> ... because it is the first day on which God worked a change in the darkness and matter and made the world. On the same day Jesus Christ our Saviour rose from the dead. He was crucified on the day before that of Saturn (Saturday); and on the day of the Sun, he appeared to his apostles and disciples.

Throughout his treatise, Justin alludes to a Day of Judgement in which evildoers will give an account before God for their lawless deeds. The apologist bravely concludes with a strict warning and a gracious invitation: 'We warn you [remember he is addressing the emperor, the most powerful person in the empire] that you will not escape the coming judgement of God if you continue in your injustice. We ourselves invite you to do that which is pleasing to God.'

Again, Justin not only wanted to defend Christianity as the only and true religion, but to disprove false charges against it. Rumors abounded that Christians were disloyal to the government (they did not pay taxes), they were cannibals (in light of the Lord's Supper formula 'this is My body and blood'), and that they were sexually immoral (i.e., they baptized naked and engaged in sexual orgies after baptisms). Justin dispelled all these myths. The *First Apology* is remarkable because it was the first non-inspired, written defense of the Christian faith. It emboldened weary and persecuted believers, modeled saving belief to future generations, and published a picture of a young faith that serious-minded believers would study for centuries.

4

The Great Persecution Under Emperor Diocletian – c. 303

FOR the next 150 years, Christianity grew to such a degree that it became a powerful minority within the Roman Empire. There is reason to think that numbers of high officials in the empire, from Paul's day forward, become Christians, perhaps even some in the imperial palace (see Phil. 1:13). Pagans were deeply suspicious and ignorantly fearful of those humble followers of Christ. There was genuine fear that Christianity would gain the ascendancy and cast out non-Christian religions in the empire. Many prominent non-Christian Roman leaders argued that something must be done to rid the empire of such an expanding and troublesome lot.

Other attempts had already been made and numerous pagan authorities had endeavored to exterminate Christianity. At first, the Jews, then Nero, Marcus Aurelius, and numerous Roman pro-consuls and legates in diverse provinces, at singular times, had tried to destroy Christianity and failed. What must be remembered, lest the wrong idea is formed, is that persecution against Christianity was neither continuous nor empire-wide. There were periods of times and places where Christians were left alone and had complete freedom and peace without any hostile interference or threat of government.

Then, in 249, Decius became emperor. He was the first emperor to undertake an empire-wide, systematic persecution of Christians. The public beginning of this persecution occurred in January 250, when Decius executed Flavian, the Bishop of Rome. Sudden deaths of other prominent Christian leaders throughout the empire followed. By early summer, all imperial citizens were required to furnish proof that they had publicly offered sacrifice to the emperor. Those that could not or did not were killed. Many were Christians who would neither betray Christ nor compromise their consciences to satisfy the demands of an unjust law. As an aside, many professed Christians expediently renounced their faith; some hid and stopped attending the Christian assemblies, and others escaped by bribing officials to 'look the other way.' These were labeled the fallen (*lapsi*) by the church. Later, when several bishops refused to receive the penitent fallen back into church membership, a sharp conflict ensued between Bishop Cyprian and the Novatians that caused a major disruption in Christianity. The first systematic persecution of Christianity ended with the death of Decius in June 251. This wicked emperor, whose reign was short-lived, also failed to exterminate the followers of Christ. Still, hatred and suspicion lingered in the empire.

Three decades later, in 284, Diocletian became emperor. He set out to stabilize and reform the empire, and he accomplished the task well. In 293, Diocletian divided the Roman Empire into the West and East. While he remained 'the' emperor over all, he made the ruler of the East an emperor also. He also designated two 'co-emperors' (one for the West and one for the East), known as 'augustus/augusti.'

Christians, for the most part, lived in peace and tranquility under Diocletian's reign. His daughter was reportedly a Christian, but his son-in-law, Galerius, was a different story. Galerius was a co-augustus under Diocletian, and for some reason, perhaps because his wife would not renounce Christ and Christianity, Galerius had a fierce hatred of Christians. Because of his unassuaged animosity towards Christianity, in 303, Galerius pressured an old and tired Diocletian to instigate a severe persecution and purging of Christians throughout the empire. Diocletian ordered it, but it was sparked and vehemently carried out by his co-augustus, top general, and son-in-law, Galerius. The next eight years became known as the 'Great Persecution.'

Because of a serious illness, Diocletian did something that had never before happened; he abdicated and stepped down from his throne. In 305, he handed over full control of his eastern empire to Galerius, who intensified the persecution with animalistic vigor.

The Great Persecution came in the form of four anti-Christian edicts (for further elaboration on these points, see Will Durant's *History of Civilization Part III*, pp. 649-652):

1. The first edict, issued on February 24, 303, ordered that all churches were to be dismantled; all Bibles, liturgical books, and Scriptures surrendered; all sacred vessels confiscated; all meetings of worship (public and private) forbidden; all Christians in imperial service forced to quit; all freed Christian slaves re-enslaved; and that no Christian could act

as an accuser or witness in the courts of law regarding cases of personal injury, adultery, or theft.

2. The second edict, which came during the summer of 303, ordered the arrest of all Christian clergy. This caused a logistical problem due to the number of pastors and believers arrested. The prisons were unable to accommodate all of them.

3. Perhaps with the second in mind, a third edict was issued on the first day of Diocletian's twentieth year as emperor. It reiterated the second edict, but added the amendment that all those imprisoned who freely sacrificed to the gods would be allowed to go free.

4. The fourth edict was issued in April 304 and seems to have been exclusively the work of Galerius. This edict marks the 'Final Solution' with regards to Christians. All citizens were required to give public sacrifice to the gods on the pain of death. Eusebius, the early church historian, describes how the next ten years of the persecution were unbearable as everyone, whether pagan, Jew, or Christian, was under suspicion.

The persecution was brought to an end almost a decade later by two unexpected sources. The first source was the rise to power and influence of Constantine, who had become co-augustus of the West (see below). The second source was something that every human being fears – terminal illness. The intervening eight years had not been kind to Galerius, who was by 311 in the grip of an unexpected and frightful cancer that would soon claim his life. He became convinced that his past behavior had come back to haunt him. With pressure put upon him by the powerful Constantine, and in the throes of death, in April 311 he rescinded his anti-Christian edicts and issued the 'Edict of Toleration.' Thus, the 'Great Persecution' ended. The great persecutor and hater of Christianity died an indescribably horrible death later that year. Christians attributed this to the heavy hand of almighty God upon him.

During this period, numberless Christians were arrested, starved, tortured, mutilated, burned, and forced into gladiatorial contests simply to amuse spectators. The records of history do not tell us how many thousands were murdered for no other reason than their faith in Christ. Unlike the soft conditions that exist in twenty-first-century Western culture, especially in the U.S., the fourth century was a time when it cost something to be a true Christian, at least within the Roman Empire. Beginning with Stephen, the first Christian martyr, and all the original apostles (except John), through the centuries countless women, men, and young people have given their lives simply because they loved and followed Christ. A later poet and hymn writer asks the searching question that each reader must seriously consider in light of this event:

> The Son of God goes forth to war, a kingly crown to gain;
> His blood-red banner streams afar; who follows in His train?
> Who best can drink His cup of woe, triumphant over pain?
> Who patient bears His cross below, he follows in His train.
>
> A glorious band, the chosen few on whom the Spirit came,
> Twelve valiant saints, their hope they knew, and mocked the
>   cross and flame:
> They met the tyrant's brandished steel, the lion's gory mane;
> They bowed their necks the death to feel: who follows in
>   their train?
> — REGINALD HEBER, 1827

47

5

Constantine the Great Converts to Christianity – 312

'THE times, they are a-changin,' as Bob Dylan strummed, describes this event. Pieces were being put into place and moves were about to be made that would forever change the world, both pagan and Christian. Here enters onto the stage one of the most controversial figures of Western civilization – Constantine the Great. His father, Constantius, was a co-augustus reigning in the West over present-day Germany, France, and England (Britannia). Because Helena his wife was of lowly birth, Constantius found it politically expedient to divorce her in 290. However, their marriage produced a son, Constantine, who would truly change the world.

Constantine entered the military early and steadily rose in rank. Part of his time was spent on the battlefield in military campaigns, and the other part was spent in Diocletian's palace, where he was both an imperial apprentice and a hostage (ensuring the obedient behavior of his father). When Galerius succeeded Diocletian, Constantine maneuvered himself out of the imperial palace and made his way to Britain to be with Constantius, his father. Constantine was given command of the legions and carried out military operations. While Constantine served with his father in Britain, his father suddenly died. When the legions heard the unexpected news of Constantius' death, they immediately saluted Constantine as Augustus, in succession to his father. Constantine was crowned Augustus on July 25, 306 in York, England. A plaque marking the spot of his coronation can be seen today under the York Minster Cathedral. This ascension in a theater-of-war was an irregular path to the imperial throne, which meant that Constantine would have to prove his right to rule on the battlefield.

In short, Constantine marshaled his legions and won more than a few strategic campaigns. He defeated several opponents and became increasingly powerful. Soon after Diocletian's abdication and Galerius' death, a fierce civil war ensued over who would become the emperor of the West. There were two surviving contenders – Constantine and Maxentius. The generals met in battle twelve miles north of Rome on the Tiber River at the Battle of the Milvian Bridge. The battle took place on October 28, 312.

The day before the battle, Constantine looked towards the sun and supposedly saw in a vision a cross of light. Over the cross were the Greek words '*by this, win,*' often rendered in the more familiar Latin '*in hoc signo vinces*' (*in this sign, you will conquer*). Lactantius recounts that Constantine purportedly heard the voice of God in the vision. Eusebius of Caesarea, an early church historian and close advisor to Constantine, reported that Christ came to Constantine in a dream that night. In both accounts, God allegedly promised the general that if he ordered the sign of the cross painted on his soldiers' shields, he would be victorious. The symbol is believed to look something like this: ☧ Constantine did as instructed in the alleged vision and won the battle, attributing his victory to the sign of the cross. Maxentius drowned in the Tiber during the battle, and Constantine became the sole and undisputed ruler or Emperor of the West.

Licinius, a military ally of Constantine against Maxentius, and one who would play a great part in the next event, succeeded Galerius as the emperor of the East. Constantine hammered out a fragile alliance with Licinius and, for over a decade, they ruled as co-emperors of the Roman Empire. Slowly, tensions increased between the two over Constantine's escalating authority and prominence. Licinius was jealous, and he prepared for war. In 324, the two met in battle, and Constantine utterly routed the armies of Licinius to become the sole emperor of the Roman Empire. Constantine then took the audacious title 'Ruler of the Entire Globe.'

Soon after the Battle of the Milvian Bridge, Constantine made his triumphal entry into Rome as the emperor of the West. He did so with the cross freshly emblazoned on his imperial banner. Contrary to the tradition of victorious Roman generals offering the customary sacrifices on the altars to the gods, Constantine went directly to the imperial palace. Not all his generals or the city's influential leaders immediately embraced Christianity, but the general populace did. Most Romans embraced the emblem overnight and began to wear it superstitiously on necklaces, rings, and other jewelry. How ironic that the cross, the emblem of Jesus' suffering and shameful death, became a charm, a symbol of good luck. At what point Constantine professed to becoming a Christian is not precisely known, but very shortly after his formal enthronement he openly demonstrated his favorable attitude toward Christians.

For Constantine, Christianity was not just a way to God, but a way to unite the empire. That is what makes his professed conversion to Christ both questionable and controversial. His mother, Helena, was a Christian. What positive influence did she exert upon his young mind and heart? There is no doubt that Constantine had some type of religious experience before the battle, but did he really believe Christ to be the eternal Son of God and embrace the second Person of the Godhead to be his Lord and Savior? Did he worship God because his heart was full of love and gratitude to Him, or because it was politically expedient? Was his life commensurate to that of a pagan or a Christian? He was not baptized until just a few days before his death in 337 and that by Eusebius of Nicomedia, an Arian bishop. Understandably, postponing baptism until one approached death was the common practice and a safety precaution of the time, lest a believer should sin in youth and lose salvation. Nonetheless, the questions regarding his conversion still remain.

Whether Constantine's conversion to Christ was genuine or not, he involved himself heartily in the affairs of the Christian church. He believed that Christ was his patron, and this made Constantine (in his thinking) the unspoken head of the church. Now the Christians had an emperor that was for them and not against them. Shortly after coming to the throne in 312, he was asked to settle a dispute among the Christians in

North Africa over who could ordain bishops. He ruled against the Donatists. Very early in his administration, the emperor sent three letters to the Roman consul in Carthage (outside of present-day Tunis), the first city of Roman North Africa. The letters contain valuable insight into Constantine's thinking. They restored in every city all church buildings that formerly belonged to the Christians; they informed the governor that funds would arrive to compensate the evicted owners of the buildings. Constantine's second letter exempted the clergy from the affairs of local government so the clergy could 'render supreme service to the Deity.' In 321, he ordered that Sunday should become a public *holiday*. Fearing the Arian controversy would tear his empire apart, Constantine called to assembly the noble Council of Nicaea that convened on July 4, 325 (see event #7).

Constantine's embracing of Christianity produced far-reaching effects upon the world. The effects are woven into the fabric of Western civilization and can be traced through the centuries. For three hundred years, the state had been the enemy of the church; now, the state became the sponsor of the church. Constantine began the process of establishing a church-state Christendom, which found its zenith in Charlemagne, and evidences of it can be seen throughout Europe and other parts of the world even to this day.

6

The Edict of Milan – 313

*A*FTER the Great Persecution ended and Constantine became Emperor and a Christian, there would be no more formal persecution against Christians and the church. In a sense, this was both good and bad: good in that Christians could publicly and freely confess their faith without fear of reprisal, and bad in that the trickle-down effect led to what many would call the adulteration of Christianity. We will examine this in more detail later.

However, while things changed immediately in Rome, everything did not change overnight throughout the empire. News and information could, and often did, travel slowly. Some remote regions of the empire had yet to learn of the monumental changes in Rome, so they maintained the previously existing state of affairs. Even when some regional governors or senior officials heard reports, they often dismissed them as mere rumors. If the unscrupulous edicts and decrees issued by imperial authorities were going to be annulled, official steps to enact positive legislation and inform the governing authorities of the changes would have to be taken.

Within a year of Constantine's conversion, a summit was called for and convened in Milan, Italy, during January 313. The Emperor Constantine, in the West, and the co-augustus, Licinius, in the East, met to confer over this very matter. How long they met and the level of their discussion is not known. No doubt, Constantine asserted his newly-acquired influence and Licinius yielded. The initial outcome of this summit was that they issued a joint statement, which has been wrongly called an edict, or an imperial decree. There had been previously issued edicts or orders for Christian toleration, but each one had been short-lived. Even dying Galerius issued one in 311. But when the regional governor or prefect died, so did the edict.

A section of the statement or agreement is cited below, as found in volume four of *Translations and Reprints from the Original Sources of European History*:

> When I, Constantine Augustus, as well as I, Licinius Augustus, met in Milan in conference concerning the welfare and security of the realm, we decided that of all things that are of profit to all mankind, those regulations pertaining to the worship of the Divinity ought rightly be our first and chiefest care, so that we might grant Christians and others full authority to observe that religion which each preferred; whence any Divinity whatsoever in the seat of heavens may be propitious and kindly disposed to us and all who are placed under our rule. And thus by this wholesome counsel and most upright provision we thought to arrange that no one ... should be denied the opportunity to give

his heart to the observance of the Christian religion ... we have conceded to other religions the right of open and free observance of their worship for the sake of the peace of our times ...

We therefore announce that, notwithstanding any provisions concerning the Christians in our former instructions, all who choose that religion are to be permitted to continue therein, without any let or hindrance, and are not to be in any way troubled or molested ... Our purpose is to grant both to the Christians and to all others ...

Moreover, concerning the Christians, we before gave orders with respect to the places set apart for their worship. It is now our pleasure that all who have bought such places should restore them to the Christians, without any demand for payment. [A provision was then made for the owners to apply to the state for compensation, which was promised.]

You are to use your utmost diligence in carrying out these orders on behalf of the Christians and so shall that divine favor which we have already enjoyed, in affairs of the greatest moment, continue to grant us success, and, thus secure the happiness of the realm.

Several things are telling about the statement. *First*, there is the acceptance of henotheism, at least on the part of Licinius, who was not a Christian. Henotheism is the superstitious belief that while there is one primary god, there is also the existence or possibility of existence of secondary or lesser gods, who usually rule over certain regions or people groups. This is seen in the statements 'any Divinity whatsoever in the seat of heavens' and 'we concede to other religions.' *Second*, it was a political act. As early as the Apostle Paul's day, the gospel had penetrated the upper strata of Roman society (Phil. 1:13). Christianity had grown to the extent that it could no longer be persecuted or ignored. If something had not been done, the unity and peace of the empire would have been threatened, even to the point of civil war. *Third*, favored and exalted status is shown to Christianity above the other religions of the empire. Constantine, just newly crowned and co-ruling with a non-Christian, did not possess the political clout to do more. He would later, but not at this particular juncture.

The jointly issued imperial statement has been misunderstood by some through the centuries. Whether the statement was an official edict is debatable. Two historical and slightly divergent documents of the statement survive, one by Eusebius of Caesarea and the other by Lactantius, a historian and close counselor to Constantine. The statement most often used and studied is by Lactantius. What is interesting about the document is that it is not in the formula of an official, imperial edict, but in the form of a letter (albeit an official one). Furthermore, it was not even issued in Milan. Shortly after the summit, Licinius, from his Eastern capital, sent the contents of the above as a letter to the governors of the eastern provinces he had just conquered. In it, he instructed them how to behave toward other religions, especially Christianity. It thus gives insight into his tolerance as a pagan rather than his belief as a Christian.

The year 2013 marked the 1,700th anniversary of the Edict of Milan. Bartholomew I, the Ecumenical Patriarch of Constantinople, traveled to Milan on May 16, 2013, the traditional date of its issuance. Pope Francis sent a cardinal to greet Bartholomew and to issue this papal declaration of thanksgiving for the Edict: 'for the importance given to the memory of the historic decision that, decreeing religious freedom for Christians, opened new paths to the Gospel and decisively contributed to the birth of European civilization.'

Why is this event world-changing? It did give freedom of religion to all, and, in particular, it recognized the legal personality of Christian churches. It subsequently allowed all properties of the churches to be returned to them, and it did mark the triumph of Christianity over persecution and pave new, unrestricted corridors for the gospel. However, it did *not* make Christianity the state religion. Pope Francis' declaration ends with a point few consider, which is essential to remember: '[it] decisively contributed to the birth of European civilization.' While the main point of the summit in Milan was to grant toleration and religious freedom to all, especially to the religion of Jesus, few, if any, in the day of its issuance, realized what a major defining moment in pagan and Christian history it was to be. It was not only a means of reprieve for early Christianity, but became a model to educate tyrants of the evil of governmental suppression and to encourage seekers of religious freedom for centuries to come.

7

The First Council of Nicaea – 325

*C*HRISTIANITY not only survived, but actually thrived during almost three centuries of external opposition and deadly persecution. Could it now survive the internal disruption that was smoldering beneath the surface of its triumph? It is often the case that an entity is not destroyed from the outside, but that deterioration comes from within. Little did the Christian church realize that after the Edict of Milan, it would shortly face an internal conflict that would threaten the very core of its existence.

Since His death, burial, resurrection, and ascension back into heaven, Christians believed that Jesus, the Son of God, was divine. His life, miracles, and teachings all substantiated their belief. The question that persisted was: How divine? What was Christ's relationship to God the Father? Did Christ come into existence at some point in eternity past, or did He always exist? Was He of a different substance or essence than the Father, or was He of the same substance and essence? Was He subordinate to the Father, or was He equal with the Father? Was He of the same power, glory, and purpose as the Father, or was He distinctly different in power, glory, and purpose? These questions may mean little to the secularist today, but they were of vast importance to the Christians of the third and fourth centuries. The doctrines of the Trinity and deity of Jesus Christ were, for them, foundational to saving Christianity.

The post-apostolic Fathers and the Apologists wrestled with these doctrinal questions without arriving at an official consensus. It was the apologist Tertullian (c. 160–220) who first coined the word '*trinity*' (Latin – *trinitas*). This helped, but still left matters unsettled. In the midst of expansive growth and scattered persecution, the theological questions and debates churned. Perhaps one of the biggest reasons for the turmoil was that the New Testament had not been formally canonized. (This issue will be discussed in event #8.) This Trinitarian controversy was causing widespread mayhem throughout the Roman Empire.

Trinitarianism was brought to a head and initially, though not thoroughly, settled at Nicaea, but it was ignited in 318 by a man named Arius (c. 250–336). He was probably a Libyan by birth. After being ordained presbyter, he was installed as pastor of the Baucalis Church in Alexandria, Egypt. Arius believed and taught that Jesus was 'more than human, but less than God'; moreover Jesus was **not** co-eternal, co-equal, co-substantial, and co-glorious with the Father. To Arius, God first created the Son, who in turn created the universe, including the world. Arius knew the power of music and embodied his theology in a book of songs called '*Thaleia*' (*banquet*), which he wrote for the common people to sing in the marketplaces and dockyards. These songs denied the eternal Sonship and deity of Christ. The followers of Arius marched through the streets chanting, 'There was [a time] when the Son was not.' The orthodox responded by marching and singing what is known as the '*Gloria Patri*' – 'Glory be the Father, and to the Son, and to the Holy Ghost; as it was in the beginning, is now, and ever shall be, world without end. Amen.' Arius was excommunicated for heresy by Bishop Alexander of Alexandria at the Synod of Alexandria (c. 320).

On the scene was another man, Athanasius (c. 296–373), a deacon and assistant/secretary to the bishop of Alexandria. A man mighty in the Scriptures, Athanasius knew from John 1:1 that Jesus was the *Word* and, not only was He the *Word* face-to-face with God; He was the *Word* who was God. Sometime after 318, Athanasius wrote his most famous book, which is still a Christian classic, entitled *De Incarnatione Verbi Dei*, or *On the Incarnation of the Word of God*. Athanasius strongly opposed Arius and would not tolerate his heresy, which he believed to be damnable.

Though Constantine was deeply troubled by the schism that reached the farthest regions of his domain, the emperor deemed the issue 'a small and insignificant question.' Nevertheless, for the peace and tranquility of the empire, Constantine knew that he must do something, or his hard-won kingdom would be split. Thus, he called for and convened an ecumenical (worldwide) council of bishops, who came from all over the empire to Nicaea to settle the divisive and destructive Arian controversy (as it came to be known). How many bishops attended? Extant lists do not give a complete number. The number could have been as few as 200 or as many as 300. Athanasius stated the number as 318, symbolically derived from the 318 armed servants of Abraham (Gen. 14:14). This last number has traditionally stood.

Constantine opened the Council on July 4, 325, with the veritable words that 'Division in the church is worse than war.' He commanded the churchmen to reach an agreement of 'one faith' that would cement the unity of the empire. Arius and Athanasius were both present, the latter attending Bishop Alexander. After extended debate covering two months, Arius' teachings were condemned, and he was excommunicated. Only two bishops disagreed with the formula that became the Nicene Creed. Ultimately, it was Athanasius who greatly influenced the outcome. Because of his love for Christ, his steadfast determination to be true to the Word of God, and his resolute character, his theology was the outstanding obstacle to the triumph of Arianism.

Three crowning doctrinal truths were advanced at Nicaea: 1) Christ was the same substance and essence (*homoousios*) as the Father; 2) Christ was **not** of a similar substance (*homoiousios*) as the Father; and 3) Christ was **not** of a different substance (*heteroousios*) as the Father. The Godhead began to be thought of more clearly and taught as co-equal: Father-Son-Holy Spirit are *One*, yet *Three*. The deity of the Holy Spirit was affirmed.

Constantine was satisfied, thinking that there was now 'one faith' solidifying his empire. However, that was not entirely the case. Yes, an orthodox faith did emerge, but there were bishops that signed the Nicene formula who were sympathetic to some of Arius' teachings. They became known as Semi-Arians. Furthermore, Nicaea raised new and more complex problems concerning the relationship between the human and divine natures of Christ. The next eighty years would uncover a latent doctrinal disunity seething in the hearts of Christian leaders that otherwise should have been united. Bishops would be excommunicated or banished, factious groups would split off of the main body, and episcopal jousting with splintered spears and battered shields occurred in prominent sectors of the realm. Instead of being a church at rest, it was now a church at war! Calm and unity would not fully arrive until Theodosius the Great ascended the imperial throne (379–395) and convened the next ecumenical council.

Though regional councils of bishops had previously convened to adjudicate theological matters and disputes, Nicaea was indeed the first ecumenical (worldwide) council of the Christian church, significant others of which were to follow. It primarily dealt with the Arian controversy and engendered a measure of doctrinal harmony by issuing its famous Creed. Not that the Fathers were diabolically conniving to invent a theological creed to bolster already-existing beliefs; instead, they were honestly endeavoring to state clearly, to the church and all heretics, what God had divinely revealed in the New Testament. Furthermore, this council did *not* invent the doctrine of the Trinity (as some erroneously claim). Rather, they initially settled the biblical teachings of the eternal Sonship and deity of Christ and the nature of the only true God who makes Himself known in three Persons (see Appendix I). Nicaea was world-changing in that its effects are still seen, and pastors, scholars, and laypersons alike continue to study meticulously its proceedings.

8

Athanasius's Easter Letter Defines the New Testament Books – 367

*W*HEN the last surviving apostle of the original Twelve (John) finished writing the Book of the Revelation of Jesus Christ on the island of Patmos, the New Testament was completed! The twenty-seven books of the completed New Testament were slowly disseminated among the churches, but had not been officially recognized by the churches (i.e., the New Testament canonized; *canon* – Greek, meaning *rule* or *standard*). Plus, there were other non-inspired letters/ epistles/books written after 100 that vied and competed with the apostolic books of the New Testament for acceptance. For example, the *Didache* (see event #2), the *First Epistle of Clement* (c. 100), the *Epistle of Barnabas* (c. 130), the *Shepherd of Hermas* (c. 150), the *Gospel of Thomas* (d. unknown), along with others, were considered by some to be equally inspired and authoritative. It was not that the churches did not have copies of the Word of God. They did, but not the complete New Testament. Some churches would have one or two Gospels, maybe Acts of the Apostles, a few of Paul's epistles, a General Epistle or two, and one or more of the non-inspired books. Another church would possess some of the same books, but have others that were different along with an additional non-inspired epistle or two. Debate arose over the question of whether such books as Hebrews, the Epistles of Peter, 2 and 3 John, and the Revelation were even inspired. Uncertainty abounded. Many arguments erupted, and much confusion plagued the churches regarding which sacred books were inspired (*'God-breathed'*) and which ones were not.

Enter onto the scene again Athanasius. (Author's note: here I am compelled to insert more biographical information about a genuine champion of the biblical and orthodox Christian faith, which has fascinated and thrilled me for decades.) After the Council of Nicaea and the death of Alexander, Athanasius was ordained bishop of Alexandria (328). His faithful, unflinching adherence to 'orthodox' Christianity (as it came to be called) both at and following the Council of Nicaea, left this Christ-centered servant with many enemies, not the least of whom was Constantine the Great himself. Shortly after his consecration as bishop, the emperor, being more interested in unity than truth, sent Athanasius the following message:

> Since you know my will, grant free admission to all those who wish to enter the church. For if I hear that you have hindered anyone from becoming a member, or have debarred anyone from entrance, I shall immediately send someone to have you deposed at my behest and have you sent into exile. (as qtd. in P. Johnson, *A History of Christianity*)

Little did the emperor realize that he had just defaulted on the very council he convened three years earlier. The emperor's threatening words were prompted by his knowledge of the bishop's insistence and enforcement that anyone who denied the Creed of Nicaea could not be admitted into the membership of the church. Allowing someone into the church that was not orthodox, Athanasius believed, was sacrilege. What was the man of God to do? Obey man or God? For Athanasius, it was an easy answer. He ignored the earthly potentate's warning and, imitating the apostolic example in Acts 5:29, obeyed the Potentate of heaven. True to his convictions, anyone who did not freely confess the Creed of Nicaea was not allowed membership in any churches of the See of Alexandria.

Constantine bore with the bishop until Athanasius' enemies persistently used political influence to have him banished and exiled in 335. Five times he was exiled, and as Will Durant observes, 'In those bitter days Athanasius spoke of himself as *solus contra mundum* [I alone against the world]' (*The Story of Civilization*, vol. 4). Nevertheless, after each banishment, truth prevailed and he was restored. Finally, Athanasius resumed his bishopric in 366, which he held until his death (373) at the age of seventy-eight. His firm stand on Holy Scripture and fierce opposition to anti-Trinitarian heresy are two reasons that the cult of the Jehovah's Witnesses is relegated to a small subculture in Christianity today!

Shortly after Athanasius's final reinstatement, the saintly bishop, weary and worn from much fighting against the heresy of Arianism, sent out his annual Easter (Festal) Letter to all the churches of his See. This, his Thirty-Ninth Festal Letter of 367, was perhaps his most influential writing. Pastoral encouragement and love, spiritual matters of general interest, and the dates of Lent and Easter were contained in the letter. Furthermore, it enunciated something else that changed and shaped the world to this very day – the completed books of the New Testament. His implied reasons for listing the books were fourfold: 1) to end the disputes about non-inspired books, such as the *Shepherd of Hermas* and the *Epistle of Barnabas*; 2) to silence the opposition to such books as Hebrews, Peter's Epistles, 2 and 3 John, and the Book of Revelation; 3) to lift the fog of confusion; and 4) to encourage the sheep of his pastoral flock to know the Word of God. The books Athanasius listed were not in the same order as the books of our New Testament, but they were the exact number and names.

What influenced and impelled this listing? When Athanasius was exiled the second time (339), he fled to Rome, where he had the protection and patronage of Bishop Julius for seven years. There he encountered the famous *Codex Vaticanus*, housed in the Vatican Library. Constans, the new emperor (remember, Constantine died in 337), commissioned Alexandrian scribes to compile the books of the New Testament (340). They arranged them in the following order: the Gospels, Acts, the General Epistles (James, 1 and 2 Peter, 1, 2, and 3 John, Jude), Pauline Epistles (including Hebrews between 2 Thessalonians and 1 Timothy), and Revelation.

He states in his Easter Letter that these twenty-seven are the final books of the 'Word of God.' After the list, Athanasius declares, 'These are the wells of salvation, so that he who thirsts may be satisfied with the sayings in these. Let no one add to these. Let nothing be taken away.' For Athanasius, the canon is now closed.

Athanasius's view was not immediately accepted by everyone; even some in Alexandria opposed it. Divergent and contrary opinions regarding inspired versus non-inspired writings swirled in both the Eastern and Western halves of the Empire. The question of the completed and 'closed' canon of Holy Scripture would continue for another three decades. Finally, the issue was formally and authoritatively settled at the Council of Hippo Regis (397). The twenty-seven books listed in Athanasius' letter were recognized as the completed and closed canon of the New Testament, and the churches were informed of the council's determination. From that point on, no other writings or epistles would be recognized as inspired books of God's Word. Can you imagine what could happen if there were not a closed canon of Holy Scripture? Abraham Lincoln's famous 'Gettysburg Address,' Winston Churchill's stirring WWII speech, 'Blood, Sweat, Toil, and Tears,' or some modern religious leader's 'prophetic word' might also be included in the Bible! It must be carefully noted that the Christian church did not inspire or invent the canonical books of the New Testament; it simply recognized and collected into one body those that were inspired (of God) and penned by apostolic writers. Yes, it was the Council of Hippo Regis that settled the issue of canonicity, but it was Athanasius's Easter Letter (367) that set in motion the process. For that letter, Christians shall be forever grateful!

9

Christianity Becomes the State Religion of the Roman Empire – 380

*T*HEODOSIUS the Great was born in Seville, Spain, and, due to his father's influence, rose through the ranks to become a general and commander of legions. When the Visigoths revolted and killed the Eastern emperor, Valens, in battle, the Western emperor sent Theodosius to the East to restore order and subdue the Germanic peoples. In the midst of a successful campaign, Theodosius fell ill of a common fever and appeared to be dying. Fearing for his eternal soul, he professed the faith of Nicaea, quickly recovered from his illness, and was baptized. Soon thereafter, in 379, he was made co-emperor of the eastern half of the Roman Empire. In 392, Theodosius became sole emperor of the empire and reigned as such until his death in 395. He was the last emperor to rule over both the Eastern and Western halves of the Roman Empire.

Two remarkable events crowned Theodosius' reign. First, immediately after his coronation, he banned divination from the entrails of animals sacrificed, forbade visits to pagan temples, abolished pagan holidays, extinguished the eternal fire in the Temple of Vesta and disbanded the Vestal Virgins, and prohibited and punished witchcraft. This, in effect, dismantled all the pagan religions of ancient Rome. Second, in February 380, along with Gratian, the emperor of the West, he issued the imperial Edict of Thessalonica, which made the orthodox (Nicene) faith the official state religion of the Roman Empire. The Edict declares in clear, unmistakable terms the following:

> It is our desire that all the various nations which are subject to our Clemency and Moderation, should continue to profess that religion which was delivered to the Romans by the divine Apostle Peter, as it has been preserved by faithful tradition, and which is now professed by the Pontiff Damasus and by Peter, Bishop of Alexandria, a man of apostolic holiness. According to the apostolic teaching and the doctrine of the Gospel, let us believe in one deity of the Father, the Son, and the Holy Spirit, in equal majesty and in holy Trinity. We authorize the followers of this law to assume the title of Catholic Christians; but as for the others, since, in our judgment they are foolish madmen, we decree that they shall be branded with the ignominious name of heretics, and shall not presume to give to their conventicles the name of churches. They shall suffer in the first place the chastisement of the divine condemnation and in the second the punishment of our authority which in accordance with the will of Heaven we shall decide to inflict. (S. Ehler and J. Worrall, trans.)

By 391, it was illegal to worship at any pagan temple or shrine within the empire. Furthermore, Theodosius banned Arian worship within the city of Constantinople, confiscated their church buildings, exiled the Arian leaders, and prohibited them from building any future places of worship within the city walls. If the semi-Arians, Arians, or Anomoeans (hyper-Arians) were to worship in any church building other than the orthodox (Nicene), they would have to do so outside the walls and limits of the city. Arianism was on the run. The tide had turned, and the persecuted then became the persecutors.

The church acquired a defender and leader in the emperor himself. Because of Constantine's initial granting of freedom of religion (#6 – The Edict of Milan) and Theodosius' going beyond that to formalizing Christianity as the state religion, emperors became the *de facto* leaders of the church. They began to construct church buildings, often very elaborate. If they did not directly preside over church councils, they at least appointed the ones who would. While others might collaborate and make recommendations for bishops, the emperors became the final appointer of bishops. Imperial acceptance or veto was indisputably final. When it came to matters of doctrine, belief, or practice, though the bishops would instruct the emperors, it was the emperors who had the final word in theology. The state and church became so blended that it was difficult to distinguish between the two, at least in the East or the Byzantine Empire.

Rapidly, the bishops realized that the state controlled the church, and who could countermand the emperors? It was Ambrose, Bishop of Milan, who rose to the occasion. A riot had occurred in the hippodrome of Thessalonica and the imperial commanders had been killed by the rioters. Ambrose, fearing imperial wrath and eradication, went to Theodosius and pleaded moderation. The emperor relented and sent word to the city that the riot had been forgiven. Later, musing on the affront to authority the rioters had shown, Theodosius sent an army to Thessalonica and slaughtered over seven thousand rioters. Ambrose heard of the atrocity and the next Lord's Day met the emperor at the door of the church with these words: 'Stop! A man such as you, stained with sin, whose hands are bathed in blood of injustice, is unworthy, until he repents, to enter this holy place, and to partake of communion.' Though Ambrose was threatened by courtiers and bodyguards, he stood his ground. Theodosius acknowledged the bishop was right and gave public signs of repentance. A bishop had successfully rebuked an emperor and boldly asserted that Theodosius was a subject of Christ and under His authority. Something remarkable had happened, as captured in the observation of Leo Donald Davis in *The First Seven Ecumenical Councils*:

> The sense of disparateness between the Christ-founded Church and the God-ordained Empire, recovered in the course of the Arian controversy under Constantius, became a permanent feature of Western Christianity even after the reestablishment of Nicene orthodoxy to favor under Theodosius, as the resounding words of Ambrose testify: 'The Emperor is in the Church, not above it.'

Nevertheless, the effects of Theodosius' Edict rippled throughout the empire. Christianity, along with its churchly hierarchy, recently officially sanctioned, would develop and play a key role in the empire's identity through the Middles Ages. If a person were a subject of the empire, that person was a part of the church, and vice versa. For centuries, the bifurcation of the two was difficult. This lack of distinction between church and state mentality exists in parts of the world even now.

Was the formal establishment of Christianity as the official state religion of the Roman Empire a good or bad thing? In the best case scenario, it was good, because Christianity was saved from being completely overtaken by heresy and, through the sword of the state, biblical orthodoxy triumphed. In the worst case scenario, it was one of the most damaging things that could have happened to the church. The imperial Edict made it popular to be a 'Christian,' which allowed political, social, and economic profiteers to fill the Church with their counterfeit professions of faith in Christ. The church became polluted with many 'false sons in her pale,' to quote the well-known hymn 'The Church's One Foundation' by Samuel J. Stone. Furthermore, the gospel of Christ that founded the church was eclipsed by the church, which shall be evident as Christianity moves forward. The wonderful apostolic message for sinners of salvation by grace alone, through faith alone, in Christ alone was, in many places and instances, replaced with a Christian institution. The issue became whether one was 'in the church,' not whether one was 'in Christ.' Biblical Christianity lost its savor and began a great decline from which segments have never fully recovered.

10

The First Council of
Constantinople – 381

*T*HE Council of Nicaea, which had been called to settle the Arian controversy, was not completely successful. By 327, Emperor Constantine the Great began to regret the decisions that were made at Nicaea. He granted amnesty to the Arian leaders and allowed the banished ones to return to their churches. Aware of the emperor's political programs for unity in the empire and his ambivalence towards absolute truth, heretics took advantage of Constantine's prevarications and became bold in their unrestricted freedom to propagate falsehood. Open opposition to the Nicene doctrine of the Trinity and the eternal deity of Christ resumed. A year later, Alexander, bishop of Alexandria and stabilizing champion of Trinitarian Christianity, died. Athanasius, a staunch Nicene, was consecrated bishop in his place. Athanasius donned the bishop's mitre and continued to be a vigorous defender of orthodox Christianity against Arianism. Remember, he was exiled five times for preaching the biblical truth of the Trinity and resisting those who twisted the Scripture. It appeared for a while that the glorious victory of Nicaea would be overthrown by the Arians and semi-Arians, which would have happened had it not been for the tireless and fearless efforts of Athanasius. Even during his exiles (consisting of seventeen of his forty-six years as bishop), Athanasius continued to write and defend orthodox truths, despite opponents on every hand.

Constantine died in 337 and was followed by a succession of emperors closely aligned with his policies. There was a brief hiatus of almost three years when Christians were forced to stop their internal squabbling and deal with an outward enemy. Julian the Apostate became emperor from 361 to 363 and set aside the favored status of Christianity for a revived paganism. His program was short-lived, as he was killed in a battle against the Persians outside of Antioch. The emperors that followed the Apostate restored Christianity's status, and the infighting continued. Another heresy emerged that further divided Christians. Apollinarius, a converted teacher of rhetoric, bishop of Laodicea, and defender of Nicaea, over-emphasized the deity of Christ to the exclusion of His human nature. 'Although he possessed a sentient human body, did the Person of Jesus the Son of God have one nature or two?' Apollinarius asked. This question generated much controversy that further threatened the empire's unity. Apollinarius posited that there was only *one* nature in Christ: the divine. Thus, he denied the reality of Jesus' possessing a reasonable soul and a human mind.

When Theodosius I, also known as 'the Great,' came to the throne in 379, he realized that Constantine's compromised unity throughout the empire was not a unity at all. Constantine's hope that Arians, semi-Arians, and Nicene orthodoxy could peacefully co-exist was seriously flawed. Something must be done ecclesiastically to create a more concrete, lasting unity within his realm instead of the superficial one that churned beneath the surface. Theodosius ordered an ecumenical council of bishops to be held in Constantinople. In May 381, 150 bishops assembled in the capital of the Eastern Roman Empire and formed the First Council of Constantinople, which is recognized as the Second Ecumenical Council of the church. Although it confirmed the Nicene Creed, it dealt with other unsettled matters stemming from the Arian controversy. The council took place from May to July. Melitius of Antioch called the council, but died shortly after it convened.

Entering the picture at this point was the great Cappadocian Father, Gregory of Nazianzus. Early in the controversy, Gregory cogently exposed the errors of Apollinarius' flawed beliefs and won the confidence of the Nicene orthodox, which had previously supported Apollinarius. In 379, he was summoned to Constantinople to combat the Arian heresies. He was a retiring and soft-spoken man, but an eloquent preacher, very skilled in the Scriptures. People flocked to hear him as he preached from the small Church of the Anastasis (Resurrection), and many were converted to Christ.

Theodosius quickly rewarded Gregory's victories by deposing the Arian bishop (Demophilus) and appointing Gregory bishop of Constantinople. Upon the death of Melitius, Gregory was elected by the bishops to preside over the council. He preached five masterful sermons, still available, entitled 'Five Theological Orations,' on the Holy Spirit as the third Person of the Godhead.

He rhetorically contended, 'Is the Spirit God? Most certainly. Well, then, is He consubstantial? Yes, if He is God.' These clear exegetical questions, so magnificently proclaimed with great oratorical force, exerted considerable influence upon the council. However, due to political infighting, for which he was not suited, and a desire for the monastic life, Gregory resigned as president of the council soon after its convening.

The council dealt with three great pressing issues: 1) the deity of Christ; 2) a mystical over-emphasis of the deity of Christ (i.e., Apollinarianism); and 3) the deity of the Holy Spirit.

In his *Christianity through the Centuries*, Earle Cairns gives insight into the thinking of Apollinaris:

> Apollinaris taught that Christ had a true body and soul, but that the spirit in man was replaced in Christ by the [Gnostic idea of] logos. The logos as the divine element actively dominated the passive element, the body and soul, in the person of Christ. He stressed the deity of Christ but minimized His true manhood. His view was officially condemned at the ecumenical Council of Constantinople in 381.

Note carefully, the Council of Nicaea had not clarified the deity of the Holy Spirit, the third Person of the Trinity. A topic of heated debate was a group known as the Macedonians, who denied the deity of the Holy Spirit. Were they orthodox or not? They believed the Holy Spirit to be an 'it' – an impersonal force – and not a person. In response, this council developed a statement of faith which included the language of Nicaea, but expanded the discussion on the Holy Spirit to combat this Macedonian heresy.

The council affirmed the original Nicene Creed as a true and accurate explanation of Scripture, issuing a creed of its own. It is called the Niceno-Constantinople Creed of 381 and was a commentary on the original Nicene formula. It expanded the third article of the Nicene Creed, which deals with the Holy Spirit. Regarding the Holy Spirit, the article states that He is 'the Lord, the Giver of Life, Who proceeds from the Father, with the Father and the Son He is worshipped and glorified.' The phrase 'Who proceeds from the Father' is seen as significant because it establishes that the Holy Spirit must be of the same substance (*ousia*) as God the Father.

The results of the First Council of Constantinople were threefold: 1) it settled the issue of one God in three Persons, a death-blow to the Arians and semi-Arians; 2) it established the true and full humanity of Christ, the second Person of the Godhead with *two* natures, who is fully God and fully man: the God-Man; 3) it declared that the Holy Spirit was indeed God (co-equal and co-eternal with the Father and Son) and the third Person of the Godhead. This council's decision regarding the Holy Spirit also gave official and creedal endorsement to the full biblical teaching of the Trinity and freed the church to fulfill her calling.

11

Augustine Converts to Christianity – 386

TIME magazine's September 29, 1986, issue allotted a full page covering the 1,600th anniversary of Augustine's conversion to Christ, his baptism, and his life. The article states that Augustine has continued to exert a 'major intellectual, spiritual, and cultural force' upon the world. Why would a secular magazine, so widely known and read, make such a claim? Many historians believe that after Jesus and Paul, Augustine of Hippo (354–430) is the most important and influential figure in the history and development of Christianity. A person cannot study Christian history without quickly encountering Augustine. How is it that this man from a remote part of northern Africa is so substantially recognized by both sacred and secular scholars? The answer lies in his life and ministry.

Little is known of Augustine's father. His mother, Monica, was a devout and godly Christian woman. As Augustine reports in his *Confessions*, early in his teen years, he became enamored with philosophy and turned from any belief in Christ and Christianity. He was consumed with lust and fell into deep sexual immorality. Finding sexual pleasures did not satisfy, he began imbibing several belief systems, eventually settling into Manichaeism. The Manichees, as they were called, were founded by a Persian named Mani around 215. Manichaeism was a sophisticated offshoot of Gnosticism: the belief in a dualist world of co-equal light and dark, good and evil. To drive out the evil contained in the physical realm, the Manichees practiced a severe asceticism, especially vegetarianism. As Augustine advanced in the sect, he saw the contradiction of its leaders as they indulged in feasts and orgies. He would later expose them in his writings. After nine years, he left the group and went to Rome with his unnamed concubine.

His mother followed after him and continually prayed for him. From Rome, he moved to Milan and (through his mother's persuasion) began to sit under the ministry of Bishop Ambrose. Augustine was impressed with the genuine piety of Ambrose and saw that he was a man mighty in the Scriptures. Under deep, unshakable conviction of sin, he had several audiences with the bishop. Ambrose's preaching continually pointed him to the Scriptures and Christ. One day while sitting in a garden, he heard children playing a game outside the wall. They kept repeating in Latin *'tolle lege, tolle lege'* ('pick up and read'). He immediately walked over to the scroll of the Word of God lying on a table and read these words from Romans 13:13a–14: 'not in orgies and drunkenness, not in sexual immorality and sensuality, not in quarreling and jealousy. But put on the Lord Jesus Christ, and make no provision for the flesh, to gratify its desires.' Instantly, he was converted, as the 'light' of the gospel infused his heart.

Some statements in Augustine's *Confessions* are glorious. Here you see a truly pious theologian who has not only a brilliant mind, but a warm heart of constant devotion to the triune God. He is controlled by the omnipotence of God sovereignly exercised (e.g., 'Grant what you command, and command what you will'), accompanied by a keen understanding of depraved human nature and the chief end of man ('This is the authentic happy life, to set one's joy on You, grounded in You and caused by You'). Portions are very moving (e.g., 'Late have I loved You … You called and … shattered my darkness …' and 'I caught a glimpse of Your splendor with a wounded heart'). No doubt his most famous quote is the following:

> And man wants to praise You, man who is only a small portion of what You have created and who goes about carrying with him his own mortality, the evidence of his own sin and evidence that You resist the proud … Yet still man, this small portion of creation, wants to praise You. You stimulate him to take pleasure in praising You, because You have made us for Yourself, and our hearts are restless until they find their rest in You.

From his conversion to his ordination into the bishopric, Augustine rose to become a powerful voice in the church. His early writings declared divine, free, and sovereign grace in salvation, especially as he opposed free will and expounded predestination. This led him into conflict with a British monk studying in Rome named Pelagius. Augustine's view of 'Grant what you command, and command what you will' especially irritated this philosophically-oriented monk. Pelagius was

Trinitarian, but denied original sin and championed an unfallen, untainted will in man. He believed that though grace is initially necessary, God is powerless without the full cooperation of man. Man, Pelagius argued, possesses the unfettered ability, by his own free will, to do anything God commands and even to live a sinless life; grace occasionally assisting.

Augustine responded that, though man is a fully responsible being, it takes almighty grace to 'tame the wild heart' (which governs the will) and bring it to a willing submission to Christ and His cross. Everything in salvation and in the Christian life, from beginning to the end, is totally of grace. He opposed free will and works-salvation and the teachings of Pelagius. Augustine expounded in the clearest way the sovereignty of God, salvation by grace alone, and predestination; thus, Augustine is known as 'the Doctor of Grace.' Pelagius was excommunicated in 417, and his teachings on free will and human ability in salvation were condemned by the universal church at the Council of Ephesus in 431 (event #13).

Two other situations that arose after the Pelagian controversy occupied the remainder of Augustine's ministry. The first is the Donatist controversy. This group developed when the *traditores* (those who had denied and betrayed Christ) returned and were received back into the church after the Great Persecution. Donatists believed that those who denied Christ during that period should not be allowed back into the church and, especially, not to hold office. Furthermore, those who were ordained by those who had denied Christ were unfit for office. A pure and separate church was their aim. Though the Donatist trouble was centered in northern Africa, its influence was felt throughout Christendom.

In 393, Augustine began his opposition to the Donatists, which continued until his death. It was his writings on the church, as he exposed the Donatist errors, that not only kept the Western church from dividing, but also laid the foundation for the development of the Roman Catholic system. He meant well but went about solving the problem the wrong way.

The other situation was the fall and sacking of Rome, the eternal city of God, by the barbarian, Germanic Goths in 410. Suddenly, the faithful were shaken. If Rome was the city of God, how could He allow this to happen? Pagans blamed the Christians because they had abandoned the ancient gods and now the wrath of the gods was turned upon the Christians. Augustine responded with his timeless classic, *The City of God*. He covered a wide range of subjects essential to Christianity, from creation to the final judgement. However, his basic thesis is that there is a city of God, which is the church (Zion) and Christ's people, and there is a city of man, which is the world system and those who willingly live in it. The city of God – not Rome – will eventually triumph over all, and a person's faith should ultimately be in the triune God as He is revealed in the face of Christ.

Augustine's life, labors, and writings quantumly influenced Western society and culture for over sixteen hundred years. Isn't it time to check out *Confessions* or *The City of God* and see how one of these books might influence you?

12

Jerome and the *Latin Vulgate* – 405

SINCE the Council of Hippo Regis, the canon of Scripture had been settled. However, a major problem existed in the church, especially the Latin-speaking West: the lack of a correct translation of the Old and New Testaments. The Jews had the Old Testament in Hebrew, but almost all non-Jews, not to mention quite a few of the Jews outside of Palestine, could not read Hebrew. That was one of the reasons why seventy scholars translated the Old Testament into Greek (c. 125–120 b.c.). This translation is known as the *Septuagint* (LXX), and anyone who knew Greek could read it, which made the Old Testament more accessible to both Jews and Gentiles.

The New Testament was written in *koine* Greek, the common trade language of the day, and was easily read by most people around the Mediterranean. Yet, some populations within the vast Roman Empire could not read Greek. Thus, there were early translations of the Septuagint and the New Testament into Syriac, Coptic, and Latin (which was quickly becoming the prevailing language of the West). Despite the zeal of the early translators of the New Testament into Latin, many did not have a good command of Greek. Hence, there were several poor-quality Old Latin translations floating around, and they often differed with each other. The differences were producing doctrinal perversions in certain regions of the Western Empire. What could be done to correct the problem?

The answer was supplied by Jerome (c. 342–420), a biblical scholar who had been converted and baptized in Rome, and made his residence there. His devotion to Christ led him to become an ascetic/monk, and though it seemed contradictory to the ascetic lifestyle, Jerome wanted to visit the great centers of Christianity. Therefore, he traveled to Antioch and Palestine (where he learned Hebrew), spent some time in Constantinople, and eventually made his way back to Rome. Jerome's godliness and erudite learning caught the attention of Bishop Damasus of Rome, who made Jerome his personal secretary. Jerome realized the problem of poor translations and offered a solution written in the Preface of the New Testament to Bishop Damasus:

> If we are to pin our faith to the Latin texts, it is for our opponents to tell us which; for there are almost as many forms of texts as there are copies. Parchments are dyed purple, gold is melted into lettering, and manuscripts are decked with jewels, while Christ lies at the door naked and dying. If, on the other hand, we are to glean the truth from a comparison of many, why not go back to the original Greek and correct the mistakes introduced by inaccurate translators, and the blundering alterations of confident but ignorant critics, and, further, all that has been inserted or

changed by copyists more asleep than awake? (P. Schaff and H. Wace, trans.)

Damasus had already warmed to the idea proposed earlier by Jerome because he wanted the Western church to be clearly Latin and to have one Latin translation that would secure his vision. He suggested that Jerome produce a new Latin translation of the entire Bible for the vulgar (common) people. Jerome vigorously set upon his task with a scholarship unsurpassed in the early church. He collected copies of the various Latin translations and listed the differences and inaccuracies for comparison of needed corrections. Most importantly, he obtained copies of the Old Testament and New Testament in the original languages and began the work. The original proposal he made to Damasus had entered Jerome's mind while in Constantinople, and he had begun some translating there in 382. However, he officially began the task in 385.

Damasus died, and because of false accusations and petty squabbles in Rome, Jerome set out to relocate. He visited Antioch, Egypt, and Palestine, hoping to find a quiet place for contemplative study and translation. He finally settled in Bethlehem, the birth-place of our Lord, and resumed his work. During his busy work of translating, he wrote extensive biblical commentaries and dispatched lengthy (sometimes eloquent, often caustic) letters to church leaders far and wide in which he engaged in theological battles and addressed burning spiritual issues of the day. He founded a monastery, where he obtained help for his daily needs, and industriously continued his work of translation. After twenty-three years of prodigious labor in 405, he produced his life's greatest achievement: the Latin *Vulgate*.

What is remarkable about the *Vulgate* (from the Latin *vulgus*, meaning *common*) is that Jerome worked alone – without the assistance of a team or teams of scholars to proof or correct his translation. There was no one to superintend his work or make suggestions. In spite of this fact, it is a rather accurate translation. Obviously, there are inaccuracies, to be expected from the labor of one fallible man, but for which he should not be severely faulted. He was plowing new ground; when such is done, there will be rocks left unmoved and roots unbroken. One such inaccuracy is Jerome's translation of *repentance* (Greek *metanoia*) to *penance* (Latin *poenitentia*); the former is a change of mind that affects actions, and the latter is an act performed. One is scriptural and the other unscriptural, which caused much misunderstanding. His mistranslation laid the framework for the Roman Catholic doctrine of Penance (i.e., people confessing to a priest in an auricular confessional).

Another issue that Jerome faced in translating the *Vulgate*, which later became problematic for the Protestant Reformers, was the *Apocrypha*. The Jews did not accept the Apocryphal books as inspired and canonical. Nevertheless, the *Septuagint* included them. What was Jerome to do? Compelled by church authorities, he also included them. However, he made it clear that he considered them *libri ecclesiastici* (church books for edification) and not *libri canonici* (church books that were inspired and canonical). No doubt, Jerome held the same belief as Athanasius on this subject. The Protestant Reformers, over a thousand years later, followed Jerome's belief and excluded the *Apocrypha* from their Bibles.

Jerome's *Vulgate* was not accepted at first. It was initially used in conjunction with the older Latin versions, but it gradually gained wider acceptance because of its excellence and superior scholarship. By the thirteenth century, Jerome's version came to be called the 'commonly used translation.' Because of the Council of Trent in 1545, ultimately it became the definitive and officially promulgated Latin version of the Bible in all the Roman Catholic Church. Highly regarded by scholars all over Christendom, the *Vulgate* was used for over a thousand years as the major source of translating the Holy Bible into other languages. Martin Luther, fluent in both the Hebrew and Greek, personally used the *Vulgate* in the pulpit throughout his ministry.

It is sad and ironic that Damasus' vision and Jerome's efforts undermined their ardent and long-term purpose of providing a common translation for the people. The *Vulgate* established Latin as the language of the church; however, centuries later, the lay people sat in worship services and heard a Bible read that they could neither understand nor apply to their daily lives. By most scholarly standards today, Jerome's *Vulgate* was flawed in certain areas. Nevertheless, Jerome's genius in translating the *Vulgate* was that he sought to go back to the original languages of Scripture (Hebrew and Greek). And for that, we shall be ever grateful to him. His desire to bring the Holy Scriptures into the common language of the people so that they could read the Word of God is to be highly commended and should be deeply appreciated by all.

13

The Council of Ephesus – 431

*T*HE Roman Empire was faced with two lethal threats at this juncture in history. One was the various Germanic peoples from the north. Many of these had embraced Arian beliefs when the Arians and semi-Arians leaders were banished into their northern kingdoms. These deposed ecclesiastics carried their heretical brand of Christianity with them and converted many in Germania. Growing in population and internally restless, Germanic hordes crossed the frozen Rhine River and began migrating south into sparse and less populated regions of the Empire carrying their heresies with them. Emboldened by their numerical advantage, they attacked Constantinople and ransacked Rome (410). Orthodoxy was again under pressure from an old heresy.

Meanwhile, plaguing the empire was the second threat of doctrinal schism and church infighting. The great Ecumenical

Councils of Nicaea and Constantinople definitively settled the biblical teaching concerning the triune nature of God: one God made known in three Persons. The new conflicts revolved around the nature and person of Christ. Certain beliefs about Christ were settled with the defeat of Apollinarianism at the Council of Constantinople; at this time a new menace concerning the Person of Christ appeared on the horizon.

Nestorius, a scholarly monk, became bishop of Constantinople in 428. His teaching brought about the next great ecumenical council – the Council of Ephesus in 431. The controversy that brought about the council began innocently when an Antiochene presbyter, brought to the capital by Nestorius, preached against using the word *Theotokos* when speaking of Mary, the mother of Jesus. For over a century, the word had been used in the prayers of the Eastern Church by such early fathers as Origen, Athanasius, and Gregory of Nazianzus, to mention a few. Its meaning, at least in the minds of the common people, was that Mary was the mother of God. Actually, the Greek word means '*God-bearer*,' and in that case, Mary was such; she carried in her womb and gave birth to God manifested in the flesh. Herein lies the problem.

By this time, two schools of theology had slowly emerged and developed among the orthodox after Nicaea. Leo Donald Davis captures precisely the overall picture:

> Just as all philosophers are said to be basically either Aristotelian or Platonist, so roughly speaking, all theologians are in Christology either Antiochene, beginning with the Jesus of the Synoptic Gospels [Matthew, Mark, Luke] and attempting to explain how this man is also God, or Alexandrian, beginning with the Word of John's Prologue [1:1–14] and attempting to understand the implications of the Logos [God] taking flesh.

It may appear on the surface today to be a simple and minor tension that is easily settled by realizing that it is not an either-or situation, but a balanced understanding and appropriation of both. For the men of that day, however, it was not that simple. The Alexandrians wanted to maintain the full deity (i.e., Godhood) of Jesus against the Arians, and they had a sturdy example in Athanasius, who insisted that only God could save. Conversely, the Antiochenes wanted to ensure the full humanity of Jesus, who was one *for* us because He was one *with* us and one *of* us; such teaching they believed was lost in the Arian controversy.

Thus, for the Alexandrians, to attack Mary as the mother of God was (in their thinking) to attack the deity of Christ. Contrariwise, to the Antiochenes, for anyone to espouse Mary as the mother of God was to deny the full manhood of Jesus. What is regrettable about the whole affair is that if good men on both sides had sat down together and amicably and biblically discussed the theological tensions, the Council of Ephesus, the following twenty years of turmoil within the church, and the next Ecumenical Council (Chalcedon) could have been avoided, and the church could have gone forward with Christ's commission. Sadly, political covetousness, personality clashes, and regional rivalries kept this from happening.

Bishop Nestorius came to the defense of his presbyter and took this issue farther. He preached and taught extensively on the subject, championing the word *Christotokos* (Christ-bearer). In his writings, he staunchly defended the Creed of Nicaea, and even clearly articulated that Christ possessed two natures (God and man). However, he became so technical in his writings defending the true humanity of Christ that he lost his way and became unclear in certain points. Simply stated, Nestorius believed that Christ was God, but only as a perfect man who was morally linked to deity. He was a God-bearer rather than the God-man. Nestorius desired to bring out the true humanity of Christ and, in the exegetical sense, he was successful. His laudable attempt to preserve intact and complete the two natures of Christ was to his credit. Nevertheless, he went overboard. The end result of his teaching was that Christ, in effect, had two natures because He was actually *two* persons. On the contrary, God is one in three persons, not four.

Cyril, Bishop of Alexandria, like his corrupt, hard, and ambitious uncle Theophilus, saw this as an opportunity to advance the See of Alexandria above the Imperial See of Constantinople. (A 'See' is the area or sphere of a bishop's authority.) He jealously attacked Nestorius by writing maligning letters to the Bishops of Rome and Ephesus and to the emperor. The controversy came to a boiling point, and the emperor called for a council of bishops to meet in Ephesus.

Amidst much church in-fighting and struggle, the Council convened in Ephesus on Pentecost Sunday 431, with 197 bishops eventually attending. A settlement could not be reached, so the emperor finally dispatched an imperial envoy, Count John, to settle the controversy. Count John adroitly navigated the troubled waters and drew up a *Formula of Union* that almost everyone eventually accepted. It reads as follows:

> We confess, therefore, our Lord Jesus Christ, the only-begotten of God, perfect God and perfect Man, consisting of a rational soul and a body begotten of the Father before the ages as touching his Godhead, the same, in these last days, for us and our salvation, born of the Virgin Mary, as touching his Manhood; the same

of one substance with the Father as touching his Godhead, and of one substance with us as touching his Manhood. For of two natures a union has been made. For this cause we confess one Christ, one Son, one Lord.

In accordance with this sense of the unconfused union, we confess the holy Virgin to be Theotokos, because God the Word became incarnate and was made man, and from the very conception united to himself the temple taken from her. And as the expressions concerning the Lord in the Gospels and Epistles, we are aware that theologians understand some as common, as relating to one Person, and others they distinguish, as relating to two natures, explaining those that befit the divine nature according to the Godhead of Christ, and those of a humble sort according to his Manhood. (as qtd. in Davis, *The First Seven Ecumenical Councils*)

The Council of Ephesus reaffirmed the biblical truth that Christ was *one* Person with two natures. It condemned Nestorius' writings, deposed him of his bishopric, and (at his own suggestion) banned Nestorius. Nestorius eventually settled in a monastery in the Egyptian deserts surrounded by rivals and enemies. Was he a heretic? Most theologians believe he was a sincere and humble believer in Christ, but muddled in his thinking. Nestorius was not heard from again for over twenty years until he sent a letter strongly affirming the *Definition* of the Council of Chalcedon of 451.

14

The Council of Chalcedon – 451

*T*HE first three centuries of Christianity's theological struggles and debates centered on the person of Jesus Christ. Was He a god or God? Did He only appear to be a man, or was He actually a man? If He was God, how could He be a man? If He was a man, how could He really be God? What kind of man was He? Did He have one nature or two? Was He two persons or one Person? These questions may appear simplistic or even irrelevant to us, but to the Christians in the early days of their religion, they were of indispensable importance, and, rightly so! They had cast the salvation of their eternal souls upon the correct answers.

We shift now to the Council of Chalcedon, which, historians have noted, came in the middle and not at the end of these Trinitarian and Christological debates. The Council of Ephesus only created a fragile and smoldering unity. Beneath the surface, agitated church leaders fumed and schemed to have their positions gain the ascendancy and become the official church doctrine of the empire.

Thus far, we have seen three heretics: Arius, who denied the deity and Trinitarian equality of the Son with the Father; Apollinarius, who denied that Christ had a real and reasonable human soul; and Nestorius, who denied that Christ was one Person. Now we are introduced to another heretic by the name of Eutyches, a distinguished celibate who was leader of three hundred monks in Constantinople. He was, no doubt, a pious man, but in the realms of theology, he was well out of his league. His aged mind often betrayed him, which made his beliefs and writings confused and tangled. Certainly, he embraced Apollinarianism as orthodox, but with a different twist. Eutyches' notions are well-summarized by Leo Donald Davis:

> [B]efore the Incarnation Christ was of two natures, but after it there was one Christ ... one *hypostasis* [substance] and one *prosopon* [person] ... He [Eutyches] repudiated the existence of two natures after the Incarnation as opposed to the Scriptures and the Fathers ... However, the flesh of Christ was not in his view consubstantial with ordinary human flesh. Yet, he acknowledged that Christ's humanity was a full humanity, not lacking a rational soul, as it was for the Apollinarians. Nor was Christ's humanity a mere appearance as it was for the Docetists. Nor were the Word and flesh fused into a mixed nature.

Does that sound confusing? It was to the early church fathers. Most scholars think that Eutyches was saying that Christ's body was not a genuine human body, but a divine one unlike any other. Swept away by an imprecise terminology and an over-emphasis on the deity of Christ, he essentially denied the real humanity of

Christ. His view is known as Eutychianism. He was defrocked, and his teachings were condemned.

Again, what is heartbreaking is that political intrigue, maliciously mingled with biblical truth and churchly activities, caused further turmoil with the church and empire. Church leaders became so jealous of ecclesiastical jurisdiction and geographical prominence that the truth about Jesus the Christ almost took second place. Once more, Alexandrian and Antiochene Christologies butted heads. Though Eutychian teaching emerged and reared its ugly head in the Eastern Church, bishops from every metropolitan center throughout the empire soon became embroiled in the controversy. Included in the number was Leo I (the Great) of Rome, who wrote a magnificent treatise balancing the exegetical truths of the Councils of Nicaea, Constantinople, and Ephesus. It is known historically as Leo's *Tome* and became the biblical and foundational teaching on the person of Christ in the Western Catholic and Protestant churches of today. Notable is Leo's uncommon precision in his beautifully balancing of truth:

> He who became man in the form of a servant is He who in the form of God created man ... Thus, in the whole and perfect nature of true manhood true God was born – complete in what belonged to Him, complete in what belonged to us ... one and the same mediator between God and man, the man Jesus Christ, should be able both to die in respect of the one and not to die in respect to the other ... Each form accomplishes in concert with the other what is appropriate to it, the Word performing what belongs to the Word, and the flesh carrying out what belongs to the flesh ... by reason of this unity of person to be understood in both natures, the Son of Man is said to have come down from heaven when

the Son of God took flesh from the Virgin from whom He was born; and again the Son of God is said to have been crucified and buried, though He suffered those things not in the Godhead itself, wherein the Only Begotten is coeternal and consubstantial with the Father, but in the weakness of human nature. (from Letter 38 in *NPNF*)

Angry at Leo's *Tome* and unscrupulously ambitious, Bishop Dioscurus (nephew and successor to Cyril of Alexandria) contrived a council at Ephesus in 449. It refused to have Leo's *Tome* read and blindly exonerated and restored Eutyches. Furthermore, it sought to establish Cyril's slogan (which he erroneously attributed to Athanasius) of 'One Incarnate Nature of the Divine Word' as the official doctrine of the church. Leo responded by gathering a synod in Rome that annulled the proceedings led by Dioscurus in Ephesus. Leo dubbed the Ephesian gathering the 'Robber Council.'

So great was the turbulence for the next twenty months that the newly crowned Emperor Marcian intervened. In September 451, he called for a council of bishops to settle, once and for all, the disunity of the empire and to write a statement of faith to that end. It convened in October at Chalcedon, just across the Bosporus from Constantinople. Over five hundred bishops assembled to correct and properly state the biblical teaching on the true nature of Christ. The bishops met in six sessions, which lasted almost the entire month and brought a relative and temporary peace to the empire.

What did this fourth ecumenical council do and what was its major accomplishment? It rejected and reversed the findings of the 'Robber Council,' deposed Dioscurus, and condemned Eutyches and his teachings. Ecclesiastical canons (laws) were passed that added to the already growing tension between East and West. However, its major accomplishment, at least for a majority, was to establish and transmit a Christology that was exegetically balanced and in beautiful harmony with the Holy Scriptures. The council set forth, in what is known as *The Definition of Chalcedon*, a glorious Christ that was complete in Godhead and complete in manhood, truly God and truly man, having two natures (for the full text see Appendix III). These two natures were brought together harmoniously in one Person with one essence by the Incarnation. Following the term 'two natures,' the bishops used a series of four Greek negative adverbs 'without confusion, without change, without division, without separation' to not only combat all the previous heretics, but to express how mysterious and incomprehensible was their subject matter. This delightful formulation and definition did not unravel every minute Christological knot, but it did establish the biblical view of all orthodox Christianity on this point since the time of the council. Unfortunately, this would be the last ecumenical council recognized by both the East and West.

EVERAL months passed before the *Definition of Chalcedon* reached the metropolitan centers and remote regions of the Roman Empire. When it reached all the churches, they realized that the fathers, in issuing the *Definition*, accomplished a feat of skill and great diplomacy while preserving truth. In affirming 'one and the same Christ,' along with the first two negative assertions ('without confusion, without change'), the fathers nodded towards Alexandria. On the other hand, strongly emphasizing the two real natures of Christ and insisting it was necessary to maintain His full humanity as well as His full deity, the second pair of negative assertions ('without division or separation') leaned toward Antioch. Most were satisfied and a little stunned, but pleased. Silence pervaded most of the Empire. However, there were two extreme groups on opposite sides of the issue. Each contended that the *Definition* made too ny concessions to the other side and did not go far enough in untying the theological knots regarding the Person of Christ. Though letters of complaints flew around, a relative peace held for a short while.

Eventually, the two extreme groups would no longer hold back, and a massive conflict erupted. For almost one hundred years, the battle raged. Once again, the point of controversy centered upon the Person of Christ. The reader may be asking at this point, 'What's the big deal? Why is it so important whether Christ did or did not have a human soul?' or 'What difference does it make if Christ was one Person or two or if He had one nature or two?' Many today think that if one simply believes in Jesus, that is all that matters. The early church fathers knew better. John the beloved apostle left specific instructions concerning belief about Christ: 'Everyone who goes on ahead and does not abide in the teaching [doctrine] of Christ, does not have God. Whoever abides in the teaching [doctrine] has both the Father and the Son. If anyone comes to you and does not bring this teaching, do not receive him into your house or give him any greeting' (2 John 9-10). As the old, but pithy, poem reminds us, 'What think ye of Christ? This is the test. If you're wrong about Him, you'll be wrong about the rest.' Though these grand controversies about the Person of Christ could quickly disintegrate into personal vendettas, political intrigue, or ecclesiastical power-grabbing, they were centered upon the right subject. It was not then, nor is it today, that simply choosing to believe in Jesus is all that matters. If one is to be saved and enter heaven at last, there must be faith in the Jesus Christ that is revealed in Holy Scripture, not the Jesus Christ of one's imagination or personal preference! The early church leaders understood this. Thus, these great controversies, of necessity, took place.

What ignited this fifth ecumenical council? The answer takes us back to the third ecumenical Council of Ephesus and the Nestorian controversy. Nestorius was wrong about Christ being two persons, but he was right about Christ having two natures (human and divine). There emerged from Bishop Cyril of Alexandria those who firmly held that Christ had only one nature, which was the divine. They did not deny that Christ had humanity, but they believed it was a *divine* humanity; it was not a thorough, genuinely human humanity such as we possess. They were called monophysites (from the Greek *mono* meaning 'one' and *physis* meaning 'nature'). The monophysites were closely aligned with Eutyches, who propounded that there was only *one* divine nature in the Incarnate Word. Outwardly, the monophysites opposed Eutyches, yet inwardly, many were sympathetic to his teachings. Without trying to confuse the reader, it could be stated that all Eutychians were monophysites, but not all monophysites were Eutychian. Monophysites refused to accept the declaration of Chalcedon, arguing that it was Nestorian, and stubbornly maintained the 'One Nature' theology.

While the monophysites were close to the orthodox position in staunchly defending the deity or Godhood of Christ, they were unorthodox in denying His actual humanity. Was Jesus truly a man subject to the same temptations and pressures as the rest of us? Did Jesus actually grow so tired and weary that He fell asleep while sailing on a boat, or did He just go through the motions of pretending to sleep (see Mark 4:38)? Did He really become hungry and actually eat to sustain physical strength, or was it again Jesus simply appearing to be a man? Did Jesus in fact think and act in the same way as other people, without sin or sinning, or was it all just a show (see Heb. 4:15)? These were questions that must be answered if the controversy was to cease.

Three dead theologians who endeavored to answer these questions almost two centuries earlier were the center of attention during the Council. They were Theodore of Mopsuestia (350–428), Theodoret of Cyrus (393–466), and Ibas of Edessa (d. 457), and their writings were known as *The Three Chapters*. Distinctly Antiochene and closely aligned with Nestorius, their writings defended a real and genuine humanity of Christ. The monophysites, desiring to shake the authority of Chalcedon, attacked *The Three Chapters*. Since it is easier to attack men who are dead than those who are alive and can answer back, the deceased theologians were easy prey. Because Emperor Justinian, like emperors before him, wanted to keep unity in the empire and reconcile the estranged monophysites, he called a council. Many questioned his theological allegiance to Chalcedon and his motives in attacking the three leading Antiochene theologians who opposed the 'One Nature' doctrine of the monophysites.

The council convened on May 5, 553, for over a month, with 165 bishops in attendance. The majority of the bishops were from the East. Vigilius, the Bishop of Rome and an outspoken critic of the 'One Nature' teaching, was conspicuously absent. The council did not repudiate Chalcedon, but by condemning the leading Antiochene theologians and their *The Three Chapters*, it issued an indirect challenge to Chalcedon. No formal creed or canons were published, but the council did produce fourteen anathemas against *The Three Chapters*.

The following year, Justinian forced the Bishop of Rome to grudgingly acquiesce to those denunciations. The West correctly understood Justinian's actions in calling the council and his ensuing actions to be a subtle attack upon Antiochene theology and the *Definition of Chalcedon*. It failed to reconcile the monophysites with the rest of the orthodox churches and was never recognized as a true ecumenical council by the West.

Why then is the Second Council of Constantinople considered a world-changing event when it failed to bring unity and left Christianity divided over the Person of Christ? First, it fueled increased division between East and West. The East, heavily influenced by Cyril of Alexandria's 'One Nature' theology, arrogantly isolated itself from those who disagreed. Rome fervently embracing Leo's *Tome* and championing Chalcedon, voiced widespread opposition, and looked suspiciously on the East. Second, it generated a split within Orthodoxy itself. Today, there are several monophysite denominations that reject the *Definition of Chalcedon* and refuse communion with the Orthodox, Roman Catholic, or Protestant Churches, though they still retain the name *orthodox*. They are the Armenian Orthodox, the Syrian Orthodox, the Coptic Orthodox, the Malabarese Orthodox (Indian in origin), and the Ethiopian Orthodox Churches. Third, it represented an unbiblical, imbalanced, and confusing view of Christ. Monophysite theologians, fearful of undermining the deity of Christ, rejected His real humanity and thus presented to the world an improper view of the Savior. These tensions are to be reckoned with even now.

16

The First Universal Pope, Gregory the Great – 590

SIMPLICITY was the hallmark of the first Christian churches. The only historical book of the New Testament, the Book of Acts, records the pattern of apostolic church government. Paul the apostle started his first missionary journey in Antioch and ended in Asia Minor. As he retraced the steps of his journey back to Antioch, he visited the disciples and churches he recently established (Acts 13–14). The human author of Acts (Luke) adds a most insightful comment: 'And when they had appointed elders [plural] for them in every church [singular] with prayer and fasting they committed them to the Lord in whom they had believed' (Acts 14:23). That pattern is confirmed in the church at Philippi: 'To all the saints in Christ Jesus who are in Philippi, with the bishops and deacons' (Phil. 1:1b NRSV). The apostolic pattern of church governance was simple. There was no multi-level hierarchy of church offices, boards, or committees. Each Christian church was governed by a plurality of elders or bishops *without* outside interference and authoritative control.

By the sixth century, the church had evolved into a monolithic episcopacy (i.e., rule from the top down by bishops). How did such a change take place? As Christianity spread, churches multiplied throughout the empire, even to regions unimaginable. The older, more established churches planted new churches, and the often-inexperienced bishops of the younger, visible churches would look to the older bishops for guidance and counsel. Eventually, the older bishops took on authority that developed into one bishop overseeing a number of regional bishops and churches, which further developed as the bishops of one region recognized an archbishop (i.e., primary geographical bishop) over a body of bishops. The episcopal system took shape as each geographical region had its own bishop or archbishop that ruled over a number of churches or bishoprics. Generally, the bishops jealously guarded their regions (called sees or bishoprics) and did not interfere with matters in other regions. This practice was maintained through the third century. Cyprian, Bishop of Carthage (martyred 258), replied to Bishop Stephen of Rome, after Stephen attempted to interfere with ecclesiastical matters in Carthage:

> For neither does any of us set himself up as a bishop of bishops, nor by tyrannical terror does any compel his colleague to the necessity of obedience; since every bishop, according to the allowance of his liberty and power, has his own proper right of judgment, and can no more be judged by another than he himself can judge another. But let us all wait for the judgment of our Lord Jesus Christ, who is the only one that has the power both of

116

preferring us in the government of His Church, and of judging us in our conduct there. (ANF vol. 5, p. 565)

The rise of bishops (episcopacy) led to an ever-present controversy among the Orthodox, Roman Catholics, and Protestants. Very early in Christian history, especially after the Council of Chalcedon (451), the Bishop of Rome assumed a primacy among the churches, to the point that today, billions around the world watch on television the election and installation of a new pope. How did this happen?

It began with the belief of a monk named Gregory. He embraced the growing consensus that because the apostles Peter and Paul were martyred in Rome under Emperor Nero (A.D. 64–67), the Bishop of Rome was (by divine right) the Head of all the [Christian] churches. Gregory crafted his belief from the writings of bishops Stephen and Leo and their commentaries on Matthew 16:18, in which they interpreted this passage to mean the church was founded upon Peter and his successors, not Christ.

Gregory was born into Roman nobility. After he became a Christian, he founded several monasteries and eventually became a monk. His piety and prudence were so well known that the Bishop of Rome summoned Gregory into diplomatic service for the church, a service he performed with distinction. Upon the bishop's death, Gregory was elected and installed as the new bishop. He became known as Gregory I (590–604). Immediately, he consolidated spiritual power and authority over other bishops in various regions. He was reputed to be a devout student of Scripture and a serious expositor and preacher. His commentary on the Book of Job, with his three-fold method of exegesis (literal, mystical, moral), became the standard for medieval preaching. He sought to reform worship and regulated the holy day celebrations of the Christian year. He loved to sing and promoted music in the church. His influence on sacred music is still in vogue, and his name is lent to the plain-song style of 'Gregorian chants.'

Since the days when Constantine moved the capital of the empire from Rome to Constantinople, the Western emperors were mostly weak and had accomplished very little. The imperial delegates from the East failed miserably to maintain Rome's dignity and strength, until the city set on 'seven hills' was overrun and sacked by the Visigoths in 410. More and more, the people looked to their Christian bishops for leadership in the governmental realm.

When the Western emperor of Gregory's time died, a great vacuum was created. Gregory stepped in and started to function in the political arena. What is most interesting is that for the first time in history, the bishop appeared as the political power, a temporal prince. He appointed governors to cities, directed complex negotiations with the Roman emperor in Constantinople, reformed the finances of both the church and state, issued orders to generals, provided munitions of war, supervised Rome's defenses and fortifications, sent ambassadors to negotiate with the Lombard king, and actually dared to settle a civil peace agreement. In these activities, Gregory went farther than any of his predecessors; he laid the foundation of a political influence which endured for centuries. It is generally recognized that the real father of the papacy is Gregory the Great. Though bishops were often called popes (Latin for *papa* or *father*) prior to his day, Gregory was the first bishop to take the title '***Pontifex Maximus***' (*maximum pope*), a term used centuries earlier and reserved only for the emperor as the head of the pagan state religion. He utilized his title and position to the extreme. Little did Gregory realize that he would be the main agent to lead Christianity, and thus the world, into centuries of darkness called the Middle Ages!

There is little agreement, much less objectivity, in Christianity today over the subject of the pope. Traditional arguments and emotional sentiments often reign over scriptural teachings. Roman Catholics determinedly believe the pope to be the successor of the apostles, especially Peter, the 'Vicar of Christ,' and the universal and earthly head of all Christian churches. The various churches within Orthodoxy, from Greece to Russia, resolutely deny this claim and believe him to be no more than one of a number of patriarchs. Despite the differences among themselves, Protestants are strongly united in their belief that the pope is a usurper and not what he claims. Most of the early Protestant confessions of faith went so far as to state that the pope is 'that antichrist,' or at least an antichrist. Largely due to the unextinguished fires set by the Protestant Reformation, many conservative Protestants understand the passages in the Book of Revelation referring to 'the great harlot who sits on many waters' (NASB) as the Roman Catholic institution (17:1-6) and the beast having 'seven heads and ten horns, and on his horns ten crowns' (13:1 NKJV) as the pope. A quick glance at Internet sites will reveal how sharply the debate continues and how intense the arguments are. Regardless of the reader's view of the pope in Christian history, the Roman Catholic pontificate cannot be ignored, and Gregory laid that foundation.

17

The Third Council of Constantinople – 680

*T*HE next world-changing event focused once more on the Person of Christ. Surprisingly, a survey of available historical resources reveals that most church history books deal very little with this Council or with the ensuing period through the Second Council of Nicaea in 787 (see event 19). This neglect by many modern students hinders the full clarification and application of the *Definition of Chalcedon*.

One may again ask, 'Why such a fuss over a less-esteemed period and small, technical details about Jesus? Isn't it enough to simply believe in Jesus?' Yes, without a doubt. However, it must be emphatically asked, 'Which Jesus?' Is one talking about the Jesus the Muslims believe in, who was nothing more than a prophet of Allah, or the Jesus the Jehovah's Witnesses believe in, who was the archangel Michael, or the Jesus the Mormons believe in, who was the firstborn son of God the Father and

God the Mother and brother to Satan, or the Jesus the early-twentieth-century liberals espoused, who was a good moral example of what it is to live sacrificially for God, or is one talking about the Jesus of the Holy Bible? While many confess the name of Jesus, not all who confess Jesus believe in the same Jesus. This is not to say that there are many Jesuses, but, contrary to postmodern thought, in order to be saved there must be faith in the Jesus that is divinely revealed in the Holy Scriptures; otherwise, the faith is not in Jesus at all, and there is no salvation. The early church fathers understood the indispensable necessity of making this point clear to the entire world.

The Second Council of Constantinople (553) was not enough to satisfy the extreme monophysites. They not only continued their battle against orthodoxy by stating that Christ the Incarnate Word had only one nature, but went further and dogmatized that the Savior had only one will: the divine will. Hence, there arose in the extended development of biblical Christology the Monothelite Controversy (Gk. *mono*, 'one,' and *thelema*, 'will'). What was the controversy all about, how did it begin, and, more importantly, what world-changing impact did it have?

The theological issues at stake in this controversy are not unlike those in the Monophysite Controversy, but added a nuance that has great bearing on human salvation. The central concern became: was Jesus a robot – an automaton – who mechanically and coldly went about doing good and accomplishing the work of salvation; or did He do so with a real, personal, passionate, God-delighting will? As the God-Man, did Jesus have a rational soul and genuine human emotions? If so, then did He not have a rational and genuine human will? The Council of Chalcedon declared that He did, but the monophysites and, subsequently, the monothelites argued that He did not. Monophysite Christology placed an emphasis on the operations or energies (*energeiai*) in Christ. They adamantly believed that there was a distinction between what a being or nature was and what it could do. Simply stated, they did *not* believe that Jesus thought, felt, or acted in the same way as other humans. The eternal Logos or Word (John 1:1), they insisted, allowed Jesus to have only one consciousness and one will, which was divine and not at all human. To the monothelites, the actions of Jesus' human body were nothing more than the manifestation of decisions taken by the divine will, the Logos. What was at stake here was not the deity of Christ, but His humanity; the reality of Jesus's authentic manhood was radically called into question.

As with almost every event and belief in Christian history, human politics played a crucial role in shaping this one. In 638, the Emperor Heraclius attempted conciliation, looking for common ground between the heterodox monophysites and the orthodox Chalcedonians. Like all political leaders, he knew religious division within a kingdom or country would eventually lead to national and cultural division, and that Heraclius did not want. Unity, not biblical truth, was his goal. Influenced by the patriarch of Constantinople, the emperor issued a position paper entitled *Ecthesis*. In it, he maintained the 'two natures' doctrine of Chalcedon, but decreed that the incarnate Christ had only one will. The West rejected the *Ecthesis*, and the East was too busy defending against Muslim encroachments to take much notice.

The next forty-two years saw unusual political and ecclesi-astical jousting and shifting of power. Emperor succeeded emperor, governors with religious authority were relocated, and bishops were deposed and restored. Division, not unity, reigned. After his father, Constans II, was assassinated in his bath, Constantine IV (668–685) became the new emperor and decided to bring the disunity to a halt. He ordered his new patriarch of Constantinople and the patriarch of Antioch to assemble all their bishops and call an ecumenical council, which convened on September 10, 680. After eighteen sessions, the bishops issued and signed a *Definition of Faith*, which was signed last by the emperor amid shouts of acclamation. They concluded their *Definition* with these words: 'Wherefore we confess two wills and two operations, concurring most fitly in Him [Christ] for the salvation of the human race' (see Appendix IV). Monotheletism, along with its spiritual father monophysitism, was condemned at the Council and, thereafter, died a quick death.

What the monothelites seemingly forgot were two important New Testament passages: John 5:30b (cf. 6:38 - NKJV) and Luke 22:42. In the first, Jesus declares at the beginning of His ministry, that 'I do not seek My own will but the will of the Father who sent Me.'(NKJV) This denotes that Jesus had a will of His own. Second, if that is not clear enough, what Jesus prayed in the Garden of Gethsemane is conclusive. Three times on that fateful night Jesus prayed, 'Father, if it be Your will, take this cup away from Me; nevertheless, not My will, but Yours, be done.'(NKJV) Yes, there was a divine will in the God-Man, but there was also a human will. The two wills did not constitute two Persons, but ratified the orthodox teachings that could be traced all the way back to Nicaea – that Christ Jesus the Lord was one Person with two natures.

The significance and glory for orthodox Christians is that Christ did *not* obey the Law and go to the cross in a numb, unthinking, and unmotivated way. He was not mechanically manipulated like someone would control a figure in a video game. Instead, in His human will, Jesus submitted to the divine will and personally, genuinely, joyfully, and willingly went to His cruel death, as a substitute on the cross, and obtained eternal redemption for those who believe. The writer of Hebrews is quick to remind us that we do not have a High Priest that cannot be touched with the feeling of our infirmities, but was in all points tempted like we are, yet without sin (see Heb. 4:15). He feels our woes and sorrows, our triumphs and joys, because God manifested in the flesh was a real Man; one willingly *of* us, willing *with* us, and willingly *for* us. This is what the Third Council of Constantinople established when it condemned the monothelites and affirmed that Christ had two wills. Never forget, Christian history teaches that a biblical Christology is not only important, but imperative to saving Christianity.

18

The Battle of Tours – 732

*W*HAT does a battle that took place almost thirteen hundred years ago in a remote mountain gap just north of the Spanish border in France have to do with Christianity? Very few in the western world have a clue. Furthermore, why is English the predominate language in the West and, indeed, the world? No matter where a person travels in the world, even to its remotest regions, there will always be found someone who speaks English. Why is Arabic not the predominate language of the world? The one answer to these questions is simple – the Battle of Tours.

The reader cannot understand the significance of this battle without knowing a little of the origin and growth of the Muslim religion. An obscure religious young man named Mohammed had a vision. He recorded his vision(s) in a book known as the *Qur'an* (*Koran*). This new faith was an unsophisticated religious system, in contrast to Judaism and Christianity, but very legalistic. His religious ideas and book caused no small stir in his native city of Mecca, capital of present-day Saudi Arabia. He and his small band of followers (mostly family members) fled from Mecca to Medina in 622. His flight is known and revered by Muslims as the Hegira. This is the traditional date of the birth of Islam. Mohammed was a crafty plotter and, by the time of his death in 632, the new faith had spread quickly throughout the Mediterranean. The object of worship in their new religion was one all-powerful, all-merciful God – Allah – and Mohammed was his prophet.

Historians acknowledge that the swift expansion of Islam is one of the most astonishing events in human history. How did it happen? Was it because of conversion through love and hope? Through skilled diplomacy and peace treaties? No! Its rapid rise came primarily by fear and cruel subjugation by the sword: one either submitted to the Muslim God Allah or was killed. The meaning of the Arabic word *islam* is *submission* or *surrender*. Much blood was shed to propagate the religion of Mohammed. Within a few decades, the Arab armies sent probing incursions into the Byzantine Empire and Persia and, finding military weakness in decadent 'Christian' societies, conquered kingdom after kingdom. Within one hundred years, Islam had control of much of northern Africa and eastern and southern Europe.

Upon the historical scene arrived a group known as the Moors. They were Islamic Saracens that led a westward and northward expansion into southwestern Europe. Islam was heady, almost drunken, with military conquest. So successful had the earlier Muslims been in expanding their religion through the power of the sword, they believed they were unstoppable and would shortly engulf the world with the religion of Mohammed. Boldly and with confident abandon, the Moors ventured from northern Africa across the Straits of Gibraltar into Spain (711). By 730, they had conquered most of Spain, except for small enclaves of resistance, and were setting their sights on the northern kingdom of the Franks (France).

In 732, a Moorish force of between 75,000 and 100,000 under the leadership of Caliph Abd-ar-Rahman advanced north toward the River Loire. The Caliph intended to pillage the riches of the Abbey of St Martin near Tours, which was the holiest and most prestigious shrine in western Europe at the time. He encountered little resistance, until he met the army of Charles, the illegitimate son of Pepin, Mayor of the palace of Austrasia, and the *de facto* ruler of the Frankish kingdom. Upon learning of the Islamic force headed towards him, Charles assembled an army of between 15,000 and 60,000 (exact numbers are not known) and marched to proverbially 'cut them off at the pass.' Charles led his troops into the direct path of the Moors and marshaled his army on the higher, mountainous grounds outside of Tours, a town near present-day Poitiers. It was if he were saying, 'This far and no farther!'

It would be an interesting battle, because the Moors were almost entirely cavalry and the Franks were almost entirely infantry. Historically, seldom has an army of foot soldiers defeated a throng of armed horsemen. Charles had all odds against him. However, he was a brilliant battlefield tactician and kept his disciplined soldiers in a virtually impenetrable phalanx. The battle began on October 10, and armed only with swords, axes, shields, javelins, and daggers, against the spears, chain mail, and slashing sabers of the mounted Moors, the Franks repelled charge after charge and actually penetrated the enemy lines. On the last day of battle, the Franks killed the Caliph Abd-ar-Rahman, and the Moors retreated. Charles prepared for surprise retaliation, but it never came. Scouts reported the next morning that the Moors had retreated into Spain, never to advance again into Europe. After the battle, Charles was given the name *Martel* (*the hammer*), probably reminiscent of Judas Maccabeus ('the hammerer') of the ancient Jewish Maccabean revolt against the Greeks.

Thus, Charles Martel defeated the Moors at the Battle of Tours in 732. What is the significance of this battle? Politically, for the Muslim Caliphs, Tours was the high-water mark of Islamic expansion into Europe. Though the Moors would eventually settle in southern Spain, and it would be another seven hundred years before they were entirely driven from the Iberian Peninsula (and Europe), it was at Tours that the tide was turned.

Militarily, most Europeans of the time fought as unarmored infantry. Tours was one of those rare instances when foot soldiers withstood and actually defeated cavalry armies. Martel did not rest on his laurels. He developed a horsed army and became the father of the mounted, armored knights in medieval times. The Hammer learned quickly and borrowed wisely from his defeated foe. With ingenuity he retooled and utilized the stirrup and mailed armor. Furthermore, he fathered the modern concept of 'strike first,' that is, 'take the battle to the enemy,' rather than wait for the enemy to attack (the conventional wisdom of the day). Also, he modeled the necessity and set the standard for a disciplined, well-trained army. The early Romans defeated many of the invading Germanic hordes because the Germanic armies were undisciplined and thought little of strategy, except that of overwhelming their enemies with numbers. Martel changed that antiquated concept!

Religiously, some modern historians have down-played the battle's importance by stating that Tours has been exaggerated in human and Christian history. However exaggerated the battle might be in terms of size of armies and days of fighting, it cannot be slighted or disdained. The overwhelming majority of historical scholars consider the battle to be 'of macrohistorical importance.' Deceased scholar and historian Edward Gibbon represented the majority opinion and contended correctly 'that had Martel fallen, the Moors would have easily conquered a divided Europe.' He elaborates on the potential results of an Islamic victory:

> [It] would have carried the Saracens to the confines of Poland and the Highlands of Scotland; ... [and later] the Arabian fleet might have sailed without a naval combat into the mouth of the Thames. Perhaps the interpretation of the Qur'an would now be taught in the schools of Oxford, and her pulpits might demonstrate to a circumcised people the sanctity and truth of the revelation of Mahomet [Mohammed]. (vol. 7, p. 13)

Does the reader now understand why this event was world-changing in Christian history? The inestimable victory of Charles the Hammer at Tours in 732 kept Islam from coming into Europe and assured the prominence of Christianity and the gospel of Jesus Christ in the western world.

19

The Second Council of Nicaea – 787

*H*OW are believers to imagine Christ in their minds? Was He tall or short? Did there appear a glow or halo about Him, or did He look like any other normal human being? Was the color of His hair dark or blond? Did He wear a beard or was He clean-shaven? What did Jesus look like? And what of Mary? Was she thin or stocky, young or old? Did she have a fair complexion or was she wrinkled with age? These were questions that lurked in the minds of people in the first few centuries after Christ's ascension; indeed, they often cross the minds of thinking people today.

Christianity was birthed and nursed with Old Testament de-nunciations of graven images ringing in its ears (see Exod. 20:4-6; cf. Ps. 115:1-8). This message roared from the pages of the Old Testament into the lives and writings of Paul and other New Testament authors (Acts 17:24-25; Rom. 1:22-25, et al). That false gods were not to be worshiped was certain; conversely, the true and living God must not be worshiped through the means of images.

This Second Commandment of the Decalogue was renounced before Christianity's very eyes by the veneration of pagan idols and images of the Greek and Roman cultures. Statues of Jupiter (Zeus) and numerous other Greek and Roman deities were scattered across the landscapes of the ancient Mediterranean world. Artisans who had been converted to Christ could be found, but the commandment restrained them from making statues, mosaics or paintings of God or Christ. The first mention of images or idols in Christian history is from Irenaeus, in his highly significant writing against the Gnostics entitled *Against Heresies*. He associates any likeness of Christ with Gnosticism. The next to mention the issue is the historian Eusebius of Caesarea (c. 265–339), a close friend and confidant to the Emperor Constantine. In his work entitled *Church History*, Eusebius describes the emperor at the Council of Nicaea as 'like some heavenly messenger of God.' Constantine's sister (Constantia) had asked Eusebius for a portrait of Christ. He writes to the Emperor in reply:

> Had she ever seen anything of the kind in a church or heard of such a thing from another? Was it not rather true that in the whole world anything of the kind was banished and excluded from the churches? Was it not common knowledge that it was only for the Christian that such things were forbidden? (Hastings, vol. 1, p. 315)

Eusebius' reply reflected the mindset of the early church, which is confirmed by the art historian Michael Gough in his *The Origins of Christian Art*: 'Very few episodes drawn from the life of Christ exist from pre-Constantinian times, and the Passion and Crucifixion seem to have been almost totally excluded.' Epiphanius, Bishop of Salamis (c. 315–403), wrote three treatises against images and sent them to his fellow bishops and the Emperor Theodosius I. Jerome would quote Epiphanius in one of his *Letters* to bolster his opposition to images.

Nevertheless, beginning in the late sixth century, Christian art made its appearance in drawings and pictures of Christ (in all stages of His life), Mary, the mother of Christ, and Mary and the Christ Child. Then, as persecution began to take its toll on the church and believers were killed for their faith, images of the more well-known martyrs (or saints, as they came to be called) appeared in various regions of Christendom. Soon, the appearance of these images spilled over into heated controversy. In the early days, the greatest supporters of using images were the unordained and, oftentimes, overly mystical monks, rather than the presbyters and theologians. Devotion was pitted against theology. Strangely enough, the emperors, who followed the teachings of the early church fathers, were those who most strongly opposed images.

Those who favored images or icons and pictures of Christ and the saints were called Iconodules (Greek – *eikon*, meaning *'image'* and *doulos*, *'servant'*). Pope Gregory and John of Damascus defended the use of images on the grounds that they were 'books' for those who could not read. It was thought that an image was to the sight what words were to the ear: a potential means of teaching in order to bring understanding and enlightenment. Christ had a physical body, they argued; therefore, He can have a physical representation. Furthermore, the defenders reasoned, images aid and strengthen devotion.

Those who opposed accused the defenders of worshiping the image. The iconodules sought to differentiate between veneration and worship, but many thought the line of distinction was too thin, as was evidenced by the habits of kissing, kneeling and prostrating before, and burning incense to the images.

Those who opposed pictures and images of Christ and the saints, in all forms, were called Iconoclasts (Greek – *eikon*, '*image*' and *klastes*, '*breakers*'). The iconoclasts had many reasons for opposing images: 1) the apostles left no drawings or pictures of Christ; thus, all pictures of Him were inaccurate and based upon human imagination; 2) pictures were means of introducing error concerning Christ's two natures and steered people into superstitious thinking and erroneous feelings about Him (e.g., the Byzantine Christ, the Anglo-Saxon Christ, the African Christ, the Asian Christ, the hippy Christ); 3) images or statues led to misguided or false worship; and 4) physical depictions of Christ were stumbling blocks to the conversion of Jews and Muslims. The iconoclasts taught that the only admissible figure of the humanity of Christ is the bread and wine in the Lord's Supper.

The theological debate was intense and rigorous. Iconodules argued that the Second Commandment was divinely set aside by Christ in His incarnation because He was the exact representation of God. Images of Christ, they affirmed, were not idols, but valid representations of a self-revealed God. To deny the use of images was to deny the incarnation. Iconoclasts also strongly affirmed the incarnation and humanity of Christ, but charged that images bypass and misrepresent the deity of Christ and cause people to be confused about His two natures.

They feared that seeing pictures of Jesus would cause people to think of Him only as a mere man.

For almost four centuries, the icon debate was unabating; it simmered slowly at first and then boiled over into a full-blown controversy in the years 725-843. It became known as the Iconoclast Controversy. Imperial decrees against image-worship, which ordered the destruction of all icons throughout the empire, were passed by Emperor Leo III in 725. Constantine V continued the policy and the Council of Hieria sustained the emperors in 753. However, the common people in general and the monks in particular strongly favored images. In 787, the Empress Irene called the seventh and last of the great Ecumenical (worldwide) Councils – the Council of Nicaea II – to settle the controversy. The council condemned the Iconoclasts and ruled in favor of images and allowed them to be venerated. Unsuccessful attempts to undo the council were made during the next fifty-five years. The controversy was finally put to rest by the Empress Theodora in 843.

The significant effects of the council caused a development in sacramental theology, an unhealthy emphasis on Church tradition, and a renewal of religious art. The Eastern Church especially flourished in iconic art and set the standard of how Christ is to be pictured in the visual arena of Christianity. Regardless of one's theological perspective on icons and images of Christ, the Iconoclast Controversy changed the world. Pictures and images of Jesus abound, even in parts of non-Christian societies. Whenever one hears the name 'Jesus,' what image comes to mind? Whatever it is, most likely the image can be traced back to the last Ecumenical Council of Nicaea in 787.

20

Charlemagne Crowned Holy Roman Emperor – 800

*T*HE Iconoclast Controversy created an even deeper distancing between the West and the East. Since the fall of Rome to the Visigoths in 410, western military power was unable to uphold its end of the empire, and the last western emperor was deposed in 476. Then, with Gregory the Great's death, popes and civil leaders became merely figureheads and could not control government or the church (so-called). The chronic disorder of the Middles Ages lay ahead.

In 754, Pope Stephen II of Rome feared there would be no help from Constantinople in the East, which was reeling because of a successful, but draining, resistance of an Islamic siege. The heat and pressure of the rapidly growing Muslim hordes was unrelenting. Therefore, Stephen did the most logical thing in his mind and traveled north to Frankland (most of present-day France and Germany) to seek help. The Franks had converted to Christianity in the seventh century, and Stephen saw in them a possible deliverer. He met with the new Frankish king, Pepin the Short, the son of Charles Martel. Stephen's intentions were to secure protection for the Western Church against the invading Lombards and reestablish papal lands taken by them and the Visigoths.

Pepin was only too ready to forge another coalition to strengthen his throne and quickly agreed to sign a treaty with Stephen. The pope honored Pepin with the title of patrician and made him the Protector of Rome. Within two years, Pepin vanquished the Lombards and captured the region around Rome, which he gave to the pope as the place of papal authority. This area of land became known as the Donation of Pepin and it lasted until 1870; afterwards, it became known as the Papal States, and the Vatican remains its capital.

Pepin died and was succeeded by his illegitimate son, Charles, who murdered the three legitimate sons of Pepin to claim the throne. Charles willingly accepted the position previously held by his father as the Protector of Rome. The insightful observation by Leo Donald Davis is of vast significance in the history of Christianity: 'The religious schism between East and West over iconoclasm had incalculable political and cultural consequences. The papacy turned from its age-old relationship with the emperor of Constantinople to a new alliance with the Carolingian dynasty of Frankland and its king Charles' (*The First Seven Ecumenical Councils*, p. 306). A new path for Christianity was emerging, and its pathfinder is most interesting.

Charles the Great, or Charlemagne, was named after his grandfather Charles Martel, the hero of the Battle of Tours (event #18). Martel was not a king, but the lord mayor of the Merovingian kings' palace, which made him the *de facto* ruler of the Franks. Pepin the Short, Martel's son, overthrew the Merovingian line and became king of a new line known as the Carolingians. Charles, who succeeded his father Pepin in 771, was an imposing figure; a great horseman and a fearless warrior. Though he gave 'lip-service' to the church, he was an outwardly ungodly man (he had ten wives and/or concubines). While he shunned educational studies and never learned to read, he realized the cultural value of education. Scholars and teachers were brought in from all over the known world to establish centers of learning and educate the Frankish people.

When he was crowned king, Charlemagne consolidated the treaties made by his father and chose a path of military advancement. This decision began thirty years of military conquest. He enlarged the borders of his kingdom east, encompassing Bavaria, Burgundy, Alemannia, and much of Italy. He further extended his domain north to include Saxony and Frisia (Holland) and Spain to the west. By the time he was finished, his kingdom stretched from the Baltic Sea to the Adriatic Sea. A large part of Europe, for the first time in its long history, had a strong and stable leadership. Charlemagne was indeed a force with whom other leaders and potentates reckoned; none bypassed or ignored him.

By 800, Pope Leo III and Christianity were in desperate straits. The Lombards had driven the pope out of Rome and into marshy Ravenna. With the division between the East and West growing wider, no help would come from Constantinople. Leo sought refuge in the kingdom of the Franks and was warmly received. Charles assembled an army and escorted the

141

pope back into Rome in mid-December to settle the disputes. At this point in Christian history, December 25 was the well-established observance of Christmas or the celebration of Christ's birth. This Christmas would take an unusual turn that would affect the West for centuries.

In the fourth volume of his *History of Civilization*, Will Durant describes how, on Christmas Day 800, as the day's principal worship service came to an end, Charles, king of the Franks, was praying before the tomb of the apostle Peter. When he arose, Leo moved toward him with a crown in his hand. Eyewitness accounts record 'the venerable holy pontiff with his own hands crowned Charles with a most precious crown' and declared Charles the 'Holy Roman Emperor.' Immediately, the crowd, who had been instructed what to say beforehand, shouted three times, 'To Charles Augustus, crowned by God, great and peace-giving Emperor of the Romans!' In chanting this, the crowd was purposefully commemorating and evoking the glory and majesty of ancient Rome. A new Rome was being built, or at least, the old Rome was being resurrected. Leo was self-serving in his action and cherished the hopes of reviving the old Roman Empire and gaining ascendancy over the East. Though done by religious hands, the act was upon a man who was neither holy nor Roman. Furthermore, while Charlemagne gave the pope his protection, he never gave him his power.

What world-changing effects did this coronation produce? Charlemagne's influence caused Christianity to be settled in Europe, albeit in a nominal form. He took the idea of a church-state, set in motion by Constantine, and stamped it upon the conscience of Europe in the concept of 'Christendom.' Hence, salvation was beginning to be understood as coming only through the sacraments of the church, as they dispensed forgiveness of sins and acceptance with God in a societal structure of equal church and state cooperation. At this point, the church was undecided on the total number of sacraments. It was not until the Fourth Lateran Council in 1215 that the sacraments of the medieval Catholic Church were established as seven (baptism, confirmation, penance, the Eucharist, marriage, extreme unction, and ordination). However, Charlemagne laid the political foundation upon which the theological sacramental system was built. Thus, if a person were a member in good standing of the state, that person was also a member of the church and accepted by God through the sacraments and vice versa. In effect, Christ and His salvation by free grace, without works, were eclipsed by belonging to the church and state. Christendom continued for over a thousand years, and strains of it still survive in Europe and various parts of the world. The title of 'Holy Roman Emperor' became a position kings coveted and schemed to obtain, not for spiritual advancement, but for political advantage. The status of Holy Roman Emperor continued long after the Protestant Reformation until Napoleon permanently abolished the position in 1806. Damaging and toxic effects of that Christmas Day in 800 polluted the streams of Christianity for the next ten centuries, deceiving the masses and turning them from the authentic spiritual life found in Christ alone.

21

Christianization of Russia – 988

RUSSIA is and always has been a gigantic country. It stretches east and west from the Atlantic Ocean to the Pacific, and north and south from the Arctic Circle to the Mediterranean Sea. It possesses ten time zones, and its cold, bitter winters and vast, unforgiving steppes have made it virtually unconquerable. The only group to achieve any success were the Mongol hordes of Genghis Khan in the eleventh century. A history professor once told his class that Russia has two generals that have never been defeated: 'General Mud' and 'General Snow'! Adolph Hitler learned this painful lesson the hard way during World War II, losing over a million soldiers in his invasion of Russia in 1941. However, Russia has been subjugated, but not with swords and guns; it was conquered by Christianity which eventually swept over the entire Russian civilization.

How did this happen? Known throughout European lands as a country of raucous paganism, Rus (as it was then called) was the least likely nation to become Christian. Pagan temples dotted the landscape, and the people were known for their debauchery, cruelty, and treachery. Traders ventured into this wild region of the world by the early part of the tenth century with the Christian message, but had little success. Olga, the widowed princess of Kiev, heard the story of Christianity, professed faith in Christ, and was baptized in 957. She sent word to King Otto I of Germany to send missionaries to her people, but they, too, had slim success. Yet, as Christians have always believed, lack of initial success does not mean permanent failure. God has a way of using the weakest means to bring about a resounding success. On the horizon lurked the most unlikely candidate to bring about gospel triumph in Russia: Prince Vladimir of Kiev, grandson of Olga.

Vladimir, who wrested the kingdom from his two brothers after a fierce civil war, was a base and Faustian man who had five wives and 800 concubines. He loved fighting and making wars, and when he was not on the battlefield, he gave himself over to hunting and feasting, which satisfied his lusts and made his people happy. Yet, he knew war and feasting was not enough and that something vital was missing. The country needed something more substantial to create a lasting happiness and to generate a national unity. Vladimir reckoned that the missing element was religion; paganism was not sufficiently fulfilling. The reports are that he sent men into different parts of the world to investigate the various religions of his day. Very soon, Judaism and Islam were ruled out because of their dietary restrictions. Vladimir loved his pork and other non-kosher foods. The search was eventually narrowed down to one: Christianity. Then the question was raised, which branch should he choose: the western Roman Catholic or the eastern Greek Orthodox? Once more the search was on as Vladimir's trusted advisors went to Rome and to Constantinople, the capital of the Byzantine Empire.

The group that went to Constantinople attended a worship service in the Hagia Sophia (Holy Wisdom Church). By this time, aided by John Chrysostom (d. 407) and John of Damascus (c. 749), the liturgy of the Greek Orthodox Church had developed into a beautiful and God-centered service of worship. Awed and filled with a breathtaking sense of the Divine, the delegation sent back this report to their Prince:

> We do not know whether we were in heaven or on earth, for surely there is no such splendor or beauty anywhere upon earth. We cannot describe it to you. Only we know that God dwells there among men and that their service surpasses the worship of all other places. We cannot forget that beauty. (trans. Cross and Sherbowitz-Wetzor)

To this day, the appeal of Eastern Orthodoxy has been its accentuation on the aesthetic, the beauty of mystery. This captured the mind and emotions of Vladimir's delegation, and they recommended the adoption of Eastern Orthodoxy as the official religion of Russia. Vladimir accepted their recommendation, was baptized in 988, adopted Eastern Orthodox Christianity as his own, and declared it to be the state religion of Russia.

Two core elements brought this about. One was spiritual and the other political. The emphasis and beauty of Orthodoxy's worship were indeed captivating. Vladimir was taken up with the worship and made it plain that in the Russian Orthodox Church, worship would be the primary focus, more than Christian living and practice. It seems that Christianity, to many average Russians, is simply liturgy. Second, the fact that the Byzantine Empire, the center of Eastern Orthodoxy, was Russia's wealthiest, most civilized, and most powerful neighbor tipped the scales of balance. A year after his baptism, Vladimir married Anna, the sister of Basil, the Emperor of the Byzantine Empire. This marriage was not only advantageous to both kingdoms, because it ensured peace for a Christian empire from its warring pagan neighbor to the north, but it solidified unity of spiritual brotherhood and political prosperity.

Baptism had a profound effect upon Vladimir. When he married Anna, he put away his five wives and all his concubines, turned from his philandering ways, destroyed idols, made laws to help the poor, set up schools to educate Russia's young, and built some of the most beautiful church buildings the world had ever seen. Many are still in existence today. Seemingly, Vladimir had become a pious and devout man. Nearing death, he gave all of his earthly possessions and wealth to the poor. He was eventually canonized by the Eastern Church and is known today as St Vladimir.

Although Christianity was now the official religion and Vladimir was a transformed man, things did not change overnight. Mass conversions did not take place as expected. Vladimir enlisted the help of monks, who have always been the most influential entity in Eastern Orthodoxy, and the new religion slowly moved forward, but not at the speed the Prince wanted. Vladimir forced many to accept Christianity, and those who refused were severely punished. The major stumbling block for full acceptance of Christianity in Russia was the Greek language. Then, two monks, Methodius and Cyril, made history. They translated the Greek liturgy into Slavonic, the national language of Russia, which was allowed by the church hierarchy in Constantinople. This radical departure from the Greek allowed Russians to participate fully in their beautiful liturgy using their native tongue, a lesson Rome would not learn for over half a millennium. It took centuries for Christianity to move from the urban centers into the far reaches of the countryside and Russian steppes. But eventually and ostensibly, Russia became a professed Christian nation.

While Christianity certainly expanded due to Russia's conversion, this did not ease the tensions that were building between the East and the West (these shall be studied in the next event). However, it did accomplish one major feat that the world will never forget. With the Bolshevik Revolution in 1917, it seemed the world, within a few decades, would crumble under Communism. Thankfully, that was not to be. In part, it was the Russian Orthodox Church that held the fabric of the Russian people together in the midst of terrible Soviet darkness and maintained a Christian consciousness that paved the way for evangelical missionaries after Communism's demise in 1989.

22

The Great Schism – 1054

*A*S noted earlier, there were growing tensions between Greek Orthodox in the east and Latin Catholics in the west. For centuries the relations between the two branches of Christianity continued to decline and grow apart, even though they were both orthodox (in the right sense of the word). They had been one great body during the first five centuries of the Church's existence, though not without differences and difficulties, but by this time their distinctions had clearly delineated them as the East and the West. Reasons for these tensions are several and, if carefully examined, the seeds of the Great Schism can be seen as early as the second century.

What are some of the reasons that brought about this great division between the East and the West? First, there was the cultural barrier of language. The New Testament was written in *koine* (*common*) Greek, and until the early part of the third century, all theological writing was done in Greek. Tertullian changed that tradition by being the first theologian to write in Latin. The West followed his lead and continued to write in Latin. One difficulty during the first four ecumenical councils was the language barrier. Latin-speaking westerners could not grasp all the nuances of Greek, and Greek-speaking easterners could not comprehend the vagaries of Latin. The West was further entrenched in its inflexible loyalty to Latin by Jerome's *Vulgate* (event #12). Misunderstanding and jumping to the wrong conclusions abounded on both sides.

Second, there were theological differences. Both branches embraced the creeds and definitions of the first four ecumenical councils and thus believed in 'one, holy, catholic, and apostolic church.' Both were devoutly Trinitarian and made equal contributions in the exegetical formulations of this truth. However, each had different emphases. Western Latins stressed the unity of the Godhead; eastern Greeks accented the threeness of the Persons. Regarding Christology, the West highlighted the incarnate, dying Christ (i.e., Christ the Victim); the East underscored the resurrected, triumphant Christ (i.e., Christ the Victor). This is still seen; the cross in Roman Catholic churches always has a statue of Christ hanging on it (the crucifix), and in Orthodox churches the cross contains no statue of Christ hanging on it. The two views of Christ are not mutually exclusive, however; each has its proper place in biblical theology. Their discord caused the two groups to go to extremes, and forget the necessity and value of the other's viewpoint. The Greek interpretation of salvation was more speculative; the Roman focused on the practical. The Orthodox viewed theology more in the context of worship and the Divine

152

Liturgy, and Roman theology stemmed more from the legal or judicial. Furthermore, the East was uncomfortable with the West's doctrine of temporary, refining punishment of believers after death, called Purgatory.

What should have been secondary 'things indifferent' (at least for them) became primary theological issues, which widened the chasm of division even more. In both branches, the central point of worship had shifted from the ministry of the Word to observance of the Lord's Supper (i.e., mass, Eucharist); in these matters, their differences surfaced and forms of worship differed. The East used leavened bread and the West unleavened. Eastern clergy could marry and have families; in the West priests could not marry. Eastern clergy wore beards, western priests were clean-shaven.

Ecclesiastical and political bickering was the next reason for division. The West believed that Rome was the sacred and eternal city of God because both the apostles Peter and Paul were martyred there. Stemming from the time when Constantine the Great united the empire and shifted the capital east to Constantinople, which was dubbed the 'New Rome,' strong tensions and rivalries existed. The Council of Chalcedon decreed that Rome was the primary See in Christendom and Constantinople the second. As moving the capital east did not sit well with the Latins, so the decree did not set well with the Greeks. There was a willingness in the East to grant ecclesiastical preference to the bishop of Rome as 'first among equals,' but there was an unwillingness to submit unconditionally to him. The East regarded him as only one of several key patriarchs. Thus, the four original Eastern patriarchates (Alexandria, Antioch, Jerusalem, and Constantinople) set into motion a scheme to create a position called the 'Ecumenical

Patriarch,' which would counter the perceived Western power play. Leaders who should have been spiritually minded and zealous for the expansion of Christ's kingdom into all the world became provincial, jealous, and petty over which was the greatest, much like the apostles in Luke 22:24-27.

Philosophical perspectives gave another cause for division. The East was mystical and speculative, desiring to stimulate meditation and discussion about ethereal realities. The West was more objective and rational, desiring to promote action and truth. As early as the late second century, Clement of Alexandria biasedly enlisted aid for Christianity from the choicest thoughts that pagan (Greek) philosophers had to offer. Tertullian, conversely, challenged the pagan cultures and philosophies of his day with his famous axiom, 'What has Athens to do with Jerusalem?'

Historians agree the 'straw that broke the camel's back' was what is known as the Filioque clause. The Niceno-Constan-tinopolitan Creed (381, see Appendix II), an expansion of the Nicene Creed, states that the Holy Spirit proceeds from the Father. From the sixth century onward, the Latin churches added and started using *and the Son* (*filioque*). The Greeks (now joined by the Russians) argued that the Latins acted unilaterally, violated the explicit canon of the council, and were in great theological error. By failing to equalize the relationships among the members of the Trinity, the Latins retorted, the East had negated the full personality of the Holy Spirit and crippled the church's understanding of the Spirit's work. Neither would give in and both were unmovable.

Two stubborn and strong-willed men brought the division to a head. Michael Cerularius became Patriarch of Constantinople in 1043 and Leo IX became pope in 1049. The four original Eastern patriarchates elected Cerularius to be the 'Ecumenical Patriarch.' Leo wanted to bring an end to the division, but he also wanted the East to submit to his absolute headship of the universal church. He dispatched a papal delegation to Constantinople led by Cardinal Humbert. Its mission was to dissuade Cerularius from becoming the 'Ecumenical Patriarch' and demand the East to recognize the *filioque* clause. Leo died while the delegation was en route to the Byzantine capital. Cerularius refused to meet the delegation upon its arrival in Constantinople, so Humbert decided, without any papal authority, to take action that was so severe that its effects are felt even to this day.

As afternoon prayers were about to begin on Saturday, July 16, 1054, Cardinal Humbert pompously marched into the cathedral of Hagia Sophia. Without paying any respects to the patriarch or the other bishops, he marched right up to the main altar and placed on it a parchment that declared the Patriarch of Constantinople, Michael Cerularius, to be excommunicated. He then paraded out of the church, shook its dust off his feet, and left the city. One week later, the Patriarch of Constantinople excommunicated the Cardinal, his delegation, and the Pope of Rome. Needlessly stubborn theological bias, carnal appetites for prestige, and ecclesiastical jockeying for power prevailed, and once again the serpent entered Christ's vineyard.

In his *Turning Points*, Mark Noll reports that, on December 7, 1965, Pope Paul VI and Patriarch Athenagoras I issued a joint statement deploring the 'vexing events' of the Great Schism and removed 'both from memory and from the midst of the Church the sentences of excommunication.' Nevertheless, the division of theological barriers, cultural diversity, and ecclesiastical distrust remains. The unhealed rupture is a reminder of the soul-damaging harm that proud, despotic, unprincipled men can do to Christianity and the cause of Christ.

23

The First Crusade Launched – 1095

*I*SLAM, the religion founded by Mohammed (d. 632), had spread rapidly throughout the Middle East. By the first quarter of the eighth century, Muslim forces had subjugated by the sword the whole of North Africa, the eastern shores of the Mediterranean (including Palestine and the holy city of Jerusalem, along with the other holy places of Christianity), and southern Spain. Islamic armies had established bases in southern Italy, greatly reduced in power and size the Byzantine Empire (the eastern half of the Roman Empire), besieged Constantinople, its capital, and threatened the rest of Christian Europe. Viking raiders had threatened northern Europe in the 800s and the Magyars (nomadic people from Asia) plundered eastern and central Europe until the tenth century. Neither group, however, had threatened the culture nor religion of Europe as had the Muslims. For over three hundred years, the holy sites of the religion of Jesus were under the domination of the anti-Christian and anti-Jewish religion of Islam. What were the Christians to do?

Because of Gregory the Great's work in centralizing and strengthening the western church, especially ending the practice of kings installing bishops and powerful clergy, the popes were able to effectively unite the popular support of Europe behind them. By the beginning of the eleventh century, the balance of power began to swing toward the West and put a halt to Islamic expansion. Still, the Holy Land remained under pagan control, and the Eastern Empire was blockaded and pillaged by Muslim armies.

In 1095, Pope Urban called for an assembly of bishops and church leaders to meet in Clermont, France. The assembly was also attended by delegates of Alexius Commenus, the Byzantine emperor, who pleaded with the pope to dispatch military assistance to help fight against the armies of Muslim Turks. Urban II addressed the assembly on November 27 and urged the warriors of Europe and all soldiers of the cross of Christ to arise and take back the sacred land where the Savior was born, lived, died, rose, and ascended into heaven. The assembly responded overwhelmingly to his call, and soon all of Europe was enthusiastically supportive, militarily and financially, of this holy endeavor, which was called a crusade. What does the word 'crusade' mean? It literally means 'going to the Cross,' and the crusaders were famous for donning a bright red cross on their tunics and shields.

Thus, Pope Urban II launched the first crusade to win back the Holy Land, especially the holy sepulcher of Christ. The First Crusade was a military expedition from 1096 to 1099 by the armies of Western Christianity to regain the Holy Lands conquered by the Muslims. To a degree, the expedition was successful, ultimately resulting in the recapture of Jerusalem and the holy sites of Christianity. An additional goal soon manifested itself as the principal objective – the freeing of the Eastern Christians from Islamic harassment. There was the hope that in so doing the breach between the Eastern and Western Church would be healed, which was really the secondary impetus behind the crusade. The First Crusade was part of the Christian response to the Muslim juggernaut and it resulted in the establishment of a Latin Kingdom in Palestine. It was followed by the second through the eighth Crusades, which are summarized as follows in Durant's *History of Civilization*:

2nd Crusade – 1147–1148:   The fall of the city of Edessa (in the Eastern Empire) into Muslim hands provoked this crusade. Bernard of Clairvaux was the primary promoter of this campaign and zealously called upon people to join it. However, no amount of piety or fabricated religious fervor could save it from being a disastrous failure.

3rd Crusade – 1189–1192:   In 1187, the Muslim prince Saladin the Great recaptured Jerusalem from the Christians. Once again, shock provoked Christian action. Three kings responded to the situation: Richard the Lion-Heart of England; Philip II of France; and Frederick I (also known as Barbarossa), the Holy Roman Emperor. This is the most famous crusade and ended with a compromise between Richard and Saladin that granted Christians access to the holy sites. However, Jerusalem was not recaptured. The Crusade did little more than generate legend and folklore in modern literature.

4th Crusade – 1200–1204:   This crusade set out to improve the gains obtained by Richard, but ended with the Crusaders sacking Constantinople (the headquarters for Eastern Orthodox) and establishing a Latin Kingdom of Byzantium, which lasted for sixty years. So much for trying to heal the breach!

5th Crusade – 1212:   This crusade was also known as the Children's Crusade. Superstitiously, it was thought that because children were pure in heart, if enough children could be mustered, they could march into the Holy Land and supernaturally conqueror it. This crusade, too, miserably failed, and tens of thousands of children were sold into slavery, drowned, or murdered.

6th Crusade – 1219–1221:   This endeavor set out to conquer Egypt on the assumption that if Egypt was taken, supplies to Jerusalem would be cut off, and the city would become vulnerable to recapture. Francis of Assisi accompanied the venture, and its only success was that Francis got to preach to the Sultan al-Kamil.

7th Crusade – 1229:   Fredrick II temporarily gained control of Jerusalem, but it was not through fighting: he negotiated a treaty with the sultan.

8th Crusade – 1248:   This last crusade ended with Louis IX of France being defeated in Egypt and dejected troops dragging themselves back to Europe. Thereafter, all enthusiasm for crusading vanished.

Militarily speaking, the crusades were a failure. The soldierly gains from fighting lasted for less than two hundred years. By 1291, the last Latin outpost in the Muslim world fell. For centuries, historians were willing to give credit to the crusades for improving Europe. Scholars argued that high standards of Eastern medicine, infusion of Greek and Muslim cultural philosophies and education (especially mathematics), luxuries of silks, spices, and Mediterranean fruits, and the exchange of ideas were the benefits of the crusades that helped eradicate the provincialism of the Middle Ages in Europe.

Modern scholarship no longer completely accepts this evaluation. These benefits would have occurred because of population growth and expanding trade without military expeditions. It is now realized that instead of enormous benefits, the crusades generated terrible consequences. Not counting the raping, pillaging, and massive loss of life, the blemish brought upon the name of Christ and Christianity cannot be erased. The expressions 'crusade' or 'crusader' were originally applied to European Christian efforts to retake the Holy Land, especially Jerusalem. Today, they bear the negative connotation of any military or evangelistic exertion by Christians against non-Christians. This is especially true regarding endeavors by Christians to win Muslims to Christ. Many Muslims still refer to Christians as 'crusaders,' and some Islamic clerics use the crusades to justify present-day jihad (holy war).

What was the final result of the crusades? Very simply, western Christianity succeeded in further driving an iron wedge between the western and eastern branches of the church, between the church and Jews, and between Christianity and Islam. Hopefully, Christianity has learned the valuable lesson taught by Paul the Apostle in 2 Corinthians 10:3-4: 'For though we walk in the flesh, we do not war according to the flesh. For the weapons of our warfare are not carnal but mighty in God for pulling down strongholds' (NKJV).

24

The Waldensian Movement – 1173

*B*Y the late twelfth century, Constantine's and Theodosius's actions had taken full effect. There was little distinction between state and church: bishops became princes and potentates, and princes were often made bishops or archbishops. Charlemagne's laws, which had given the church favored status, allowed the church to seize lands and forcibly extract taxes. By so doing, the church became rich and powerful.

As the church increased its wealth, Gothic architecture emerged in the form of massive cathedrals and lavishly adorned church buildings. Fat, wealthy bishops ascribed the magnificent structures to the devotion of the people; but in reality, they were due to the arrogance and ostentation of the church hierarchy. It seemed the bishops had forgotten about the founder of their religion, the humble carpenter from Nazareth who had no earthly place to lay His head.

Latin was the language of the church and university. The development of philosophical, scholastic theology demonstrated the intellectual dominance of the university, while the average person could barely read and write. It seemed the leadership had forgotten that the master Teacher walked among common people and taught the poor plainly and openly on mountains and in deserts.

The Crusades revealed a military strength forged by church-state cooperation that not only fought off Islam, but also kept the people under control through fear. Those in authority had forgotten that the God-Man never carried a sword.

These worldly achievements did not go unnoticed by the everyday people. They felt alienated by what they perceived as a church corrupted by wealth and power. The Savior's call to poverty of spirit and humility went unheeded. Where was the simplicity of apostolic Christianity?

As always, there was dissent among some within the church and some outside. Within the church would emerge the 'mendicant orders' of monks who renounced property, took vows of poverty and chastity, and traveled about preaching and taking care of the poor and destitute. These monks depended directly on the charity of others for their livelihoods. The two most recognized mendicant orders were the Dominicans, or Black Friars (founded by Dominic de Guzman), and the Franciscans (founded by Francis of Assisi). However, before either of these orders was formed, there arose two groups who reacted against the opulence and richness of the church: the Cathari, also known as Cathars or Albigensians, and the Waldensians.

The Cathars went outside the church and devised an intensely spiritualistic religion that opposed most things physical, especially the incarnation of Christ. Though they were popular among the poor and attracted many followers from the south of France, they were condemned as heretics by the church and brutally persecuted by church and state. The Dominicans were initially formed to counter them.

Some are trend-setters without realizing it. Such were the Waldensians. This group originated in the late 1100s through the influence of Peter Waldo of Lyon, France. Little is known about his life, except that he was a wealthy merchant who gave up most of his wealth and preached poverty. He quickly gained a sizable following that became known as 'the poor men of Lyons.' Waldo had no desire to leave the church, only reform it. Robert Godfrey carefully notes that Waldo's 'critique of the church adopted neither the radical love of poverty in itself as Francis [of Assisi] had done nor the radical spiritualizing of the Cathars.' For the most part, the 'poor men of Lyons' were moderately educated and could read their Bibles. What they found in the Word of God was a wonderful but simple picture of Christ and Christianity. With some money left over, Waldo had the Bible translated into the language of the people. The Waldensians, as they became known, would pack their mules with Bibles and distribute the Bibles through the Alps of Switzerland and northern Italy. Stopping wherever they were received, they preached a simple understanding of the Bible. This preaching brought them into conflict with the church.

The Waldensians were ordered to appear before the archbishop of Lyons, who commanded them to stop preaching. They replied with the words of scripture: 'We must obey God rather than men' (Acts 5:29). They were promptly excommunicated, but that did not stop them or the movement. In

1179, the Waldensians sent a delegation to Rome to appeal to Pope Alexander II. The Pope was impressed with their simple poverty and said that they could preach if the area bishop gave them permission. This, of course, would not happen. More French and Italian believers, disgusted with the worldliness of the church, joined them, and this incurred the wrath of both the church and state. The Waldensians were persecuted and mercilessly slaughtered; entire villages in the Piedmont region of Switzerland were plundered and destroyed, their women raped and children killed, along with other unspeakable atrocities committed against them. Yet, they continued freely distributing Bibles and preaching the gospel.

It must be remembered that they, like the Reformers, did not wish to leave the church, but to remain and have its approval to preach the Word. They were forced out of the church and, by today's evangelical standards, were never heretics. Eventually, they rejected the authority of the pope and the Roman Catholic institution. Along with a positive proclamation of the gospel, the Waldensians preached against notions of purgatory, prayers for the dead, worship of saints and relics, the trappings of clergy vestments and holy water, saints' days, and other Roman Catholic beliefs. They believed that the Holy Bible *alone* – not the pope or church – was the sole authority of faith and practice and from that conviction they would not yield. They were Trinitarian and firmly held to the eternal Sonship of Christ and His substitutionary atonement. They believed in salvation by grace alone through faith alone in Christ alone and many, though not all, eventually began to practice baptism by immersion. They were champions of the priesthood of believers and individual soul liberty.

In 1207, Pope Innocent III offered the Waldensians universal amnesty if they would submit to the Catholic Church. Some returned, but others did not. Condemned as heretics by papal bull in 1214, the pope directed the Inquisition against them. Again, indescribable persecution ensued. Despite the inquisitors' best efforts, the Waldensians could not be eradicated. They continued to grow and exist until the Protestant Reformation. Sometime in the late 1520s, a delegation of the Reformers was sent to meet the Waldensian leaders; William Farel, the Protestant Reformer from Geneva, was among them. The Reformed delegation read the Waldensian confession of faith and declared them to be orthodox and Reformed. The Waldensian churches, the oldest evangelical churches in existence, were then absorbed into Protestantism. It was not until 1870 that the Waldensians received full civil rights in Italy. Today, there still exist Waldensian churches in Italy and Valdese, North Carolina.

Their major contribution to Christian history may seem insignificant by today's standards, but it was earth-moving in their day. This contribution was their dissemination of the Word of God in the common language of the people. They believed the common people had the right and must have available to them the Word of God in their own language. Through their 'muleteers,' they sacrificially sowed the seed of the Word of God in many parts of Europe, including Germany, Austria, and Holland. Numerous church historians strongly believe the Waldensians sowed the seed that blossomed into the Protestant Reformation.

25

John Wycliffe and the Lollard Movement – 1381

*H*OW could a man be so hated that forty-three years after his death his body was dug up, the remains burned, and his ashes scattered into a river? He certainly must have been an evil, monstrous man, right!? No, he was John Wycliffe, a Scholastic philosopher, theologian, translator, church reformer, preacher, and professor at Oxford University, whom many consider to be the 'Morning Star of the Reformation.'

What is his story, and what was world-changing about him? At this juncture of the Middle Ages, the Western church had grown immensely prosperous. But, with the prosperity, it had become a formal, sterile, and lifeless institution rather than the dynamic, fruitful, life-giving body of Christ. In *World Christians: Living on the Wavelength of the Great Commission,* Sundar Krishnan recounts an anecdote concerning Thomas Aquinas (1225–1274): when invited to the Vatican and shown the incalculable riches of the vault and treasury of the Roman Pontiff, the curator smugly observed to the great theologian that the Church can no longer say, 'Silver and gold have I none' (KJV) (referring to Acts 3:6). Aquinas responded, 'And no longer can she say in the name of Jesus Christ, rise up and walk.' What the Waldensians discovered, John Wycliffe more fully realized: the Church had lost its spiritual power and was trusting in itself instead of its Head and Lord. His attacks on the clergy and attempts to reform the Church would bring about his demise. But before his death, he would put into motion ideas that would shake the world.

Born in the North Riding of Yorkshire, England, in 1330, Wycliffe's family was wealthy and owned sizeable territory. He received an excellent classical education and was known to study at Oxford by 1345. In the middle of the twelfth century (c. 1150), two of the greatest universities in the world were founded: the University of Paris and Oxford University. Oxford would be the center of Wycliffe's controversies. Two men powerfully shaped his life and theology: William of Ockham and Thomas Bradwardine, Archbishop of Canterbury. Ockham (of Ockham's Razor fame) stimulated Wycliffe's interest in natural science, mathematics, and logic, and Bradwardine's book *On the Cause of God against the Pelagians*, which was a gallant resurgence of the Pauline-Augustine doctrine of grace, influenced his religious studies.

Wycliffe's conflicts with the church began with his addressing the enormous wealth and massive amounts of land that it owned. England's nobility resented the church's quest for power and wealth, but continued to bequeath to it in hopes of purchasing divine favor in the afterlife. The church, many believed, had become a business rather than the soul-saving organism Christ died for it to be.

The dukes and lords found a friend in Wycliffe. It seems that he argued for Parliament to confiscate the papal lands in England, or at least to control them, so that the clergy and monks would not be encumbered in their eternal, spiritual duties by managing temporal, physical wealth. He became rector of Lutterworth in 1374, which was in close proximity to Oxford, and that position allowed him to preach in the church, teach at the university, and write. From there, Wycliffe wrote most of his *Tracts and Treatises* (translated by Robert Vaughn for The Wycliffe Society), which contained twelve treatises totaling thirty-two chapters. They reflect his mature thoughts on the authority of Holy Scripture, the way of salvation, and his mounting estrangement from Roman Catholicism. Observe that after his death, all of Wycliffe's Latin and English writings were collected and compiled into one volume entitled *Summa Theologiae* (*a summary of theology*).

Wycliffe believed that most of the monks were irredeemably corrupt and that the moral degradation of the priests nullified their ministry and polluted the sacraments. He thought that all clergy and monks should, like the apostles, live simple lives of poverty. Infuriated clergymen attacked him. When news of Wycliffe's beliefs reached Rome, the pope issued a bull (ban) against him. John of Gaunt, the Duke of Lancaster, granted him protection. It must be noted that at this time there were two popes vying for the official recognition of the Roman Catholic Church, one in Rome and the other in Avignon (see HISTORICAL NOTE below).

Wycliffe's beliefs set forth in the *Summa Theologiae* were advanced for his time. The later Reformers would drink deeply from his theological well and use his biblical arguments. In his

Tracts and Treatises, he condemned the sale of indulgences, the irrational worship of saints and holy relics, and the doctrine of transubstantiation (the belief that the bread and wine of the Eucharist became the actual body and blood of Christ). He denounced the power of the priesthood to forgive sins and the use of the auricular confessional, saying it 'was not ordered by Christ and not used by the apostles.' He challenged the supremacy of the pope and made the vague reference to him as antichrist.

Wycliffe's passion and love for the Holy Scriptures caused him to biblically conclude that a person is made right with God (justified) by faith alone, although he was not as articulate as Martin Luther who would appear two hundred years later. 'Trust wholly in Christ,' he taught, and 'rely altogether on his sufferings; beware of seeking to be justified in any other way than by his work.' Conceivably, his most ardent belief was that the Holy Scripture possessed authority over the pope and the church and they must submit to its authority, not vice versa. Coupled with his belief in the supremacy of the Scriptures was his conviction that the common people should have the Word of God in their own language. Latin was the language of the university and, worst of all, the church. Farmers, stonemasons, milkmaids, nursing mothers, and uneducated shopkeepers all went to worship and understood very little, if anything, of what they heard.

Wycliffe stated in one of his treatises:

Those Heretics who pretend that the laity does not need to know God's law, and that the things which priests have told them is enough, do not deserved to be listened to. For the Bible is the faith of the Church, and the more widely it becomes known the better it will be. Therefore since the laity should know the faith, it should be taught in whatever language is most easily understood. (Loserth, p. 74)

When his critics retorted that the Scriptures in the hands of the laity would cause the pearl of the gospel to be scattered and trodden underfoot by swine, Wycliffe countered, 'Englishmen learn Christ's law best in English. Moses heard God's law in his own tongue; so did Christ's apostles.' He set out to translate the entire Bible into English from Jerome's Vulgate. John Wycliffe was the first to translate the Bible into English (albeit from the Latin). As sections were translated, he enlisted itinerant preachers to travel throughout England preaching and distributing the Word of God. These preachers became known as Lollards, deriving their name from the region where Wycliffe had his strongest support. Their broadcasting of the Scripture in English across the land brought many people to saving faith in Christ.

Wycliffe survived many attempts at excommunication. He suffered a stroke in church and died December 31, 1384, before his translation was completed. His good friend John Purvey is responsible for the version of the Wycliffe Bible we have today. The Lollard movement was driven underground, but they stealthy continued their gospel work until the English Reformation, despite harassment by the Catholic authorities. Notwithstanding the papal suppression of Wycliffe's teachings, they continued to infiltrate the minds and hearts of the English people. In frustration and hate, the pope ordered Wycliffe's body exhumed, burned, and the ashes scattered on the River Swift, which flowed through the parish of Lutterworth. An observer of the event later recorded, 'Thus the brook hath conveyed his ashes into Avon; Avon into Severn; Severn into the narrow seas; and they into the main ocean. And thus the ashes of Wycliffe are the emblem of his doctrine which now is dispersed the world over.'

HISTORICAL NOTE:
Papacy begins 'Babylonian exile' in Avignon (France) – 1309

Disputes between the papacy and the French King, Philip IV, resulted in the election of a French archbishop, who promptly seized the title of Pope and relocated the papal court to Avignon in France. The Avignon papacy, sometimes called the 'Babylonian Captivity of the Church,' lasted from 1309 to 1379. During a seventy-year period, a total of two popes simultaneously ruled Roman Catholicism, and at one juncture, there were three.

This period reflected a growing loss of power for the papacy and resulted in direct challenges to papal authority, ending the claims asserted by Pope Innocent III (at the height of the medieval period) that the church had all authority over secular matters. By the end of the fourteenth century, church and state emerged as clearly defined entities that operated within their own spheres. This period, and these developments, set the stage for what we know today as the 'separation of church and state.'

26

Johann Gutenberg and the First Printed Bible – 1456

*F*ROM the earliest days of the history of mankind, people have tried to draw sounds and transfer their phonetic images onto physical objects that could be understood by others. Pictographs in caves and hieroglyphics on clay tablets illustrate the point. Handwriting began to appear on animal skins and then paper (papyrus), after it was invented by the Egyptians, sometime around 3500 B.C. Handwriting was the normal mode of drawing sounds and transferring those images into messages for thousands of years. It was a slow, and oftentimes, painful process.

Now, fast forward to the twentieth century. How many readers have used a typewriter? Who can remember those days of ribbons and carbon whiteout? Certainly in this day, almost everyone has used a computer, sent a text on a smartphone, or written something on an iPad or tablet. Who is to be credited with these concepts of mechanical writing? Was it Henry Mills, who created a strange machine in 1714 that made letters on a piece of paper by pecking certain keys? Was it Pellegrino Turri, who supplied a typing machine to a blind countess in 1808, whose letters have been preserved in historical archive? Was it Steve Wozniak, who along with Steve Jobs formed the Apple Corporation and sold the first Apple computer on April 1, 1976 for $666.66? No, none of the above can take credit. Time must be turned back almost 600 years to find the answer. The answer will also reveal what performs mechanical type actually has to do with the history of Christianity.

Moveable type was probably invented in China during the Song Dynasty by Bi Sheng (c. 960–1127). Sheng began by making Chinese characters of earthen clay and moved on to carved wooden pieces. Because of the enormous number of characters in the Chinese language (more than 3,000) and the extreme difficulty of accurately arranging them to print the correct message, his innovation did not catch on with the Chinese business world. His process was too expensive and labor-intensive. A short while later, the Koreans tried something similar during the Goryeo Dynasty (c. 1230), but their efforts also came to an end. Simple handwriting or a more flamboyant style called calligraphy remained the preferred method of visual communication in Asia. But when Marco Polo returned from his adventures in the Far East, he brought Bi Sheng's ideas of moveable type to Europe.

During the Middle Ages, only universities and enormously wealthy people owned books. Churches had Bibles, but they were usually chained to the pulpits. Some have thought the chains were to keep the people ignorant of the Word of God.

That was not the case. Since there was no public education, the average person could not read, even if that person had a Bible. No, the chains primarily kept robbers from stealing the Holy Scriptures. Books of all sorts were very expensive, especially Bibles. A monk or a group of monks could take two years to hand-copy a Bible. Even if the average person could read, the cost of materials and manpower to produce a Bible made it far beyond his means to purchase one. With the arrival of Marco Polo's far-eastern knowledge and the creative ingenuity of a young German, that would quickly change.

Johann Gutenberg (c. 1398 – February 3, 1468), a German goldsmith and entrepreneur, lived in the mining town of Mainz. For years he had toyed with the question of how to mass-produce literary works without the arduous task of copying by hand. Remember, it often took a year or longer for copyists to generate a copy of the Bible, especially if it was decoratively colored and ornate. Gutenberg had an idea and borrowed money to experiment on his new hypothesis of technology. His experiment turned into reality as he manufactured and introduced a machine that changed the world of publishing: the printing press.

Though the Chinese invented the primitive model of moveable type, it was Gutenberg who perfected it. With his innovations of casting reusable letters and his principles of mass production, Gutenberg made printing books functional and affordable. His invention of mechanical moveable type and the printing press started the Printing Revolution, which is widely acknowledged as the most important event of the modern era.

For some time, Gutenberg's printing associates in Mainz kept the techniques of his invention a secret. Despite every attempt to conceal, such knowledge could not be sequestered indefinitely. Before long it was pirated, and within thirty years every major European nation had at least one printing press. The advent of the rapid production of books created an environment for learning. Within a century, public schools would be started. The average person would be taught to read and write. Illiteracy, for the most part, would be eventually eradicated. Knowledge, which had trickled like a small stream for centuries, quickly turned into a rushing river and flowed throughout Europe and into the known world. The rapid sharing of information and ideas had begun.

Little did Gutenberg fathom that his printing press would play a monumental role in the emergence of world-changing events. It fed the growing Renaissance as it allowed knowledge and ideas to be more readily accessible. It influenced the scientific revolution, which laid the material basis for our modern knowledge-based economy and the spread of learning among the masses. It fueled the Protestant Reformation, which enabled Martin Luther's *Ninety-Five Theses* to be widely circulated in a matter of weeks (see #28). Luther also utilized the cheaply printed broadsheet to promulgate his beliefs. Those broadsheets evolved into the modern-day newspaper. In 1997, *Time-Life* magazine chose Gutenberg's printing press as the most important invention of the second millennium. In 1999, the *A&E Network* ranked Johann Gutenberg number one on its list of the most influential people of the second millennium.

What is most significant about Gutenberg's printing press was the first book he printed. It was neither a literary classic, nor a book of science or mathematics or medicine, but the Holy Bible. His first printing was 180 copies of the Latin Bible.

Rather than taking a year or two, he needed only a few weeks to produce them. The Bible was on its way to being mass-produced.

The printing press paved the way for 'every ploughboy and serving maid' to have a copy of the Bible in his or her own hands. No longer would the priest or university scholar have sole access to the Scriptures, which would be studied and debated only among the educated elite. Common people learned to read, and more often than not, the first book they turned to was the Holy Bible. The secrecy that had so long enshrouded the sacred pages of God's Holy Word was lifted. The hearts of God's people, like those of the disciples on the Emmaus Road (Luke 24:32), began to burn within them as they studied the Bible. Hearty, brave souls risked their lives, violated the suppressing orders of church hierarchy, and dared to translate the Scriptures (like the Waldensians and Wycliffe before them) from Latin into the common vernacular of the people. They wanted others to know about the glory and magnificence of Christ and the joy of His saving gospel. They desired that every person be granted access to the full revelation of God, in order to understand His way and will for all creation. All who own a Bible or have one in the home should thank God this very moment for Johann Gutenberg.

27

Erasmus Publishes Greek New Testament – 1516

*H*AVE you ever heard the expression 'It's all Greek to me'? For centuries, after the days of the early church father Tertullian, Latin dominated the Christian world, and the original (Greek) text of the New Testament was laid aside. Except in the East, Greek, through which the holy apostles communicated the very words and message of Jesus Christ, was a forgotten language. A few classical scholars in major universities taught Greek, but none seriously considered its value. Latin was the language of the day, and thus Latin would forever remain, or so most scholars thought.

Erasmus of Rotterdam, a Dutch humanist and classical scholar, would change that forever. Humanism in Erasmus' day was a Renaissance cultural movement that turned away from medieval scholasticism and revived interest in ancient

Greek and Roman thought. It also had a special interest in the downtrodden of the state and in educating the poor.

Desiderius Erasmus (c. 1467–1536) was born in Rotterdam, the illegitimate son of a priest and (probably) his housekeeper. Both loved and cared for him until their deaths, but Erasmus could not erase the stain of his illicit birth. His father made sure that he received the highest education in the best Latin school located in Deventer, Holland; the quality of his education is evident in the pure Latin style of his writings. It was there for the first time ever that Greek was taught at a level lower than university, and to those of an early age. Erasmus quickly mastered Greek, which propelled him into prominence.

Ordained at twenty-five, he never engaged in pastoral ministry, but confined himself to being a man of letters. While in Paris, Erasmus was exposed to corruption within the church, and he addressed this degeneration in his writings. The following statements from J. A. Froude's *Life and Letters of Erasmus* reveal the extent of the church's abuses:

> What would Jerome say could he see the Virgin's milk exhibited for money … the miraculous oil; the portion of the true cross, enough if they were collected to freight a large ship? Here we have the hood of St Francis, there Our Lady's petticoat, or St Anne's comb, or St Thomas of Canterbury's shoes … and all through the avarice of priests and the hypocrisy of monks playing at the credulity of the people. Even bishops play their parts in these fantastic shows, and approve and dwell on them in their rescripts [official notices].

In 1503, Pope Pius III died and was succeeded by a warlike man, who, instead of taking the name of a saint, took the name of a pagan emperor – Julius II. Erasmus watched with grief Pope Julius' triumphal entry into Florence at the head of the army that had conquered Bologna. Speaking on Matthew 24:23, Erasmus relayed the account: 'I saw with my own eyes Pope Julius II, at Bologna, and afterwards at Rome, marching at the head of a triumphal procession as if he were Pompey or Caesar. St Peter subdued the world with faith, not with arms or soldiers or military engines' (Proude, *Life and Letters*, p. 122).

Furthermore, Erasmus believed strongly that the laity should have access to the Holy Scriptures in their own language. In his *Paraclesis* (*Exhortation*), which prefaced his 1516 edition of the New Testament in Greek, he firmly states his beliefs – shocking for the time – regarding laity' s access to Scripture:

> And truly I do greatly dissent from those men, which would not that the Scripture of Christ should be translated into all tongues that it might be read diligently of the private and secular men and women. Others propound, as though Christ had taught such dark and insensible things, that they could scant be understood of a few divines. Or else as though the pith and substance of the Christian religion consisted chiefly in this, that it be not known. Peradventure it were most expedient that the counsels of kings should be kept secret, but Christ would that his counsels and mysteries should be spread abroad as much as is possible. I would desire that all women should read the gospel and Paul's epistles, and I would to God they were translated into the tongues of all men, so that they might not only be read, and known, of the Scots and Irishmen, but also of the Turks and Saracens.

Needless to say, the church did not take warmly to his sentiments. For years, Erasmus worked on an updated Latin translation of the Bible. When he published it, he also included a parallel Greek text. Johan Hausschein (also known as Oecolampadius, Greek for 'light of the house') assisted Erasmus in preparing the Greek for the New Testament portion. Erasmus had, at most, twelve Greek manuscripts to use in translating – whereas today, at least 5,000 are at our disposal. None were very old, and all were incomplete. When sections were missing in his Greek manuscripts, he used the Latin and translated it into Greek. By today's standards of textual criticism, this Greek compilation was somewhat inferior. Nonetheless, it was the first attempt to create a Greek New Testament in over 1,000 years, and it enabled pastors, theologians, and scholars in Western Christianity to go back to the Word of God in the original language. From this, many of the early Reformers were able to correctly grasp the great doctrines of Scripture, empowering the Reformation.

In the 1930s, A. T. Robertson, Greek scholar *par excellence* and author of the massive 1,450 page tome *A Grammar of the Greek New Testament: In the Light of Historical Research*, made this correct observation: 'The Greek New Testament is the New Testament. All else is translation. Jesus speaks to us out of every page of the Greek.' Erasmus realized this over 400 years before Robertson, and Robertson acknowledges this when he quotes from Erasmus' preface to his Greek New Testament:

> These holy pages will summon up the living image of His [Christ's] mind. They will give you Christ Himself, talking, healing, dying, rising, the whole Christ in a word; they will give Him to you in an intimacy so close that He would be less visible to you if He stood before your eyes.

There is no doubt that Erasmus loved Christ, but he was truly an enigma. While highly critical of the church, he was a timid soul and refused to leave it. He remained loyal to papal authorities and 'played it safe' so that he might be enabled to continue his pursuit of writing. At the start of the Protestant Reformation, both sides at times laid claim to him. He died in Basel in 1536. Although a loyal Catholic, nowhere in all the accounts of his death is there intimation or mention that he received the last rites or even asked for a priest or confessor. Durant, in volume six of *The Story of Civilization*, affirms that he died 'without the sacraments of the Church.'

Two major accomplishments resulted from Erasmus' Greek New Testament. The first was a widespread revival of the study of the New Testament in Greek. Latin lost favor, and the original language of the New Testament gained the ascendancy in theological studies. This allowed people to communicate directly with Christ and the apostles without the intermediary of a translator. 'It's all Greek to me' was no more. The second notable achievement was an unintentional one. It involved an intense controversy with an Augustinian monk over grace and predestination and whether the will of man was absolutely free or in bondage to sin. Shortly after Erasmus published his Greek New Testament in 1516, that German monk began to read the Book of Galatians in Greek and slowly came to understand justification by faith alone more clearly. The spark that lit the flame of the Protestant Reformation was struck. That monk was none other than Martin Luther.

28

Martin Luther Posts His
Ninety-Five Theses – 1517

NOW a millennium and a half old, the Christian church had changed drastically from the days of its founder, Jesus of Nazareth, and its greatest promoter, Paul the Apostle. Sacramentalism, the belief that grace and salvation are conveyed through religious rites or sacraments, was the mainstay of Christianity. The average person who professed to be a Christian simply thought that being baptized, living a pretty good life, going to church, and partaking of the Eucharist (at least twice a year) would eventually assure him or her a place in heaven. Granted, perhaps one would have to spend a few hundred years or more in Purgatory, but sooner or later, as long as no mortal sin was committed, a person would go to heaven. Most people in Europe were content to live and die resting in this belief. However, some were not.

One who was not content with this belief was Martin Luther, an Augustinian monk, who struggled deeply with 'how to be right with God.' Luther was born in 1483 in Eisleben, Germany. His father wanted him to study law and sent Martin to the University of Erfurt. One day, while riding in a thunderstorm, he was thrown from his horse and barely escaped death by lightning. He believed this was a sign from God and determined to enter the priesthood.

As Luther studied the Scriptures, he became aware and convinced of three things: his own persistent sinfulness, God's unswerving holiness, and his total inability to remedy his condition. Desperate to be right with God and find peace, he travelled to Rome in 1510. He was positive that he would find what he was looking for in the Eternal City and that peace with the holy, eternal, triune God was waiting for him in that sacred capital of God. What did he find?

Contrary to his dreams and hopes, Luther found a city that was far from holy. It was filled with unimaginable sins of every sort. Not to be deterred, he climbed Pilate's stairs, where Christ supposedly walked, kissing and repeating the Rosary at every step. Disgusted over the decadence and sexual immorality among the priests – numerous illegitimate children of priests and nuns ran in the streets – Luther left Rome incurably disillusioned, never to change his mind and never to return. He later noted '... the knavery, the horrible sinfulness and debauchery that are rampant in Rome ... If there is a hell, Rome must be built on top of it; for every kind of sin flourishes there ...' (as qtd. in Oskar Thulin, *A Life of Luther Told in Pictures and Narrative*).

When Luther returned to Germany, his mentor, Johannes von Staupitz, the head of the Augustinian monastery, wanted him to pursue a doctorate in theology. Martin had done so well in that field of study before he went to Rome that Staupitz reasoned this discipline would surely heal his troubled soul and bring relief. Strangely enough, Staupitz also provided one of the cornerstones of Luther's faith by urging him to trust in the goodness and mercy of God and not rely on any type of effort or work to earn salvation. Luther did as his mentor directed and again took up biblical and theological studies. He received his doctorate in theology in the year 1512 and immediately started lecturing at the University of Wittenburg.

The year 1516 was a crucial turning point in Martin Luther's personal life and academic career. At that time, Luther, despite his mentor's assurance that a benevolent and loving God existed, was in constant torment over the state of his soul. He devoted himself to fasts, flagellations (i.e., beating his body with whips and wire), long hours in prayer, pilgrimages to sacred shrines to Mary and the saints, and constant confession of sin in the auricular confessional. The more he tried to be holy and do works for God, it seemed, the more aware he became of his sinfulness.

One day, as he was preparing for his lectures, Luther was reading the Psalms and Paul's epistles of Romans and Galatians, in particular from Erasmus' Greek New Testament. He came upon a series of phrases by Paul that read, 'The just (or righteous) shall live by faith.' As Luther contemplated the passage, suddenly, the unconnected dots in his mind connected. He began to understand what Paul was saying and correctly interpreted the phrase to mean that not only will the just live by faith alone, but he will receive this righteousness by faith alone.

Luther apprehended and was instantly persuaded from Scripture that a person's good works or deeds could **not** earn that person a place in heaven, much less guarantee it. The *only* way a person could be right with a thrice-holy God was through the imputed righteousness of Jesus Christ, who lived the perfect life of obedience that Luther could not live and died the required death for sin that Luther should have died. He came to believe what is known as justification. Furthermore, Luther was now certain that righteousness or justification was received by faith *alone*. With joy, Luther believed and taught that salvation is a gift of God's grace, received by faith and trust alone in God's promise to forgive sins for the sake of Christ's death on the cross. This, he believed, was God's work from beginning to end.

Soon thereafter, a situation occurred that Luther would not tolerate and could no longer bear. A monk named Johann Tetzel came into the area selling indulgences to raise money to finish building St Peter's cathedral in Rome. An indulgence was a grace or a pardon/forgiveness for sin that one could purchase with money, not only for oneself, but also for dead relatives. Tetzel's indulgences purportedly promised forgiveness of sins, past, and future. Nothing else was required except legal tender. No repentance. No confession. No faith. No satisfaction or works of penance. Just cash on the barrel was all that was needed. This practice violated the official dogma of the church, but it raised too much money to face any objection by the pope or archbishops.

Tetzel had organized quite an efficient money-making campaign. He scheduled local priests to lead his processionals into a town. He then, usually in the town square, preached sermons that depicted the parishioners' dead relatives screaming and writhing in agony from the flames of purgatory. 'Can you hear your dead relatives screaming out in pain in purgatory while you fiddle away your money?' Like a good marketer, Tetzel had a jingle to go along with his indulgences' sale. It went something like this: 'As soon as the coin in the coffer rings, a soul from purgatory springs.' Tetzel's approach was grounded in undisciplined emotionalism, pure and simple, and the people could not resist. Money poured in from the rich and poor.

Luther was outraged and so terribly provoked that he sat down and wrote a series of theses in which he questioned a number of traditions and practices, or abuses as he saw them, in Roman Catholicism. On October 31 (All Hallows Eve), 1517, Luther nailed his *Ninety-Five Theses* to the university church door in Wittenberg. He wrote these theses only to stimulate thought and discussion, hoping people would turn to the Holy Bible to find answers. The rest, as they say, is history! The Protestant Reformation had begun, and within weeks the flames of biblical reformation spread throughout Europe. So influential did Luther become that the world-famous American civil rights leader of the 1960s, Martin Luther King, Jr., as his father before him, was named after this great German Reformer!

29

The Diet of Worms – 1521

*B*ECAUSE this event is so closely related to the previous event, many historians merge them into one. However, I believe they should not be merged, but are best viewed as two separate – though related – events. They occurred four years apart and should thus be studied in that light: one event led to the other. To understand the Diet of Worms, you must realize that a 'Diet' was not a weight loss program, but a parliament called to settle a particular issue.

Though posted with the intent to invite discussion and debate, Martin Luther's *Ninety-Five Theses* caused no small stir and attracted the immediate attention of the Roman Catholic hierarchy. Many believe that Luther naively thought the Pope and Roman curia (administrative body) would agree with him. His objective was not to disrupt or leave the church, but to reform it. The *Theses* had just the opposite effect. Criticism came from many corners. Tetzel debated him, and later the infamous scholar, Johann Eck, declared Luther to be a heretic. On June 15, 1520, Pope Leo X issued a papal bull (decree) entitled *Exsurge Domine* (*Arise, O Lord*), in which he stated, 'A wild boar from the forest has invaded the Lord's vineyard.' Of course, he was referring to Luther and his attacks upon Roman Catholicism. The bull outlined forty-one purported errors found in Martin Luther's *Ninety-Five Theses* and other writings. (Pictures and woodcarvings soon appeared throughout Europe depicting Luther as a wild-eyed pig running with tusks slashing left and right through a vineyard.) Pope Leo demanded that Luther retract his alleged errors within sixty days.

Luther, however, was undisturbed. When he received the bull, he prayerfully considered what he should do. On December 10, 1520, Luther called a gathering of students in front of the Wittenberg Church. A huge bonfire was roaring. Luther stepped forward, read the papal bull to the assembled crowd, threw it into the fire, and watched it burn. It was reported that he then thundered (referring to the Pope), 'Because you have confounded the truth of God, today the Lord confounds you. Into the fire with you!' Word of Luther's actions quickly spread. Some scholars suggest this was the actual day the Protestant Reformation began. Soon thereafter, on January 3, 1521, Leo issued another papal bull in which he excommunicated and condemned Luther to the fires of hell.

Undaunted by the excommunication, Luther was infused with a new enthusiasm and became more confident and bold in his faith and beliefs. He describes his new-found joy this way:

Night and day I pondered until I saw the connection between the justice of God and the statement that the just shall live by his faith. Then I grasped that the justice of God is that righteousness by which through grace and sheer mercy God justifies us through faith. Thereupon I felt myself to be reborn and to have gone through open doors into paradise. The whole of Scripture took on a new meaning ... This passage of Paul became to me a gate to heaven. (as qtd. in R. H. Bainton, *Here I Stand*)

Energized in his new life, Luther wrote tracts, treatises, and books, which were translated into many languages and materialized all over Europe. University students and tradesmen alike read and met to discuss these ideas. It is believed that the Protestant Reformation in England started in a place near Oxford called the White Horse Inn. There students discussed and disseminated Luther's bold biblical beliefs. The winds of reformation and change were blowing.

An infuriated pope directed the Holy Roman Emperor to call a diet, a special parliament to address Martin Luther and the effects of the Protestant Reformation. Emperor Charles V commenced the Imperial Diet of Worms on January 28, 1521. Luther was summoned by the Emperor to appear before the Diet. Prince Frederick III (or the Wise), Elector of Saxony, obtained an imperial agreement that if Luther appeared, he would be given safe passage to and from the meeting.

The reason Luther was summoned was to give him an opportunity to either renounce or reaffirm his views. When he appeared before the assembly on April 16, Johann Eck, an assistant of the Archbishop of Trier, acted as spokesman for the emperor and pope.

Eck presented Luther with a table stacked with copies of his books and writings. Eck then asked Luther if these were his works, to which Luther answered in the affirmative. Eck than asked him if he still believed what these works taught. Luther humbly requested time to think about his answer. He was granted a twenty-four hour extension. Through the afternoon and night, Luther prayed and consulted with friends and mediators.

The next day, he presented himself before the Diet once again. When Eck put the same question to Luther, as the day before, the reformer apologized for the harsh tone of many of his writings, but said that he could not reject the majority of them or the teachings in them. He was ordered to recant. Then, surrounded by the Holy Roman Emperor, great heads of state, and powerful religious leaders from all over Europe, Luther respectfully but boldly stated, 'Unless I am convinced by proofs from Scriptures or by plain and clear reasons and arguments, I cannot and will not retract, for it is neither safe nor wise to do anything against the conscience. Here I stand. I can do no other. God help me. Amen' (see *Luther's Works: Career of the Reformer III* for additional discussion). He immediately turned and left the room unmolested. The Diet continued its deliberations, but Luther left for Wittenberg the next day.

On his return to Wittenberg, it was reported that Luther had been kidnapped by violent highwaymen and his whereabouts were unknown. 'The rest of the story' is that his protector, the German prince Frederick the Wise, actually kidnapped Luther and hid him in Wartburg Castle for several months. Frederick did this to protect Luther from his growing cadre of enemies. It was at Wartburg Castle that Luther began translating the Scriptures into German (using Erasmus' Greek New Testament) and organized the Reformation. He was convinced the church had grown so corrupt that it was beyond repair.

Calls to recant came from many quarters, from friend and foe alike. When called upon to recant, recant this German monk did, but not in the way many may have wanted. In a letter to his friend Spalatin he wrote, 'Previously I said the pope is the Vicar of Christ. I recant. Now I say the pope is the adversary of Christ and the apostle of the Devil' (as qtd. in *Here I Stand*). There would be no turning back.

The Diet ended, and an official decree called the Edict of Worms was issued on May 25, 1521, by the Holy Roman Emperor Charles V. Its content was unmistakably clear:

> For this reason we forbid anyone from this time forward to dare, either by words or by deeds, to receive, defend, sustain, or favour the said Martin Luther. On the contrary, we want him to be apprehended and punished as a notorious heretic, as he deserves, to be brought personally before us, or to be securely guarded until those who have captured him inform us, whereupon we will order the appropriate manner of proceeding against the said Luther. Those who will help in his capture will be rewarded generously for their good work. (qtd. in D. Teems, *Tyndale: The Man Who Gave God an English Voice*)

A sincere monk, who had earnestly struggled with how to be just and right before a thrice-holy God, read the Greek New Testament and discovered in reading that salvation was by grace *alone*, through faith *alone*, in Christ *alone*, to God *alone* be all the glory. This ignited the Protestant Reformation, and the world has not been the same since.

30

The Anabaptist Movement Begins – 1525

*T*HE Protestant Reformation had firmly gripped Europe. Though Martin Luther was the spark that lit the flame, he stood on the shoulders of significant and unusual predecessors. Among these predecessors are men with whom this volume will not interact, yet they must be mentioned. Of course, the Waldensians and John Wycliffe were considered in events # 24 and #25, but also important were Jan Hus, Jerome of Prague, and Savonarola (in Italy). Each sowed seeds that Luther would harvest.

Historically, the Reformation took place in four movements: Lutheran, Reformed, Radical Reformation, and English Reformation. However, when the dust settled, Protestantism in continental Europe took the shape of three prominent figures. Luther led one group, John Calvin another, and Huldrych (Ulrich) Zwingli led the third group in Zurich, Switzerland.

Out of the third group sprang the Anabaptists (the Radical Reformation). How did they begin and what is their historical significance?

Three main theories exist as to how the Anabaptists began. One common notion is the 'Trail of Blood' theory, which holds that there was a historical line of succession from the Anabaptists all the way back to the apostles; and that Anabaptist and Baptist churches are the only true ones. Popularly held by many today in the southern United States, this belief was propagated by J. M. Carroll (brother of B. H. Carroll the founder of Southwestern Baptist Theological Seminary) in his widespread booklet entitled *The Trail of Blood: Following the Christians Down Through the Centuries* (American Baptist Publishing Co.: 1931). This notion simply cannot be sustained by historical fact as Tom Nettles (*The Baptists*, vol. 1) and James McGoldrick (*Baptist Successionism*) have shown. Another thought is the 'Zwichau Prophets and Thomas Müntzer' theory, which is a possibility, but not likely the case. The Zwichau Prophets were a fanatical group that emerged in 1522, led by Thomas Müntzer and located near Wittenberg. They rejected the authority of Scripture and were governed by Spirit-wrought 'prophetic words' and apocalyptical beliefs that the end of the world was immediately at hand. The first Anabaptists had knowledge of Zwichau, but no connection.

The most likely beginning of the Anabaptists is described in the 'Swiss Origin' theory. Zwingli was a Roman Catholic priest who was converted to Christ and Protestant beliefs, probably in late 1517. One year later, in December 1518, he was called to be the stipendiary pastor of the Grossmünster Church in Zurich. Zwingli gave his first sermon on January 1, 1519, immediately departing from the standard practice of preaching on the Gospel lesson of a particular Sunday. He mounted the pulpit with Erasmus' Greek New Testament in hand and began to read through the Gospel of Matthew, giving interpretation and commentary as he read. He continued this style of preaching, going through the Gospels, the Acts of the Apostles, and the Epistles, until his death. He only deviated to address quickly certain issues and subjects. This method of preaching became known as *lectio continua* (*continuous reading*). He brought great reform to the church and the city and created no small stir throughout Europe with his style of preaching.

Young humanists, who were greatly affected by Erasmus, soon heard of Zwingli and drifted into Zurich, where they found a safe haven. Zwingli saw an opportunity to influence these young men for the gospel and took them under his wing. He introduced them to Erasmus' Greek New Testament, and their study made them zealous for reform (Conrad Grebel is a case in point). As they read and studied the Greek New Testament, they began to question certain practices, especially the baptism of infants. They doubted if it could be found in the New Testament. Clashes between Zwingli and the radical humanists ensued, which caused them to be isolated, and later persecuted.

Preserved in *The Large Chronicle of the Hutterian Brethren* is a moving account of events that took place during a blustery winter night in the home of Felix Manz. On January 21, 1525, several men had trudged their way through driving sleet and snow to arrive at Manz's home for prayer and discussion. According to an eyewitness account, anxiety 'so pressed within their hearts that they fell to their knees and called upon the

Informer of Hearts to give them his divine will.' When they finished praying, George Blaurock stood up and 'besought Conrad Grebel for God's sake to baptize him with the true Christian baptism [based] upon his faith and knowledge.' Blaurock knelt down, and since there was no ordained minister 'to perform such a work,' Grebel took a bucket of water and a dipper and baptized him in the triune name. Blaurock rose and proceeded to baptize all those present. According to William Estep in his *Renaissance and Reformation*, this act of 'believer's baptism' signified the official break with mainstream Protestantism. Soon thereafter, because they believed in the baptism of adult believers only, they were given the name of *Anabaptists (re-baptizers)*.

There are three interesting points that must be made with regard to this account and the group's subsequent designation as Anabaptists. The first was the mode of baptism they utilized. Contrary to what most think, the first Anabaptists did not immerse on that bitterly cold winter night. Instead, they poured or effused, which is the standard mode of baptism for almost all anabaptistic groups today. Second, they thought their label as Anabaptists was misinformed. Since they did not accept infant baptism, they did not believe they were re-baptizing anyone; they were simply baptizing. Third, they believed their practice of believer's baptism could be traced back to the early church, which was a radical break with not only Protestantism, but almost 1,300 years of Christian history. Thus, the Anabaptists have often been called the 'stepchildren' of the Reformers. That is why they are called the 'Radical Reformation.'

The primary leaders of the Anabaptist movement were Conrad Grebel, Felix Manz, and George Blaurock. Others that followed were Pilgram Marpeck, Menno Simons, and Balthasar Hubmaier. Because they emphasized an experiential Christianity over a doctrinal one, their opponents accused the Anabaptists of being non-theological. Most of the above-mentioned leaders were persecuted and killed within three years of that fateful meeting in Manz's home in 1525. Thus, while it is true they did not have time to produce a thorough systematic theology or an in-depth confession of faith, they did write. Volumes of their writings remain. Early on, Hubmaier was their most prolific writer. He always ended his treatises with these words: 'Truth is immortal.'

For the most part and with few exceptions, the Anabaptists were orthodox and held to the historic creeds of the early church. Furthermore, they embraced justification by faith alone and the sole authority and rule of Scripture. However, their view of the rule of Scripture alone led them to strongly disagree with both the Roman Catholics and the Reformers on a number of points. That believers should join the church voluntarily rather than being born into the church was intrinsic to their system. This led to baptism (effusion/pouring) of adults only upon a confession of faith, rather than infant baptism. They rejected the nominal Christianity that surrounded them and called for a radical commitment to discipleship, which entailed holiness of life lived in full conformity to Christ and coupled with a radical nonconformity to the world. They preached a separation of church and state and declared that the state had no authority to interfere whatsoever with the body of Christ. In days that had recently witnessed the Inquisition, they embraced a full liberty of conscience and an ethic of love, which included nonresistance, refusal to serve in the military, and a total rejection of war of any type or the use of force.

It must be noted for the record and contrary to the thinking of many evangelical Christians: modern-day Baptists did *not* descend from the Anabaptists. Present-day Baptists came out of the English Separatist Movement, which was basically the Puritan Movement that broke from the Church of England entirely.

What, then, is the primary significance of the Anabaptists? They facilitated the dismantling of the church-state infrastructure erected by Theodosius I and set the stage for the 'free' church movement. Their spiritual heirs and blood-line descendants are the Mennonites, Hutterites, Amish, and various worldwide Brethren groups.

31

William Tyndale and the First English New Testament – 1526

*A*LTHOUGH John Wycliffe was the first to translate the Bible into English, his translation still carried
the problem of being translated solely from Latin. The Latin
Vulgate, rather than the Greek text, was the apparatus from
which Wycliffe worked. Furthermore, Wycliffe's Bible was
suppressed and not readily available to most who could read.
Because of the initial grassroots distribution of Wycliffe's Bible,
a law was passed declaring that possession of an unlicensed
copy of Scripture in English was punishable by death. People
were afraid to have a Bible.

Meanwhile, in the same year as the Anabaptist movement
began, across the English Channel, a thirty-one-year-old man
was about to shake the English-speaking world. His name
was William Tyndale (1494–1536). Tyndale was a scholar and
translator who became a leading figure of the English Protestant

Reformation. He was a gifted linguist and fluent in German, French, Italian, Spanish, Latin, Hebrew, and Greek, in addition to his native English. What is his story?

Tyndale was born in Gloucester, and by the age of sixteen, he began his studies at Oxford (1510). Due to Scholasticism, philosophy had become more important than the Word of God, and, at that time, no one could teach theology without a Master's degree. Upon attaining his Bachelor's degree, Tyndale moved to Cambridge and obtained his Master's degree at the age of twenty-one. This allowed him to be ordained and teach theology. Biographer David Daniell notes that Tyndale grumbled that this Scholastic tradition of obtaining a 'heathen learning eight or nine years and armed with false principles ... clean shut the understanding of the Scripture.' Hungry to know the Bible, he continued his studies, especially Greek. Erasmus (event #27), who taught Greek at Cambridge from 1511–1512, profoundly affected Tyndale with his belief, set forth in the preface to his New Testament: 'Christ desires his mysteries be published abroad as widely as possible. I would that [the Holy Scriptures] were translated into all languages, of all Christian people, and that they might be read and known.'

The more Tyndale studied the Word of God, the more he desired that the common person be able to read it. By 1523, a fire had been lit in his soul that would be extinguished only by his death. Foxe, in his *Book of Martyrs*, described an argument with a 'learned' but 'blasphemous' clergyman who had asserted to Tyndale, 'We had better be without God's laws than the Pope's.' Swelling with passion, Tyndale responded, 'I defy the Pope, and all his laws; and if God spares my life, ere many years, I will cause the boy that driveth the plough to know more of the Scriptures than the Pope himself!' He set out to do just that. He travelled to London to request help from Bishop Tunstall, a classical scholar who had assisted Erasmus with his New Testament. Snubbed by the Bishop, Tyndale left for Europe, determined to translate the Bible into English. He was convinced that the way to God was through His Word and that Scripture should be available even to common people.

Tyndale arrived in Germany and travelled to Wittenberg, where he was influenced by Martin Luther. There, in 1524, he began the work of translating the New Testament into English. The first edition was published in January 1526 and was smuggled into England and Scotland where it was distributed among the masses. By October 1526, Bishop Tunstall condemned the translation and ordered copies to be burned publicly. The public torching of Scripture troubled even the 'faithful.' With printings being done in Worms and Antwerp, Tyndale's New Testament flooded England. The more the English people read the Bible, the less of Roman Catholicism they believed to be biblical. In 1529, Cardinal Wolsey condemned Tyndale as a heretic.

Not satisfied with the New Testament in English, William set out to translate the Old Testament, but he did not know Hebrew. Anti-Semitism abounded, and the Act of Expulsion had driven most Jews out of England. Even the Jews on the continent kept a low profile. Nevertheless, Tyndale found a tutor, learned Hebrew, and began translating the Old Testament. (Unfortunately, he was only able to complete about half of the Old Testament before his death.) For nine years after the publication of his New Testament, Tyndale was hounded throughout Europe. In 1530, he wrote a treatise opposing Henry VIII's divorce from Catherine of Aragon and proposition of marriage to Anne Boleyn. The infuriated Henry demanded the Holy Roman Emperor, Charles V, hunt down and arrest Tyndale and ship him to England.

Eventually betrayed by a devious Henry Phillips and arrested in Antwerp in 1535, Tyndale was imprisoned in Vilvoorde Castle (near Brussels) and treated inhumanely for sixteen months. While in prison, he continued to translate the Old Testament and wrote a small treatise entitled 'Faith Alone Justifies before God.' He was tried on a charge of heresy in August 1536 and condemned to death. The traditional date of his death is October 6, 1536. He was tied to a cross in the center of town, strangled to death with a hangman's rope, and then burned. Before strangulation, he was given opportunity to recant (which he would not do), pray, and say his farewell. His last words were 'Lord! Open the King of England's eyes.'

What was his crime, and why was he hunted all over Europe like an animal? Simply this: he had given the English-speaking peoples their first Bible translated (from the Greek) into their own language. For this, he was brutally killed.

Why were the Roman Catholic leaders and the secular magistrates so afraid for the ordinary people in the streets to have the Holy Bible? Tyndale believed he knew the answer: if they had direct access to God's Word, the people would be liberated from the spiritual bondage of an apostate church and brought into the glorious liberty of the children of God. Desiring that the common milkmaid and ploughboy would know the glory of God in the face of Jesus Christ and possess the joy of justification by faith alone, Tyndale was the first to translate considerable parts of the Bible into English for lay readership.

His was the first English translation to extract directly from Hebrew and Greek texts, and the first to take advantage of the new medium of the printing press, which allowed for its wide distribution. Tyndale's Bible was the first English Bible of the Reformation.

More so than William Shakespeare, William Tyndale is often referred to as the 'Architect of the English Language' because he created or recorded more phrases used in English today than any other person. Among words unique to Tyndale, as listed by David Teems in *Tyndale: The Man Who Gave God an English Voice*, are *Jehovah*, *Passover*, *atonement*, and *mercy seat*. He also appears to have coined such phrases as *the powers that be*, *my brother's keeper*, *the salt of the earth*, *a law unto themselves*, *filthy lucre*, *it came to pass*, *gave up the ghost*, *the signs of the times*, and *live and move and have our being*. Scholars estimate that 85 per cent of the New Testament and seventy-five per cent of the Old Testament books he translated were carried over by later translators into the Authorized King James Version of 1611 (see event #34). Without a doubt, he shaped the way English is spoken, thus influencing the world's major language.

Within four years of his martyrdom, by direct order of King Henry VIII, four English translations of the Bible were published in England, including Henry's *Great Bible* (1539). They were followed by the Geneva Bible (1560), the Bishops' Bible (1568), and the Roman Catholic Douay-Rheims Bible (1582). All were based on Tyndale's ground-breaking work. Indeed, Tyndale's dying prayer was answered: the Lord opened the King's eyes!

32

John Calvin Publishes First Edition of *The Institutes of the Christian Religion* – 1536

*I*F Luther was the 'Prophet' of the Protestant Reformation, Calvin was the 'Professor.' Whether one excoriates him or blesses him, John Calvin cannot be disregarded in either world or Christian history. Though hated, despised, and misrepresented by some, this great, influential Protestant Reformer of Geneva has also been well loved by many. In March 1536, Calvin published in Basel a slim volume of only six chapters, prefaced with a letter to Francis I of France, in which he defended the Protestants against their enemies. It was a short summary of the Christian faith, which became popular among the Protestants as both an able exposition and a forthright apology for the Reformed faith. This short and powerful book is known as *The Institutes of the Christian Religion*.

Who was John Calvin? He was born in Noyon, France, on July 10, 1509, to Gerard Cauvin. Calvinus was the Latinized form of his name, from which we get 'Calvin.' His father was a notary public employed in the comfortable service of the Bishop of Noyon.

From early childhood, John was most liberally educated. He studied at Paris and made considerable achievements. His father intended his son to study theology with the goal of Calvin's becoming a priest in the Roman Catholic institution. With that goal in view, his father procured for him two ecclesiastical benefices (a church office fixed with capital assets that provided a living), which were used to support him during his university studies. Gerard became disgruntled with the Church and transferred John's study from theology to law. From Paris, Calvin went to Orleans and attained a Doctor's degree in Law. He then went to Bourges and quickly cultivated a love for sacred literature. By the time he returned to Paris at age twenty, he had mastered Greek and Hebrew. Studying the Scriptures in the original languages would profoundly affect him for years to come.

Watching Protestant believers burned at the stake in Paris moved Calvin deeply. Through the faithful witness of his cousin, Pierre Robert Olivet (aka Olivetan), and a fervent reading of the Holy Scriptures, the light of God broke in upon his heart and made him a new creature in Christ Jesus. His conversion to an evangelical faith in Christ was in late 1533 or early 1534. Never does Calvin speak of himself in any of his theological writings (over sixty volumes of commentaries, treatises, and sermons), except in two instances. One is in his treatise to a Catholic cardinal, Sadoleto, and the other is in the preface of his commentary on the Psalms, in which he briefly described his conversion:

God drew me from obscure and lowly beginnings and conferred on me the most honorable office of herald and minister of the Gospel ... What happened first was that by an sudden conversion he tamed to teachableness a mind too stubborn for its years – for I was strongly devoted to the superstitions of the Papacy that nothing less could draw me from such depths of mire. And so this mere taste of true piety that I received set me on fire with such a desire to progress that I pursued the rest of my studies more coolly, although I did not give them up altogether. Before a year had slipped by anybody who longed for purer doctrine kept on coming to learn from me, still a beginner and a raw recruit. (*Calvin's Commentaries*, vol. 4)

Through an unusual series of providences, Calvin ended up in Geneva, where he exercised a fruitful ministry of Reformation for twenty-three years until his death in 1564. The Presbyterian Church can trace its roots back to Calvin and Geneva.

Why did Calvin write the *Institutes*? He gives eight reasons, but they can be summed up in two main points. The first was a defense of Protestants. All kinds of charges of sedition and heresy had been leveled against the Huguenots, and many Protestants had been burned at the stake by the order and decree of King Francis I:

And this was the cause which induced me to publish my *Institutes of the Christian Religion*; first in order to reply to the lying accusations spread by the others and to clear my brethren, whose death was precious in the sight of the Lord; and then that, since the same cruelties might very soon be practiced against many poor persons, foreign nations might at least be touched with some compassion and solicitude for them. (*Institutes*, vol. 1)

The second was to be a theological introduction to the Bible so that common people might know and understand the Holy Scriptures. Additionally, it was to teach sound theology in order to train men for the gospel ministry. Calvin gave insight into his heart's desire with these words in his preface 'To the Reader': 'My object in this work is to so prepare and train students of sacred theology for the study of the word of God that they might have an easy access unto it, and be able to proceed without hindrance.'

The first edition of the *Institutes* consisted of six chapters:

    i.   An exposition of the 10 Commandments

    ii.   An exposition of the Apostles' Creed

    iii.   An exposition of the Lord's Prayer

    iv.   An exposition of the sacraments

    v.   An exposé of false sacraments

    vi.   A treatise on church government

The final edition consisted of four books under the following heads:

    i.   Book One, The Knowledge of God the Creator

    ii.   Book Two, The Knowledge of God the Redeemer in Christ, First Disclosed to the Fathers Under the Law, and Then to Us in the Gospel

    iii.   Book Three, The Way in Which We Receive the Grace of Christ: What Benefits Come to Us from It, and What Effects Follow

    iv.   Book Four, The External Means or Aids by Which God Invites Us into the Society of Christ and Holds Us Therein.

The *Institutes* went from six chapters published in 1536 to eighty chapters (under the four Books or headings listed above) in the final and definitive edition issued in Latin in 1559 and French in 1560. Oxford theologian Alister E. McGrath gives an insightful assessment of the Reformed Church's success in his *A Life of John Calvin*:

> Lutheranism never really recovered from the false start given to it by Melanchthon; the intellectual domination of Protestantism by theologians of the Reformed tradition is due to both the *substance* and *structure* of Calvin's final edition of the *Institutes* ... to study Calvin is not merely to study the past – it is also to gain a deeper understanding of the present. Modern western culture continues to be shaped by memories of the past. Although Calvin lies buried in an unmarked grave somewhere in Geneva, his ideas and influence live on in the outlooks of the culture he helped to create.

From its initial printing, the *Institutes* established Calvin as a theologian. Church historian Philip Schaff observed that Philip Melanchthon, himself the prince of Lutheran divines and 'the Preceptor of Germany,' emphatically called John Calvin 'the theologian.' Quickly, the *Institutes* became the textbook of the young Protestant faith and of Reformed theology and the subsequent formative structure for all dogmatic and systematic theological books. Furthermore, perhaps more than any other book, *The Institutes of the Christian Religion* shaped western civilization. Regardless of one's feelings toward the man, Calvin's *Institutes* are well worth reading. Why not read the book and get to know John Calvin better? It could very well change your life.

33

The Council of Trent Convenes – 1545

*T*HE Protestant Reformation caused great division within Christianity, which, essentially, in the West, was Roman Catholicism. The Reformers' original intent was not to divide the church, only to reform it. Yet, from their actions, fresh winds started blowing throughout Renaissance Europe, dissolving the stale, soul-withering air of the Middle Ages. Entire nations were converted to biblical Christianity, and Protestants were spreading their faith, little by little, into all parts of the world. John Calvin even ventured to send out of Geneva to Brazil a missionary party of seventeen people to convert the peoples there. Five months later, this entire Calvinist missionary team, under the leadership of Pierre Richier and Guillaume Charpentier, was massacred by the Jesuits. Persecution and death could not stop the Reformation, as throngs of people departed from the icy monolith of Rome to the warm freedom of Christ alone. With the hemorrhaging of the Catholic faith, what was the ecclesiastical hierarchy to do?

Notwithstanding the gross corruption they saw, not all left the Roman Catholic institution. Paul III, a reform-minded pope, appointed a commission of cardinals to assess the situation. The cardinals' report was straightforward and candid. Worldliness and immorality were rampant. Many clergy obtained their offices through simony or bribery and were rich and lazy. The monastic orders were rife with sexual immorality of unmentionable sorts. Prostitutes filled the holy city of Rome, some even to serve Vatican officials. The abuse of the sale of indulgences left multitudes of the faithful cynical toward the church and skeptical of its teachings. Drastic action, the cardinals reported, must be taken, or the church would bleed to death with self-inflicted wounds.

Pope Paul III decided to fight back against the Reformation. The Pope called for a council in 1537, but political bickering postponed it for eight long years. Eventually, an ecclesiastical council was called that lasted from December 13, 1545 to December 4, 1563, and which required another eight years for the prelates to settle issues and make canonical determinations. What Rome did during those eight years is known as the Counter-Reformation. It consisted of twenty-five sessions during three separate periods. Accounts of the Council record that latent political rivalries publically surfaced, and most sessions were poorly attended. Despite the internal squabbling, the Council managed to enact canons, or laws, that brought about change.

The results of the Council of Trent (i.e., Counter-Reformation) were several. First, the teachings of Martin Luther, John

Calvin, Ulrich Zwingli, and the rest of the Reformers were condemned as heresy.

Second, it was forever established that only the Catholic Institution could interpret the Holy Bible and that its interpretation of the Bible was final. The official Church feared, no doubt, Tyndale's prediction about every ploughboy reading and studying the Scriptures for himself. Any Christian who substituted his or her own interpretation over the Church's was counted a heretic. Also, the Bible *and* Church Tradition (not mere customs, but the ancient tradition that made up part of the Catholic faith) were declared equally authoritative. *Sola Scriptura* (*Scripture alone*), the watch cry of the Reformers, was deemed heretical. The Word of God was not to be translated in the languages of the people, and Jerome's Latin Vulgate was the only version of Scripture that was allowed in public worship or scholarly writing.

Third, due to the controversy over Martin Luther's doctrine of 'justification by faith alone,' the relationship of faith and works in salvation was clearly defined. Justification, according to Rome, was righteousness imparted and declared to be obtained upon the basis of faith *and* good works, as opposed to the Protestant (and biblical) doctrine of righteousness imputed and received by faith alone. Under Rome, justification and saving faith was treated as a progressive work, making no distinction between justification and sanctification. The idea of man's will being in bondage to sin and sinners unable, within themselves, to respond to grace was also rejected. Additionally, the council insisted, one could be in grace and saved and then fall from grace and be lost again. To have assurance before death that one was justified and going to heaven was anathematized as a damnable heresy.

Other Catholic practices that drew the ire of the Reformers but were adamantly reaffirmed by the council included indulgences, pilgrimages to Rome and sacred shrines, prayers to the saints, the veneration of relics, and the worship of the Virgin Mary. Abuses of them, especially the sale of indulgences, were forbidden.

The greatest weight in the Council's decrees was given to the sacramental system. The seven sacraments were reaffirmed, in contrast to the two that Protestants embraced. The Eucharist, or Lord's Supper, in which Christ said 'do this in remembrance of me' was declared to be much more than a memorial. According to the Council's decree, the sacrament of the Mass was pronounced to be a true propitiatory sacrifice; in other words, Christ is crucified again each time the Mass is held to make atonement and take away sin. The bread and wine consecrated in the Eucharist are transformed into the actual, physical body and blood of Christ. The term 'transubstantiation' was purposefully used by the Council to convey that Christ is transformed and is 'really, truly, and substantially present' in the consecrated forms. The sacrifice of the Mass was to be offered, not only for the living, but also for the dead in Purgatory. Church leaders confirmed the practice of withholding the cup from the laity.

The Catholic priesthood saw itself as taking the place of the Old Testament Levitical priesthood. Christ, Trent decreed, conferred upon priests in these New Testament days a sacerdotal power to actually forgive sins. The auricular confessional was validated. Furthermore, the performance and the saving power of the sacraments did not depend upon the holiness of the priest or the consent of the people.

In the decrees on marriage, the excellence of the celibate state was reaffirmed, concubinage condemned, and the validity of marriage made dependent upon its being performed before a priest and two witnesses. In the case of a divorce, the right of the innocent party to marry again was denied so long as the other party was alive, even if the other party committed adultery.

In the last session, the doctrines of purgatory, prayers to the saints, and the veneration of relics were reaffirmed, as was also the efficacy of indulgences as dispensed by the Church, according to the power given her. However, there were some cautionary recommendations and, again, a ban was placed on the *sale* of indulgences.

Did the Council of Trent succeed? Yes and no, depending upon a person's point of view. For the Catholics, it settled ecclesiastical dissent within the Roman institution for a while. For the Protestants, it sealed the split and permanently prevented any possible hope of reconciliation. Worst of all, in the minds of the Protestants, it degraded the person of Christ and His propitiatory, saving work upon the cross, undermining the doctrine of salvation by grace alone, through faith alone, in Christ alone by supplanting it with man's works and moral 'goodness.' If good works can save and make a person right with God, the Reformers contended, Christ died in vain! If a person can contribute in any part to salvation, there is no need for a Savior to actually save. Protestants saw that the Council of Trent would blind minds and hearts to the glory of Christ and thus have eternal repercussions. Among the majority of conservative, Bible-believing Protestants today, the issues with Catholicism have not changed.

34

The *King James Version* of the Bible – 1611

*T*HE Authorized King James Version (AV or KJV) is an English translation of the Bible produced by the Church of England. Translation started in 1604, and it was published in 1611. Although it is now over four hundred years old, it is perhaps the most beautiful of all English translations of the Holy Bible and is still the most widely accepted and used in the English-speaking world. Why was it produced, and what gave it that enduing and lasting quality?

Queen Elizabeth died without an heir, and her nearest blood relative was the son of Elizabeth's cousin and bitter rival, Mary Queen of Scots. His name was James VI of Scotland, and he was of the royal House of Stuart. The Stuarts possessed a high view of the monarchy that has been termed 'the divine right of kings.' For the Stuarts, that meant that not only did they rule by God's divine authority, but also they were accountable to no earthly authority. James was crowned King James I of England, Ireland, and Great Britain in 1603, and he carried this 'divine right' mentality from Scotland into England.

Part of James' title as monarch was the 'Defender of the Faith.' The Church of England, less than seventy years old, was in turmoil. Two parties, the Bishops and the Puritans (Reformed), vied for control in the Church. James was raised a staunch Presbyterian in Scotland, and the Puritans hoped his rearing would incline him to their side. James, however, deplored his Presbyterianism, and as the Faith's Defender, he had his own ideas. Before his arrival in England, the Puritan party presented James with a Millenary Petition that supposedly was signed by a thousand men. The Petition requested a moderate change in the Church of England, which was much to James' dislike. The Reformed party being too numerous to ignore, he agreed to a meeting with them in Hampton Court. He rejected all of their propositions, except one. He approved a new translation of the Bible.

James had two reasons for approving a new translation. One, he detested the commonly used Geneva Bible because of its Calvinistic bias, its frequent usage of the word 'tyrant,' and a footnote on Exodus 1 that commended the Hebrew midwives' disobedience to Pharaoh (both contrary to his belief in rule by 'divine right'), and, as petty as it may seem, because the populace loved it. Two, the Bishops' Bible, which was the official Bible of the Church of England intended to replace the Geneva Bible, was not received by the ordinary people.

In 1604, King James I commissioned a new translation of the Bible. Fifty-four men were appointed as translators, although only forty-seven were known to have taken part in the actual work of translation. Interestingly, from the preface written by the Puritan Miles Smith (1554–1624), it may be questioned whether a new translation was intended. Miles states that it was the translators' 'endeavor to make a good one better, or out of many good ones, one principled good one.' F. F. Bruce noted that between Tyndale's New Testament and the printing of the KJV, there were ten stepping-stone English translations of the Bible (for more detail, see his *History of the Bible in English*).

At the outset of their work, the translators were organized into six groups, assigned portions of the Bible to translate, and issued fifteen guidelines to follow. The translators met respectively at Westminster, Cambridge, and Oxford, with two groups at each location. One group of ten at Westminster was assigned Genesis through 2 Kings, and another group of seven had the letters of Romans through Jude. At Cambridge, one group of eight worked on 1 Chronicles through Song of Solomon, while another group of seven handled the Apocrypha. Oxford employed one group of seven to translate Isaiah through Malachi and another group of eight occupied themselves with the Gospels, Acts, and the Revelation. The initial translation was completed by these six groups in 1608, which was then sent to a special review committee. This committee worked on it for another two years. Miles Smith wrote the Preface and, last of all, it was reviewed by Archbishop Bancroft. In December 1610, it was handed over to the royal printer, Robert Barker, and published in 1611.

As was typical with the translations that preceded it, the KJV translators used the Hebrew Masoretic text and the Septuagint for the Old Testament. For the New Testament, they used the 1526 Greek text of Erasmus, the 1550 Textus Receptus of Stephanus, and the 1589 Codex Bezae. The standard Greek and Latin texts were used for the Apocrypha. In the Preface, the translators humbly acknowledged and addressed several things: they answered those who questioned the need for a revision of the English Bible when there were already several available; they commended earlier English translations and affirmed that they built upon them (note: four-fifths of Tyndale's New Testament was carried over into the KJV); they admitted their limitations as translators and their use of variant readings; they addressed the usefulness of a variety of sources for further revisions; they pointed out the need for Scripture to be translated into the everyday language of the people and that translations should be current; and, finally, they observed that even the poorest translation is still the Word of God. These acknowledgements suggest that the men who collaborated on this translation were both honest and godly.

Acceptance of the text and translation by biblical scholars was slow to develop. Hugh Broughton, the most highly regarded English Hebraist of his time (excluded from the panel of translators because of his utterly uncongenial temperament), issued in 1611 a total condemnation of the new version, especially criticizing the translators' rejection of word-for-word equivalence. The Puritans, at first, opposed the translation, but by the 1650s, they accepted it more fully, because it was written in the common vernacular of the people. Since its initial translation, it has been revised five times, in 1629, 1638, 1662, 1762 (by Cambridge University), and 1769 (by Oxford University). A copy of the original '1611' KJV is vastly different from the KJV of today, and the original is often difficult for modern readers to grasp.

The 'plain style' beauty of the language, coupled with its usefulness through the centuries, makes the KJV inestimable in value. It has been memorized and quoted more than any other translation of the Scriptures in English. F. W. Faber said of the translation, 'It lives on the ear, like music that can never be forgotten, like the sound of church bells, which the convert hardly knows how he can forego.' Sir Winston Churchill spoke of the value of the KJV without hesitation: 'The scholars who produced this masterpiece are mostly unknown and unremembered. But they forged an enduring link, literary and religious, between the English-speaking people of the world.' Ironically, Richard Dawkins, a leading twenty-first-century atheist, when asked why he wanted to participate in the quatercentenary celebrations of the Authorized Version, gave this reply in an interview:

> You can't appreciate English literature unless you are steeped to some extent in the King James Bible. People don't know that proverbial phrases which make echoes in their minds come from this Bible. We are a Christian culture, we come from a Christian culture, and not to know the King James Bible is to be, in some small way, barbarian. (to see the full segment, visit GoodPersonTest.com's channel on YouTube)

There is available online an excellent one-year Bible reading program, which can be easily followed in just fifteen minutes a day http://www.oneyearbibleonline.com. Would it not be good for each person reading this book to read through the entire King James Version in a year and experience the beauty and warmth of the most famous English translation of the Bible that has literally shaken the world?

35

The Synod of Dort – 1618

*T*HE Synod of Dort was a National Synod held in Dordrecht in 1618–1619 by the Reformation churches of the Netherlands and Low Countries. Dort is a colloquial English term used today for the town of Dordrecht. The Synod was called to settle a serious controversy in the Dutch churches sparked by the rise and spread of a theological system of belief that became internationally known (and is known even to this day) as Arminianism.

Arminianism, which the Synod would eventually condemn, had as its foundation a manmade philosophy (originating out of Pelaganism) that begins with human reasoning and logic (for in-depth description, see B. R. Brees' *Pelagius: Life and Letters*). Arminians argued that they were beginning with the Scriptures, but the Reformed theologians believed that the bottom line of Arminian beliefs was a series of philosophical presuppositions and a refusal to receive God's *absolute* sovereignty (i.e. to let God alone be God).

Jacob Arminius, who studied theology in Geneva under Calvin's successor Theodore Beza, was a professor of theology at Leiden. He opposed the basic ideas of the Reformation of the *absolute* sovereignty of God and the almighty working of God's grace. After the death of Arminius in 1609, his followers presented objections to the *Belgic Confession* and the teachings of John Calvin, Theodore Beza, and their followers. These objections were published in an alternative document entitled *The Remonstrance of 1610* and presented to the national church leaders of the Netherlands for their consideration. Therefore, Arminius' proponents were known as Remonstrants (remonstrate: from Medieval Latin, to forcefully oppose). This was the first collectively organized attack within Protestantism against the principle doctrines of the Protestant Reformation.

As an alternative to the Calvinist doctrines of the *Belgic Confession*, *The Remonstrance* contained five articles that vastly differed with the Reformers on the doctrine of salvation. When biblically, theologically, and thoroughly examined in their detailed minutiae, the articles of the Remonstrants can be summarized as follows: 1) man, not God, is ultimately sovereign in salvation; 2) man's will, though in 'the state of apostasy,' is not totally bound, affected, or tainted after the Fall, but is absolutely free (The Remonstrants did acknowledge that despite 'the energy of his free will,' mankind nevertheless needed the grace of Christ); 3) election is based on foreknowledge of a person's foreseen repentance and faith and, consequentially, good works; 4) a universal atonement was made for all the sins of all people in every age, in that 'Jesus Christ, the Savior of the world, died for all men and for every man, so that He obtained for them all, by His death on the cross, redemption and the forgiveness of sin' (Theologically speaking, this is incipient universalism); 5) while God's grace is needed in order for a person to be saved, the grace of God is 'not irresistible.' Thus, in the matter of salvation, man can ultimately resist almighty God (though, theologically speaking, if God can be ultimately resisted, this actually makes man stronger than God); 6) and the very real possibility of a believer's final lapse (fall) and loss of God's salvation by 'becoming devoid of grace.' Simon Episcopius (1583–1643) was the chief spokesman of the thirteen representatives of the Remonstrants who were summoned before the Synod in 1618.

The first meeting of the Synod of Dort was on November 13, 1618, and the final meeting (the 154th) was on May 9, 1619. All of the sessions were held in the Great Church of Dordrecht. Voting representatives from the Reformed churches in eight foreign countries were invited (including Bishop Joseph Hall from England). Altogether, eighty-nine pastors and theologians formed the Synod of Dort (recommended reading on this topic includes *Acta of the Synod of Dordt, Crisis in the Reformed Churches*, and *The Articles of the Synod of Dordt*).

With great eloquence, Simon Episcopius, the spokesman for the Remonstrants, began the Synod debate by stating his objections to the misunderstood doctrine of reprobation. In so doing, he feebly argued that he and the Remonstrants were within the bounds of Reformed orthodoxy, but hoped to prejudice the minds of the ministers against the other articles of the Calvinistic system. Quickly and properly, the Synod reminded Episcopius that they had not convened with the intent of putting on trial the long adopted and well-loved

Belgic Confession. Instead, the Synod had gathered to give the Remonstrants an opportunity to defend themselves against the accusation of departing from the Reformed faith, to justify their change of doctrinal opinions, and to produce scriptural support for their opinions.

The Remonstrants (Arminians) would not yield to this procedure, because it would ultimately destroy their entire structure of argument. Session after session, the Synod leaders reasoned and pleaded with Episcopius and the Remonstrants to defend their published doctrines with exegesis and precepts. The Arminians *refused* to do so and were compelled to voluntarily withdraw from the Synod. Seeing the obstinacy of the Arminians, their reliance upon philosophical and speculative arguments, and their refusal to produce exegetical, biblical supports for their beliefs, the Synod had no other recourse but to proceed without them.

After almost six months of prayerful deliberation, the Synod produced a five-point response to the five points of the Remonstrance. This response is known as *The Canons of Dort*: five main articles that confess the biblical and Reformed faith. Each of the five points contains two parts, a positive exposition of truth and a rejection of listed errors. The following are the five main articles:

    i.   The First Main Point of Doctrine
           Divine Election and Reprobation The Judgment Concerning Divine Predestination Which the Synod Declares to Be in Agreement with the Word of God and Accepted Till Now in the Reformed Churches, Set Forth in Several Articles

ii.   The Second Main Point of Doctrine
       Christ's Death and Human Redemption Through It

iii-iv. The Third and Fourth Main Points of Doctrine
       *Human Corruption, Conversion to God, and the
       Way It Occurs*

v.   The Fifth Main Point of Doctrine
       The Perseverance of the Saints

Even though the *Canons'* first point deals with divine election
and reprobation, the opening two articles under the first 'head'
set forth a beautiful free and unfettered offer of the gospel:

> ARTICLE 1. As all men have sinned in Adam, lie under the
> curse, and are deserving of eternal death, God would have
> done no injustice by leaving them all to perish and delivering
> them over to condemnation on account of sin, according to the
> words of the apostle: 'that every mouth may be silenced and
> the whole world held accountable to God' (Rom. 3:19 NIV).
> And: 'for all have sinned and fall short of the glory of God'
> (Rom. 3:23). And: 'For the wages of sin is death' (Rom. 6:23).

> ARTICLE 2. But in this the love of God was manifested,
> that He 'sent his one and only Son into the world, that
> whoever believes in him shall not perish but have eternal life'
> (1 John 4:9, John 3:16).

The *Canons of the Synod of Dort* end as follows:

> Finally, this Synod urges all fellow ministers in the gospel
> of Christ to deal with this teaching in a godly and reverent
> manner, in the academic institutions as well as in the churches;
> to do so, both in their speaking and writing, with a view to
> the glory of God's name, holiness of life, and the comfort of

anxious souls; to think and also speak with Scripture *according to the analogy of faith*; and, finally, to refrain from all those ways of speaking which go beyond the bounds set for us by the genuine sense of the Holy Scriptures and which could give impertinent sophists a just occasion to scoff at the teaching of the Reformed churches or even to bring false accusations against it.

May God's Son Jesus Christ, who sits at the right hand of God and gives gifts to men, sanctify us in the truth, lead to the truth those who err, silence the mouths of those who lay false accusations against sound teaching, and equip faithful ministers of his Word with a spirit of wisdom and discretion, that all they say may be to the glory of God and the building up of their hearers. Amen. (*emphasis added*)

Rather than being cold, hard, soul-hating, anti-evangelism, anti-missionary Calvinists, the Synod of Dort demonstrated that they were otherwise. It successfully repelled the first organized attack within Protestantism and held fast to the apostolic and Reformed faith. In producing the *Canons of Dort*, the Synod provided a warm and wonderfully balanced teaching tool, not just for the Reformed churches, but for all evangelical churches around the world. It is known and widely-used today from the darkest parts of Africa to the balmy islands of the Pacific.

36

John Bunyan Authors
The Pilgrim's Progress – 1678

*W*HAT is the most published book in the world apart from the Holy Bible? Is it the writings of Confucius or Socrates or, perhaps, the Qur'an (Koran)? It is none other than *The Pilgrim's Progress* by John Bunyan. Second to the Holy Bible, it is regarded as one of the most significant works of secular and Christian literature of all time. It has been translated into more than two hundred languages and is being translated into other languages even now. With such unprecedented appeal, it bears the distinction, unlike many classics before it, of having never once been out of print. Kings, presidents, religious leaders of all sorts (including popes), philosophers, educators and more people than can be numbered, have been influenced and affected by this wonderful spiritual allegory.

In a 1957 edition of *The Pilgrim's Progress*, Alexander M. Witherspoon, distinguished professor of English at Yale

University, wrote an introductory essay as the preface in which he made an extraordinary claim:

> Part II, which appeared in 1684, is much more than a mere sequel to or repetition of the earlier volume. It clarifies and reinforces and justifies the story of Part I. The beam of Bunyan's spotlight is broadened to include Christian's family and other men, women, and children; the incidents and accidents of everyday life are more numerous, the joys of the pilgrimage tend to outweigh the hardships; and to the faith and hope of Part I is added in abundant measure the greatest of virtues, charity. The two parts of *The Pilgrim's Progress* in reality constitute a whole, and the whole is, without a doubt, the most influential book ever written in the English language.

Who was John Bunyan and what is 'the most influential book ever written in the English language' all about?

Bunyan was a nonconformist Baptist pastor who lived in Bedford, England (1628–1688). He was a tinker (a mender of pots, kettles, and pans) and did not have a university education. However, he was a godly man who loved the Word of God and preached Christ and His salvation in a clear, remarkably simple manner. He was not a part of the established Church of England and was imprisoned for refusing to submit to the laws of the land regarding the established church. He spent approximately twelve years of his life in prison (1660–1672) for violations of the Conventicle Act, which prohibited the holding of religious services outside the authority of the established Church of England. Bunyan could have avoided imprisonment by submitting to the Conventicle Act, but he chose instead to go to prison in protest of illegitimate laws and to advocate for religious freedom to preach the gospel. He is but one of many throughout history to protest by way of incarceration. Bunyan, who had previously written his spiritual autobiography, *Grace Abounding to the Chief of Sinners*, began his immortal Christian allegory while in Bedfordshire jail. He entitled it *The Pilgrim's Progress from This World to That Which Is to Come*. It was officially published on February 18, 1678.

The Pilgrim's Progress opens with a quaint but delightful poem called 'The Author's Apology,' wherein Bunyan states his reasons for writing the book 'in the similitude of a dream.' The narrative tells a story about a man 'clothed with rags' who lives in the City of Destruction (earth) with his wife and family. While reading the book of God, the man realizes that he has a large burden upon his shoulders and back. He is deeply troubled because of this burden and struggles with how to be rid of it.

One day, he encounters a man who introduces himself as Evangelist. Bunyan gives a pleasant description of him as 'a man who had his eyes up to heaven, the best of books was in his hand, the law of truth was written upon his lips, and *he stood as if he pleaded with men*' (emphasis added). When asked how to get rid of this burden, Evangelist points Pilgrim to 'yonder wicket-gate,' which would eventually lead him to a hill far away on which stands a cross. Pilgrim returns to his wife and children, tells them of the cross, and entreats them to go with him to that far-away hill. At that time, they are reluctant to go with him, so Pilgrim determines to go alone.

On his journey, Pilgrim first arrives at the House of the Interpreter, where he understands things more clearly, and then, at last, he comes to the cross. It is there that Pilgrim's burden falls away and he becomes a *Christian*. The book is about his 'progress' after leaving the City of Destruction and his exciting and adventure-filled journey towards the Celestial City (heaven), which is an allegorized picture of the Christian life. It is filled with colorful characters along the way – villains and heroes, scoundrels and brave souls – not the least of which is a man named Ignorance. Ignorance typifies all nominally religious people in the world.

Part II, published six years later and added to the first, introduces the reader to Christian's wife, who earlier chose to remain in the City of Destruction. Christiana, her four sons, and a maiden named Mercy come to see their burdens and start their pilgrimage to the Celestial City. They visit the same places Christian visited, exhibiting the same adventurous spirit. However, there are additional locations on their journey, such as Gaius' Inn, and new heroic characters, such as Greatheart; and a longer time is taken to reach the City. Marriage of the sons and subsequent childbirths, along with other normal affairs of life, extend the chronicle. Many scholars believe Bunyan had a point to make in his prolonged narrative: women, children, physically handicapped, and even mentally challenged people can be heroes in the struggle of life and the Christian faith. Human frailty is no barrier to coming to faith in Christ and journeying to heaven.

The book has a wonderful cadence and is saturated with Bible verses in a simple yet effective style of prose. Filled with unpretentious vitality and beauty of language, its robustness and charm immediately grab the attention, regardless of whether the reader is a university graduate or a kindergartener. Referring to Bunyan, John Owen, the prolific Puritan and Vice-Chancellor of Oxford University, said he would trade all of his education and learning to be able to touch the hearts and minds of people like that 'tinker of Bedford.' Samuel Johnson, English writer, essayist, poet, literary critic, lexicographer, and claimed by the *Oxford Dictionary of National Biography* as 'arguably the most distinguished man of letters in English history' said of Bunyan's masterpiece, 'This is the great merit of the book, that the most cultivated man cannot find anything to praise more highly, and the child knows nothing more amusing.' Charles Spurgeon, the famous Victorian pastor of the 5,000-member Metropolitan Tabernacle in London, read the book one hundred times and affirmed, 'Next to the Bible, the book I value most is John Bunyan's *The Pilgrim's Progress.*'

Bunyan ends Part I with holy angels carting Ignorance away from God and closes with these words: 'Then I saw that there was a Way to Hell, even from the Gates of Heaven, as well as from the City of Destruction. So I awoke, and behold it was a Dream.' What does Bunyan mean by this ending? Does it seem confusing? If the reader has never experienced this enriching and exciting book, buy it and read it immediately. You will discover the answer and not regret it!

37
The Apex of Protestant Confessionalism – 1689

*T*AKING its cue from Paul in 1 Timothy 3:16 ('Great indeed, we confess, is the mystery of godliness ...'), the Christian church has always been a confessing religion of creeds (from Latin *credo* – 'I believe') and confessions of faith. Very quickly, Christianity realized the value and purpose of confessions of faith. Confessions were used to publicly declare and affirm what Christians believed, enabling them to defend the truth revealed by God against slanderous accusations. Confessions also served as a standard of fellowship, which allowed the Christian churches to 'keep the unity of the Spirit in the bond of peace' (Eph. 4:3 KJV). They enabled the visible bodies of believers to follow apostolic instruction and maintain discipline by 'marking them that caused divisions and occasions of stumbling, contrary to the doctrine that you have been taught; avoid them' (Rom. 16:17).

By establishing confessions of faith, the churches were able to evaluate those men who professed to have an internal call of Christ into the gospel ministry. A person's orthodoxy could be determined by his adherence to the early and time-honored creeds and confessions. And for Christianity today, confessions contribute to a sense of historical continuity. Christianity is not a religion that has only been around for a century or two, but can trace its origins all the way back to the early days of the apostles, and before that, to the beginning of creation. This secures for the Christian a consciousness of historic connection. Early Christian churches and believers boldly confessed their faith before a watching world.

Confessionalism in Christianity continued to grow through the centuries, but it flourished with the Protestant Reformation. Many have completely misunderstood the term 'Protestant,' thinking that it was simply a protest against Roman Catholicism. Originally, the word had a far more positive meaning than its perception today. The infinitive form of the verb to 'protest' was a transitive verb meaning to affirm, to declare, to set forth a position (e.g., to protest one's innocence or to protest one's love). In volume 3 of his *2000 Years of Christ's Power*, N. R. Needham captures the idea well: 'The first Protestants were not only *protesting* against medieval Catholic errors; they were also "protesting the gospel," declaring the positive truths of Scripture which medieval Rome had neglected, obscured, distorted, or denied.'

What are the major Protestant confessions of faith?

The Augsburg Confession (June 1530) was the first official Protestant confession of faith. It was written by Philip Melanchthon in Latin, later translated into German by Justas

Jonas (1532), and became the doctrinal confession of all Lutheran Churches.

The Confession of Faith (*Confession de la Foy*) was written in November 1536 by John Calvin for the citizens of Geneva and the Swiss churches. It prepared the way for many other confessions, especially *The Belgic*, *The Second Helvetic*, and those listed below.

The Belgic Confession of Faith (*Confessio Belgica*, 1561) was written by Guido de Brès for the Reformed churches of the Low Countries (today divided into Belgium and the Netherlands).

The Thirty-Nine Articles (1563) is the set of doctrinal formulae accepted by the Church of England (Anglican) and other Episcopalian bodies worldwide.

The Second Helvetic Confession (1566) was based upon the *First* (1536) and written by Heinrich Bullinger. It was a mature statement of Reformed theology for the latter part of the six-teenth century and was translated into Dutch, English, Polish, Italian, Magyar, Turkish, and Arabic.

The Canons of Dort (1619, see event #35).

The Westminster Confession of Faith (1643–1646, adopted by Parliament in 1647) was written by an assembly of 151 ministers and theologians initially convened by the British Parliament to revise *The Thirty-Nine Articles*. Over the course of twenty-seven months, the Confession was produced, and upon its completion, it was immediately established as the definitive statement of Presbyterian doctrine in the English-speaking countries, and now in the entire world.

The Savoy Declaration of Faith and Platform (1658) was written along the lines of the *Westminster Confession* by the most influential divines (theologians) that Congregationalism (i.e., Independency) could boast. They were Thomas Goodwin, John Owen, Philip Nye, William Bridge, Joseph Caryl, and William Greenhill. All except Owen had actively participated in the Westminster Assembly. This Declaration set the standard for Congregationalism to this day.

The London Baptist Confession of Faith (1689) also followed the format of the *Westminster Confession*. It was probably written by Nehemiah Coxe and William Collins, the elders at London's Petty France church. The Baptists, more than other Protestant groups, suffered greatly (Bunyan being one example) and for years were either imprisoned or heavily fined. Other nonconformists, such as Presbyterians and Congregationalists, suffered, but not as badly. Upon the Glorious Revolution of 1688, when William and Mary were brought from the Netherlands to the throne of England and the Protestant faith of the Reformation was secured, the non-conformists (including Baptists) were granted full freedom of worship and expression. Though the Confession had been published unsigned and in circulation since 1677, it was formally issued, signed, and adopted by all the Particular Baptist churches of the United Kingdom in 1689.

In the same vein as the Westminster Confession, differing only in baptism and church government and a slight nuance in covenant theology, the Baptists stated a summary of their beliefs in the '1689.' Its historical significance is that it was the most thorough and complete doctrinal statement of Baptists and set the standard of doctrinal belief, church practice, missionary endeavors, and family worship for almost two hundred and fifty years. It is without equal in Baptist confessions and articles of belief. Charles Haddon Spurgeon, perhaps the greatest Baptist preacher of all time, had this to say in reissuing the '1689' to his church, the Metropolitan Tabernacle in London, in October 1855:

> This ancient document is a most excellent epitome of the things most surely believed among us. This little volume is not issued as an authoritative rule or code of faith, whereby you are fettered, but as assistance to us in controversy, a confirmation in faith, and a means of edification in righteousness. In this confession, the members of our church will have a body of divinity, of concise, scripturally based doctrine; and, by means of scriptural proofs, they can be ready to give a reason of the hope that is in them … Cleave fast to the Word of God, which is here mapped out to you. (as qtd. in L. Drummond, *Spurgeon, Prince of Preachers*)

What is so important about these early Protestant confessions of faith? What world-changing effects did they have? Why should they even be mentioned, much less remembered? Are not confessions of faith outdated and antiquated, some question. Furthermore, were there no other significant confessions of faith and articles or statements of belief published after these?

Yes, other confessions of faith would be written and would be adopted by various denominations in the decades and centuries that followed. However, in one form or another, all would take their lead from these formative Protestant confessions, which taught a robust Christianity that converted pagan societies from their damagingly superstitious worldviews and brought light to darkened continents. In spite of this, there is a sad note to be observed about all the Protestant confessions of faith from 1689 onward. While following the basic pattern of the early Protestant confessions, there ensued a tragic lessening and watering-down of those creedal statements. They became less precise and more broad and accepting of beliefs that the apostles and Reformers would have rejected. The result has been that in some parts of Christendom today there is a non-descript, feeble Christianity that is more descriptive of the cultural pressures of a particular geographic society than the hearty, robust 'faith of God's elect' (Titus 1:1). Sadly, this anemic Christianity has little respect from the world, slight influence upon the world with the gospel, and negligible impact upon post-modern, western society and culture. On a positive note, there is an encouraging return in many parts of Christianity to these early confessions of faith and a new generation of believers is sensing a fullness of satisfaction in their souls instead of the leanness of a modern-day Christianity.

38

The Great Awakening Peaks – 1740

*T*HE Enlightenment period of history that sprang from the Renaissance had created a dark and vocal skepticism about God, the Holy Bible, and many other matters pertaining to the Christian religion. After Roman Catholicism's ignorant condemnation of Galileo, science was rebounding and making headway in an increasingly educated society. Judeo-Christian ethics and morality were sharply debated and on the decline. With the exception of a few pockets of evangelical fervor in the American colonies, Christianity on both sides of the Atlantic had become cold and formal. The status quo of society exhibited little life or zeal for the gospel. Most were content with being Christian in name only. Many Christian ministers were unconverted and did not even believe the Bible or the faith they were paid to proclaim. The Christian ministry was generally viewed by the populous as another professional vocation, a status in high-fashion circles, instead of a divine calling from heaven. Culture deemed Christianity to be irrelevant or unnecessary. Anglican bishop J. C. Ryle noted that it was one of the darkest times in English history since the Protestant Reformation (for an overview of the period, see Ryle's *Christian Leaders of the Eighteenth Century*). Would biblical and apostolic Christianity survive? Or, would it slowly drift into the backwaters of Western civilization?

God, as He always does in the history of redemption, began to do something. In this case, His action came in the form of a momentous spiritual awakening. Historically known as the Great Awakening, it was a mighty, Spirit-wrought revival that swept both sides of the Atlantic, especially the American colonies, in the 1730s and 1740s. The Awakening left a permanent impact on British and American Christianity. It came about by powerful preaching that produced in listeners an acknowledgement of personal guilt, a high view of Christ, and a sense of their need for a real and personal experience of salvation in the Savior. Once more, the Christian church had relevance.

Pulling away from ritual and ceremony, the Great Awakening made religion intensely personal to the average person. It fostered a heart-felt understanding of sin and spiritual guilt, esteemed redemption in the cross of Christ, and produced divine regeneration and new life by the Holy Spirit. The newness of life found by many encouraged heart introspection and a commitment to a new standard of personal holiness.

The Great Awakening brought Christianity to African slaves who had been forcibly stolen from their native lands and sold by their own people, causing an upheaval in New England that challenged established church-state authority. It incited rancor and division between old traditionalists, who insisted on enforcing rituals that many thought were lifeless, and the new revivalists, who did not entirely reject the rituals, yet strongly preached personal faith and devotional allegiance to Christ. It had a major role in reshaping Protestant churches and denominations in the colonies, especially Congregational, Presbyterian, Dutch Reformed, and German Reformed denominations. It gave birth to the Methodist denomination in England, which sprang out of Anglicanism, and transported Methodism into the American colonies, where its circuit-riding preachers caused it to thrive. When the dust had settled, the small and persecuted Baptists were the greatest recipients of the revival's benefits, with their adherents springing up all over the colonies and expanding into the Western frontier. For some reason, the Great Awakening had little impact on established Anglicans and Quakers. Unlike the Second Great Awakening, which began around 1800 and reached out to the unchurched, the First Great Awakening focused on people who were already church members. It radically changed their rituals, piety, and worldviews.

There were several major characters involved in this great movement of God's Spirit, many of them unknown to present-day Christianity (e.g., Daniel Rowlands, Howell Harris, Lady Selina-Countess of Huntingdon, and John Fletcher, to name a few). More wellknown are John and Charles Wesley, advocates of Arminianism and sinless perfectionism in their theology, who founded the Methodist societies that later became the Methodist Church.

The Wesley brothers are a story in themselves. Their piety and tireless labors, their zeal for lost souls and organizational skills to reach them, their ministries of compassion, and their hymn-writing, which has enriched the church for centuries, are feats deserving of fuller treatment. However, the two greatest personalities were George Whitefield and Jonathan Edwards.

Whitefield was born in England and received a Bachelor's degree from Pembroke College at Oxford University, where he came under the influence of John and Charles Wesley. Though he was a baptized member of the Church of England, through these Methodist Society meetings, Whitefield came to understand that he had never been born again. After an intense period of soul struggle, he came to repentance and saving faith in Christ and embraced Him as his Lord and Savior. Immediately, a fiery desire to preach the gospel to the lost welled up inside him.

Soon thereafter, Whitefield was called and ordained into the ministry of the Anglican Church. His Calvinistic theology coupled with his unorthodox methods, especially that of preaching in the 'open air' (e.g., at coal mines as miners exited work) and other unhallowed locations such as barns and city plazas, brought him into conflict with local church leaders and ecclesiastical authorities. He was forbidden by bishops in many regions to preach in Anglican churches. Still, he persisted in his unique approach, crossing the Atlantic Ocean thirteen times. (He died in America, September 30, 1770, and is buried beneath the pulpit of the First Presbyterian Church of Newburyport, Massachusetts.)

Whitefield had a dynamic and passionate delivery and often preached to crowds of 30,000 in the open air. The American inventor and statesman Benjamin Franklin once measured the distance and documented that he could hear Whitefield preaching one mile away. Whitefield modeled a wonderful example of combining the proclamation of the sovereignty and electing grace of God with a full and free offer of salvation to all who would repent and believe upon Christ.

Jonathan Edwards was a Congregational minister in Northampton, Massachusetts. A truly converted and pious man, he was one of the most brilliant intellectuals the United Sates has ever produced. His grandfather was the patriarch Solomon Stoddard, who was of the blue-blood stock of New England.

Called by many the pioneer theologian of revival, Edwards' most famous work (among many) is his sermon 'Sinners in the Hands of an Angry God,' which was preached in Enfield, Connecticut, in 1741. When detractors belittled this great awakening of God, Edwards defended it in a treatise entitled *A Narrative of the Surprising Work of God*, which dealt with sudden and surprising conversions.

Whitefield and Edwards were friends, and each promoted the Great Awakening in his own way, one as an evangelist and the other as a pastor/scholar. Edwards was elected president of Princeton University in 1758 and died one month later from the ill effects of an experimental smallpox vaccination.

The following facts are significant to remember about the Great Awakening: 1) It rescued the United Kingdom from a lifeless and dead Christianity; 2) It emphasized individual religious experience over established church tradition, thereby decreasing the importance and weight of the clergy in many instances; 3) New denominations arose and older ones grew in numbers as a result of the emphasis on individual faith and personal salvation; 4) It created a never-before-seen sense of urgency in evangelism, especially directed to those who had never heard the gospel of Jesus Christ or to those who were ambivalent to its saving power; 5) It unified the American colonies and gave them an awareness of identity (separate from England) as spiritual fervor spread north to south and east to west through the work of itinerant preachers and organizers of outdoor revivals. This unification was greater than had ever been achieved previously in the colonies and set the stage for the American Revolution. Furthermore, it laid the groundwork for the modern missionary movement (event #40).

39

Robert Raikes Promotes Sunday Schools System – 1780

*F*OR many churches and denominations, Sunday School has become an established institution. It is the medium through which the elementary teachings of the Bible are often-times first introduced. Diverse and interesting characters are made familiar to children, exciting narratives of great feats and daring exploits of redemptive history are recounted, salvation's story in Christ is traced from Genesis to Revelation, and moral and ethical lessons are instilled into minds. Some churches and denominations count their size and strength by their Sunday Schools' enrollments and consider it their primary tool for evangelism and outreach to non-Christians.

Though the early church had its schools of catechesis and John Calvin started the first school opened for free public education, 'Sunday School' is a relatively modern phenomenon. How did it come into existence?

Though the Renaissance and the Protestant Reformation brought the world out of the darkness of the Middle Ages, over time western civilization had not, practically speaking, caught up to the noble theories and biblical principles each generated. England is a good example. Most of the common people were poor and ignorant. Only the rich and affluent could attend the higher institutions of learning or universities. The average person worked in the fields or in the unskilled occupations, and shops sustained the general infrastructure of society. While there is nothing dishonorable whatsoever about plowing or working with the hands, these jobs did not allow the average person to obtain an education.

Furthermore, most children usually worked to help support their families and followed in their parents' footsteps. A vicious cycle of ignorance, poverty, and crime often prevailed among many working-class and uneducated families. Debtors' prisons were filled with illiterate adults, who left illiterate children on the streets. It was rare for a child to break this endless cycle.

In the mid-1700s, there were no child labor laws, and many children from poor families were sent to work at an early age (of six or seven years), often working ten to twelve hours or more a day with meager pay. Six days a week people worked, allowing Sundays for the parents to recuperate and the children, unfortunately, to cause mischief and, in some cases, to commit crimes. Sundays, therefore, became a dreaded day for Sabbath-breaking among the shopkeepers and people in the cities. Also, given the short life expectancies of that era, a large proportion of street children were orphans left to their own devices to survive. Charles Dickens gave insight into the times in his novel *Oliver Twist*. Something needed to be done to curb the tomfoolery and crimes of the children.

One person who was deeply concerned about children running rampant and getting into trouble was the open-minded editor of the *Gloucester Journal*, Robert Raikes. He was moved with compassion at seeing waifs (poor, homeless, or fatherless children) running through the streets and causing havoc on Sundays.

Raikes addressed the matter in several editorials, but seemed to get no public support. Some even ridiculed his notions. Not to be deterred by mockery and lack of public sympathy, he devised a scheme whereby he would gather some children in a home and teach them the basics of reading, writing, math, and the Bible. Since Sunday was the best time for the children to meet, Raikes gave it the name 'Sunday School.' Privately, he found a few sympathetic readers (mostly women) who were willing to assist him and give his plan a try.

The first attempt in a woman's kitchen did not go well. The children were too rambunctious and undisciplined. Nevertheless, Raikes persevered and made several more attempts in different homes. He learned from the mistakes of each attempt and refined the process. This pioneering individual is credited with saying, 'The world marches forward on the feet of little children.' His belief paid off: if you gain a child, you have gained a whole life. What commenced as an experiment to remedy an unwholesome situation slowly began to achieve success. He reported his modest endeavors and results in his newspaper, and the people started taking notice.

The first Sunday School was probably set up early as 1769 by Hannah Ball, who had been converted under the preaching of John Wesley, in High Wycombe, England. Another one was run by Thomas King, a Dissenter in nearby Dursley. However,

Robert Raikes was the first person to conceptualize and set up Sunday School as an educational system with the Bible as its primary textbook.

The best people he could find available to help as teachers were church lay people. The curriculum was simple: reading, writing, 'rithmetic, and the Bible. Once the children began reading, Raikes progressed to the catechism. At the outset, the people who worked with the children were paid from Raikes' own funds.

Then, as more people came to see the benefits of Raikes' work, prominent people began to assist him financially. Queen Charlotte heard of his work and invited him to a private royal audience. Impressed and deeply moved, she lent her patronage to the system, which garnered massive sponsorship from the nobility and upper class. John and Charles Wesley embraced the system and incorporated it into their new movement of Methodism, which transported it to the American colonies. William Fox, a rich London merchant who thought along the same lines, decided to bestow his benefaction upon Raikes' plan and founded in 1785 the Society for the Support and Encouragement of Sunday Schools in the Different Counties of England. Within seven years (1787), there were approximately 250,000 children enrolled in Sunday schools in England. It is estimated that fifty years later, 1.5 million children and 160,000 teachers were participating in Sunday Schools worldwide.

Of course, changes have occurred within the Sunday School system from Raikes' day to ours. First, the teachers ceased being paid, and their work became strictly voluntary. Churches embraced the concept and used lay volunteers to do the work. A Sunday School teacher was an honorable and well-respected position in society, and a Sunday school superintendent was looked upon with esteem. Second, public education developed and assumed the responsibility of teaching children to read. This alleviated a major burden for the Sunday Schools; therefore, they dropped the '3 Rs' and started concentrating their efforts solely on teaching the Holy Scriptures.

Robert Raikes' work laid the groundwork for Sunday Schools to become national institutions in England, the United States, and, through missionary endeavors, all parts of the world. The effects of this system have been phenomenal. Today, there are multitudes of publishing companies that print Sunday School materials almost exclusively. Numerous curricula covering every book, genre, subject, historical event, and person of the Bible are available in every major language in all parts of the world. Missionaries from the United Kingdom and the United States have established Sunday Schools on every continent and many islands, and in some of the remotest regions of the planet. Where would most Christians in western civilization be in their Christian lives without Sunday Schools and their subsidiaries – Vacation Bible Schools and Bible Clubs?

Most believers can trace their first knowledge of the Bible and Jesus to the Sunday School teachers who lovingly and patiently taught them. Sunday Schools have been a human instrument to spread the knowledge and learning of the Bible and the mighty, saving acts of the triune God in an unbelievable fashion, and Robert Raikes is to be thanked!

40

William Carey and the Modern Missionary Movement – 1793

*H*OW does a cobbler, born in a rural area near North-hampton, England, who had no formal theological education, fit into Christian history? Watching him grow up or visiting his workshop, one would have never guessed that he would start a movement that would affect the entire earth or that he would become known as the 'Father of Modern Missions.' How did it all begin?

William Carey was born in 1761, and at the age of fourteen he was apprenticed to a cobbler (one who repairs shoes rather than makes them). What was unusual for an apprenticed trades-man of Carey's sort was that he taught himself Latin and later Greek, with the help of a college-educated villager. Converted at the age of eighteen, he left the Church of England and was eventually baptized, licensed, and ordained to preach among the Calvinistic or Particular Baptists. (Particular in this context does not mean odd or strange, but refers to a belief in particular redemption or a definite and limited atonement.)

Repairing shoes by day and studying in his spare time, Carey supplied pulpits in the area churches. The more he studied the Word of God, the more burdened he became for the nations and peoples of the earth that had never heard the gospel of Christ. Beside his shoe-repairing bench, he hung a carefully drawn map of the nations of the world as they were then known. He began to catalogue the various nations and people groups, along with the fauna and flora of each geographical region.

In Carey's day, there was very little missionary activity among the Protestants, the Moravians excepted. Two books kindled a flame for missions in Carey's heart: *An Account of the Life of the Late Rev. David Brainerd* by Jonathan Edwards and *The Last Voyage of Captain Cook*. In 1789, Carey was called to pastor the Particular Baptist Church in Leicester. He was convinced that something must be done for the unevangelized heathen in other lands. With the burden of missions percolating in his mind and soul, three years later (1792) Carey wrote and published *An Enquiry into the Obligations of Christians to Use Means for the Conversion of the Heathen*.

The book consisted of five parts. Part One argued that Christ's last command to make disciples of all nations (Matt. 28:18-20) was not for the apostles (or clergy) only, but the entire church. Part Two chronicled a history of missionary activity, beginning with the apostles. Part Three contained almost thirty pages of astounding statistics for every country in the known world. Part Four answered objections to missionary endeavors. Part Five proposed that a missionary society be formed by the Particular Baptist denomination to carry out this task and supplied practical answers as to how it could be supported. This volume became the seminal textbook for gospel missions and has since been read by every student of missionary history.

In that same year, Carey was appointed to preach the annual convention sermon of the Northhampton Baptist Association. On May 30, 1792, he preached his now-famous missionary sermon, which has been called the 'Deathless Sermon.' He took as his text Isaiah 54:1-3, in which the LORD cheers His ancient people to 'enlarge the place of your tent.' Urging his fellow ministers to form a missionary society for the conversion of the heathen, in his conclusion, he drove home the point that they must 'expect great things from God; attempt great things for God.'

The association's annual convention ended with the following resolution recorded in its minutes: 'Resolved, that a plan be prepared against the next ministers' meeting at Kettering for forming a Baptist Society for propagating the Gospel among the Heathens.' In Kettering, four months later on October 2, 1792, the 'Particular Baptist Society for Propagating the Gospel among the Heathen' was founded. It later became the Baptist Missionary Society. The alleged account of John Ryland, Sr. telling Carey to 'Sit down, young man … If God wants to save the heathen, he will do so without your help or mine' has been proven a fabrication and a myth. No such verbal transaction occurred.

With the resolute backing of such Baptist notables as Andrew Fuller, John Sutcliff, and John Ryland (Sr. and Jr.), Carey sailed for Calcutta, India, in April 1793. History was in the making. From Calcutta, he and his missionary team later moved to the Danish colony of Serampore, which remained the base of his missionary labors. For over forty years, Carey preached the gospel, often in meetings in the streets where they sang hymns, distributed literature, and preached a gospel message from the Bible.

It was seven years before they saw the first convert, a Hindu named Krishna Pal. Carey translated the Word of God into Bengali, evangelized, planted and pastored churches, founded Serampore College to train indigenous gospel ministers, established schools and medical facilities, served as professor of Sanskrit, Bengali, and Marathi languages, supervised and edited translations of the Scriptures into approximately forty languages and dialects, produced a massive Bengali-English dictionary, worked for social reform among the caste systems of India (that brought abolition of sacrificing children to Hindu gods and burning widows on their husbands' funeral pyres), and founded the Agricultural and Horticultural Society of India. Whew! Is there a need to say anything more?

Carey always reminded others that he was simply a cobbler called to preach Christ's gospel. He did not believe himself to be especially gifted. He often told his co-workers that while he could not do many things, the one thing he could do was 'plod.' And plod he did! In the face of cultural opposition, sickness and disease, the deaths of wives and family members, desertion among the mission team members, a fire that destroyed years of translation work, and a myriad of other obstacles, Carey plodded. Through his tireless labors and passion to carry the gospel to those who had never heard, people from England and the United States were inflamed with a vision to make Christ known to the ends of the earth.

The first missionary from America, Adoniram Judson, was directly influenced by Carey to go to Burma as the first Christian minister to carry the gospel to that land and people. Countless missionaries can trace the initial stirring in their hearts to go to the mission field back to accounts, either read or heard, of Carey's indefatigable labors in India.

When Carey died in June 1834, he had spent forty-one years in India without a furlough, which is unthinkable to missionaries today. Can the Calvinists and Reformed, who believe in unconditional election and particular redemption, have a fiery zeal and genuine burden for lost souls? Carey is proof positive that they can and do.

F. Deauville Walker reports in his *William Carey: Father of Modern Missions* that, as he was nearing death, Carey said to his missionary friend, 'Mr Duff! You have been speaking about Dr Carey, Dr Carey; when I am gone say nothing about Dr Carey – speak only about Dr Carey's Savior.' These last words exemplified his vision for the supremacy of the glory of the triune God in all missionary work.

At the time of Carey's funeral, the Baptist mission could only count approximately seven hundred converts in a nation of untold millions. But do not allow numbers to deceive you. William Carey, by expecting great things from God and attempting great things for God, laid the foundation for evangelization of the unreached peoples of the earth, for Bible translations in languages where there are none, and for gospel-oriented social reform, which challenges the evil cultural practices that are contrary to the Holy Scriptures. He truly deserves the title by which many of us know him: 'Father of Modern Missions.'

41

William Wilberforce and the Abolition of British Slave Trade – 1807

*T*HE Toronto Film Festival did something unusual in September 2006: it showed a Christian film. *Amazing Grace*, which was released in the United States in February 2007, is about the life and labors of William Wilberforce (1759–1833). The film's release in the States was intended to coincide with the two hundredth anniversary of anti-slavery laws passed in the British Parliament. The movie was a hit, and for most people of the twenty-first century, it was their first knowledge of the events that led to the abolition of slavery in Western society.

Slavery is a despicably evil institution of fallen cultures and has been in existence since the first century of human history. Traces of slavery in Lower Egypt from six thousand years ago were uncovered in archeological findings. The Code of Hammurabi (c. 1800 B.C.) contained the first written rules to govern slavery. All of the ancient civilizations practiced slavery, including India, China, Israel, Greece, Rome, the Islamic Caliphates, *and* Africa. It is reckoned that Athens, in the height of its glory, had over eighty thousand slaves. While the Bible neither commends nor condemns slavery, to Christianity's own chagrin, some of the earliest Christians were both slave owners and slaves (e.g., Philemon and Onesimus, Philemon 15–16). How terrible that one person should own and sell another person, as if that person were nothing more than common goods or chattel!

Slavery existed in the dark continent of Africa for centuries. Muslim traders discovered, in their coastal trading expeditions on both sides of the massive continent (the Indian Ocean side and the Atlantic Ocean side) that African tribes enslaved those they conquered. These Muslim buyers purchased slaves from African chiefs and sold them elsewhere. Portuguese traders initiated contact with sub-Saharan Africa and its Muslim traders in the fifteenth century. The Portuguese purchased slaves from the Muslim agents and transported them to Europe, which proved to be quite lucrative. Soon Spanish and English traders, followed by the Americans, became involved in this profitable business, and black African slaves quickly populated the white European and American landscapes. It is assessed that between 45,000 and 50,000 souls were bought and sold each year during the active slave trade.

All of this would be changed by a man named William Wilberforce.

Wilberforce was born into a wealthy merchant family. He grew up idle, but was brilliant and witty. He graduated from Cambridge, where he became friends with William Pitt (the Younger, later to become prime minister). While at Cambridge,

Wilberforce became proficient at cards and dice and was the darling of the theater and horse-racing societies. He had political ambitions, and at the age of twenty-one was elected to Parliament as a member of the Tory Party. By his own admission, he did nothing his first years in Parliament. Taken up with his 'own distinction,' he was an eloquent and clever orator. That gave him the fame and popularity that he would need in the years to come. However, his life and ambitions were about to change.

James Ramsey, a minister and former slave-ship surgeon, published a book against slavery in 1784. Wilberforce probably met Ramsey the previous year and discussed slavery for the first time then. Meeting with Ramsey, and reading his book, deeply stirred Wilberforce. Around his twenty-fifth birthday, Wilberforce began to have serious and deep spiritual struggles. Though a member of the Anglican Church, something was missing; genuine Christianity, he knew, was more than a comfortable and cultural social club.

On Easter Sunday of 1786, after months of intense sorrow and agony of soul, Wilberforce came to an authentic saving faith in the resurrected Christ. His life radically changed, and, imitating the apostolic description of 2 Corinthians 5:17, life took on meaning. He quickly became a part of the evangelical wing of the Church of England. The group included the famous John Newton, a former slave trader – even once a slave himself and the author of the world-renowned hymn, *Amazing Grace*. (Interestingly, in 1797, Wilberforce would write a derisive critique of nominal Christianity entitled *A Practical View of the Prevailing Religious System of Professed Christians*. It became a bestseller.)

Thomas Clarkson called upon Wilberforce in early 1787 and presented him with a copy of his own book on human trade, entitled *Essay on Slavery*. This was the first time the two met, but it would not be the last. They formed a friendship and collaboration that would endure for over fifty years. It was Clarkson who initially prodded Wilberforce to oppose slavery, until the prodding was no longer needed. Wilberforce quickly recoiled against the evils of slavery and began to use his political clout to influence his apathetic colleagues against it. His task was not an easy one, due to much sympathy for slavery in England. The free labor force of the slaves was financially beneficial for the country, and contributed to the financial prosperity of many. Greed, Wilberforce learned, can easily blind people to what is right and true. Nevertheless, he persevered and joined the 'Clapham Sect,' which was a group of evangelical Christians whose goal was to persuade businesses and government of biblical principles and thus act accordingly.

Having mustered a sufficient level of support among society and political strength in Parliament, Wilberforce began his legal quest to abolish slavery. Bill after bill was presented in the House of Commons, and each was voted down. With each failure, however, came an incremental increase of support as the eyes of Parliament and the voters were slowly opening.

Early in 1807, the rise of public sentiment could not be contained. Under William Pitt's early leadership and then Lord Grenville as prime minister, coupled with Wilberforce's political navigation, Parliament passed a law to abolish the slave trade on March 25, 1807. In reality, this did not abolish slavery, but only the active trade of enslaved people. Thankfully, though, a breakthrough change had been made. It would still take another twenty-five years before slavery was completely abolished in the United Kingdom.

Parliaments then, like parliaments and congresses today, are mostly governed by expediency rather than principle. Wilberforce knew that Parliament needed to be drastically reformed and that that would take time. He continued to garner public support and, despite failing health, persisted in reforming England's governing body. Finally, with a reform-minded Parliament in place, in April 1833, he drafted his last petition to completely abolish slavery. It was debated for three months, and after its third reading in the House of Commons, it was passed on July 26, 1833. The good news was immediately rushed to his home. William Wilberforce died three days later on July 29, 1833, his life's mission completed.

Wilberforce's conviction eventually carried the day in the United States, despite a great Civil War (1861–1865). While his anti-slavery beliefs have been implemented in many parts of the world, it must be remembered that the abominable practice of slavery still exists. According to the BBC (quoting Canadian author Richard Re), 'Conservative estimates indicate that at least 27 million people, in places as diverse as Nigeria, Indonesia, and Brazil, live in conditions of forced bondage. Some sources believe the actual figures are ten times as large'. This does not account for the sex-slave trade that is rampant worldwide and, oftentimes, is happening unnoticed right under the public eye.

What is the answer? Wilberforce was partially right: the establishment of legislation and the swift, decisive enforcement of these laws are major components of the solution. However, legal solutions alone will not remove the greed and corruption of the human heart. Christianity's message of the saving power of God revealed in the gospel of Jesus Christ, which William Wilberforce personally experienced, is the ultimate answer that will truly set people free.

42

Charles Finney and *Lectures on Revivals* – 1835

*T*HE decade of the 1830s was revolutionary in Christian history. Novel ideas and practices were launched, but there were three that forever changed the face of Christianity. First, a new form of eschatology originated at a prophecy conference in Edinburgh through a 'prophetic utterance' of Margaret MacDonald (1830). MacDonald claimed that Jesus told her the church would be raptured out before the Great Tribulation, and dispensationalism was born.

Second, a new cult was started in Palmyra, New York, by Joseph Smith. A protracted 'revival of religion,' as Smith described it in his autobiographical *History of Joseph Smith, The Prophet, By Himself,* was taking place in the region. (Interestingly, the revival was conducted by Charles Finney.) Smith wanted to know which church to join, so he went to a nearby grove to pray. As he prayed, 'an angel of light' (see 2 Cor. 11:14) appeared and told Smith that he was to join no church because 'All the churches are wrong, their creeds are an abomination, and their professors are corrupt.' He claimed he was given 'golden plates written in Reformed Egyptian' that he translated into the *Book of Mormon*. Thus, on April 6, 1831, the Church of Jesus Christ of the Latter-day Saints (Mormonism) was organized.

Third, Charles Grandison Finney (1792–1875) refined a novel method of evangelism that had originated a few years earlier in the frontier camp meetings. This innovative form of evangelism was termed 'new measures' because they were totally new to Christianity. Christ, the apostles, the early church Fathers, the Reformers, and the great evangelists never used it. Finney's use of the new measures changed the face of evangelical Christianity.

Born in Connecticut in 1792, the youngest of fifteen children and the son of a farmer, Finney never went to college. Apprenticed to a lawyer, he passed the law exam and was admitted to the New York state bar. During his early career as a lawyer in Adams, New York, he was critical of Christianity and religious dogma. Noticing numerous Bible references in his law books, Finney started attending church services conducted by a friend.

This friend urged Finney to read and study the Bible. The more Finney read the Bible, the more convinced he was of its truth, and he soon came under a conviction of personal sin. After a period of intense soul struggle, he professed conversion to Christ in 1821 and joined the Presbyterian Church. Refused entrance into Princeton Seminary, he began theological studies under his pastor. He was ordained in the Presbyterian Church in 1824.

For the next eight years, Finney conducted 'revivals' along the northeastern seaboard and saw unusual results. He placed great stress on human responsibility and the freedom of man's will. His meetings were noted for their emotionalism and excitement. 'Mankind,' he stated, 'will not act until they are excited' (see Finney's *Lectures on Revival of Religion*). When he finished preaching, he invited people to come to the front and sit in what he called the 'anxious seat' and 'pray through' until the Lord saved them. This practice Finney invented was afterward termed the 'altar call.' Later, it became known as the 'invitation system.' These new tactics brought Finney into conflict with his Calvinistic Presbyterian denomination.

When the revivals cooled in 1832, Finney took the pastorate of the Second Presbyterian Church in New York City. His Pelagian doctrine was so obvious that calls for his defrocking from the Presbyterian ministry were numerous. He remained in New York and in 1834 developed a series of lectures on revival. In them, he borrowed heavily and enlarged upon the condemned teachings of Pelagius (see event #11). Realizing his beliefs were diametrically opposed to the beliefs of his denomination, he eventually resigned from the Presbyterian ministry in 1837.

Meanwhile, in 1835, Finney was invited to join the faculty of a newly established college in Ohio. He resigned his pastorate and became the first professor of theology at Oberlin College. There, he published his *Lectures on Revivals of Religion*.

The book contained twenty-two chapters. Hitherto unpublished and articulating a theology generally unknown by the masses, his book revealed his extremist beliefs. What were some of his aberrant views?

In the opening of the first chapter, Finney made this shocking statement: 'Religion is something [for man] to do. It is not something to wait for.' Granted, he affirmed that God 'influences' mankind by His Spirit, but in the end, salvation was entirely up to man. He rejected the biblical teaching of total depravity and, along with Pelagius, believed that the human will was completely unaffected by the fall of Adam and was absolutely free. Because he believed the will was untainted after Adam's original sin, Finney taught that people had the innate ability to create within themselves a new nature. Later on, he developed his belief that Christians could reach a state of sinless perfection.

Like Pelagius, Finney denied the imputation of Adam's sin and guilt onto the human race. Finney also denied the substitutionary, penal atonement of Christ. His belief was that Christ's death actually paid the ransom and penalty for *no* person's sins; it only publicly demonstrated what their sins deserved and what they would receive if they did not repent. The cross simply allowed God to forgive people if they repented, believed, did good works, and persevered. This doctrine of the atonement is known as the governmental view. Robert Reymond notes, 'But this is just to eviscerate the Savior's work of all its intrinsic saving worth and to replace the Christosoteric vision of Scripture with the autosoteric vision of Pelagianism' (*A New Systematic Theology of the Christian Faith*).

For Finney, not only was salvation a work of man, but revival was also a work of man. Contrary to Jonathan Edwards, the Wesleys, and George Whitefield, who preceded him, Finney unequivocally stated in his *Lectures on Revivals* that 'a revival of religion is not a miracle ... it is not a miracle, or dependent on a miracle, in any sense. It is a purely philosophical result of the right use of the constituted means – as much so as any other effect produced by the application of means.' If people met God's conditions, he taught, they could bring about real revival. If people prayed and advertised and the preacher properly 'excited' the people, genuine revival would occur. These beliefs, among many others, are explained more fully in his book.

In 1851, Finney became president of Oberlin College, where he served until he resigned in 1866. It was during his tenure as president that he developed what is called Oberlin Theology, which had as its hallmark the teaching of sinless perfection. He continued his evangelistic and revival campaigns until his death in 1875.

The reason Finney and his *Lectures on Revivals of Religion* are listed as a key event in Christian history is not for the good they caused, but for the paradigm shift they brought to evangelical Christianity worldwide. Hailed as a hero who saved the church by some and the recognized Father of Modern Revivalism by all, Finney ushered in a destructive upheaval. He caused the focus of Christianity to be turned from Christ and the objective truth of God to man and his subjective experience; evangelicalism went from a doctrinal-oriented, Christ-centered theology to an experience-oriented theology, from God-centeredness to man-centeredness.

Today, over 70 per cent of Americans profess a 'born again' experience, which generally occurred through some form of Finney's invitation system. Yet, there is little evidence of saving impact upon the culture or society. Most churches have more people on their membership rolls than in attendance. Both membership and attendance are declining. And, as usual, America is quick to export its products, both material and spiritual, to every corner of the earth, as it has done with

Finney's teaching and practice. Christianity in the western world is in a crisis. A major part of the reason Christianity is in a mess lies at the feet of Charles Grandison Finney and his new measures, which have been spread all over the world. An excellent evaluation of Finney's impact can be found in Nancy Almodovar's *Pelagius' Return to American Evangelicalism.*

43
Julius Wellhausen and the Documentary Hypothesis – 1885

*U*NTIL the nineteenth century, most Christians and biblical scholars believed in the inspiration and inerrancy of the Bible and that Moses was the human author, who wrote under the direct movement of the Holy Spirit, of the first five books of the Bible, known as the Pentateuch. Regarding this, there was certainly no question in the mind of the apostolic church. Furthermore, almost all within Christianity, except a few radical skeptics, believed the Bible to be the full revelation of God Himself to the world He created. Julius Wellhausen (1844-1918) drastically changed this.

Wellhausen was a German biblical critic who was part of a group of liberal scholars that were firmly convinced of Theological Naturalism. Theological Naturalism is the view that the natural realm is the only sphere of reality, ruling out any possibility of a God who performed supernatural wonders or did miracles. They did not deny that there was a God; they just denied that He did supernatural things in the world.

According to the thought of Wellhausen and his liberal associates, the supernatural stories and miracles were fictive and folklorist myths that needed to be demythologized. Rather than approaching the Bible as the divine Word of God, they approached it as if it were *only* the word of man that *possibly* had divine elements within it. In order to understand the Bible, they reasoned, it must be deconstructed or taken apart section by section. Then each section must be scrutinized with linguistic precision until the real truth is discovered and the myths dispelled. People will then be able to separate truth from fiction.

Building upon the groundwork laid by others, Wellhausen is most credited with formulating what is known as 'documentary hypothesis' or the JEDP theory. The essential claim of this theory is that the first five books of the Bible were written not so much by Moses, but by four people (at least) or groups of people, whom they called *redactors*. These redactors wrote at varying periods of Israel's history.

The basic premise of Wellhausen, and those who followed him, was that the Jewish religion was not a divine revelation, but a natural evolution of the development of the Israelite nation. In Israel's early and formative stages, Judaism was a very primitive religion, not unlike the various religious groups around them. As the nation grew more cultured, its leaders, especially the religious ones, felt the need to fill in the supposed gaps of their records and make their historical development flow more smoothly. This rendered the Old Testament orderly, and the Jewish religion appeared conclusively divine; thus, it became more attractive to readers and inquirers. They believed the redactors had good intentions and sought to ascribe to Israel a higher status and sophistication among the nations.

The pattern of Wellhausen's documentary hypothesis is seen in the following acrostic:

J = Jehovahist redactors – those who wrote in Judah from 950–850 B.C. These redactors favored the name of Jehovah or Yahweh in their writings, and their additions are scattered throughout the Pentateuch, from Genesis to Numbers.

E = Elohistic – those who wrote in the northern kingdom of Israel from 850–750 B.C. These redactors favored the name of El or Elohim, and their insertions are scattered throughout Genesis to Numbers.

D = Deuteronomic – so named because they included redactional supplements found mostly in the Book of Deuteronomy. These redactors set the framework for the rest of the Old Testament.

P = Priestly – primarily redactor priests who tidied up the 'messy' parts of formal temple worship concerning sacrifices, rituals, laws, and most of the genealogies of the Old Testament. Supposedly, written from the 600s–500s B.C.

The documentary hypothesis scholars started with the Torah or Pentateuch and, eventually, proceeded through the rest of the Old Testament. The historical Old Testament books fell under their criticism, followed by the Prophets. For more information on this topic, see *The Documentary Hypothesis and the Composition of the Pentateuch: Eight Lectures,* by Umberto Cassuto.

A classic example of the documentary hypothesis' deconstruction of the Bible is its view of the book of Isaiah, which came under their diabolical analysis. Instead of the ancient and time-honored belief that Isaiah was written by one Isaiah, son of Amoz of Jerusalem, the unbelieving academics postulated that the book was written by Isaiah, who wrote chapters 1–39, and a second (*deutero*) Isaiah, who wrote chapters 40–66. Later came the hypothesis of a third (*trito*) Isaiah. This theory states that the son of Amoz wrote chapters 1–39, *deutero*-Isaiah wrote chapters 40–55 near the end of the Babylonian Captivity, and *trito*-Isaiah (probably multiple authors) wrote chapters 56–66 shortly after Israel's return from Babylonian exile.

It seems that the scholars who formulated these theories forgot Jesus' words in John 12:38-41, where He quotes from the early and latter sections of the book of Isaiah and attributes both to the same Isaiah, not to two or three Isaiahs. This multiple-Isaiah theory revealed that the higher-critical scholars granted no special credence to Jesus' word, probably seeing Him as just another man speaking from limited knowledge, if not outright superstition.

Wellhausen's work, along with the other liberal scholars, set the stage for the theological liberalism that marked the first part of the twentieth century. Many universities and seminaries rapidly embraced Wellhausen's documentary hypothesis and trained future ministers in this belief. This led to a trickle-down effect as young ministers were called to churches and passed on their philosophies to the people. Doubts about the authenticity and authority of Holy Scripture spread quickly.

Churches that once were champions of orthodox Christianity became citadels of unbelief. The cherished beliefs bequeathed by the hard-fought and valiant efforts of the early Fathers were swiftly jettisoned, almost as if they never existed.

Wellhausen's theories were not without their critics. Noted Greek scholar A. T. Robertson, though appreciative of the advances in linguistic understanding, notes the University of Chicago professor Paul Shorey's sharp critique of Wellhausen's 'higher criticism' movement:

> He [Shorey] speaks of 'the need of rescuing scholarship itself from the German yoke.' He does not mean 'German pedantry and superfluous accuracy in insignificant research – but ... in all seriousness from German inaccuracy.' He continues about the 'disease of German scholarship' that insists on 'sweat-boxing' the evidence and straining after 'vigorous and rigorous' demonstrations of things that do not admit of proof. (*A Grammar of the Greek New Testament*)

Most of Wellhausen's theories have been disproved by modern scholarship, but long before his opponents prevailed, the damage had been done. Battles were fought over the inspiration and inerrancy of the Bible (event #45), as evidenced by the 'Conservative Resurgence' in the Southern Baptist Convention, which started in 1979 and ended with the publishing of *The Baptist Faith and Message 2000*. Conservatives and, later, fundamentalists considered Wellhausen and his cohorts to be instruments of Satan that caused people to doubt the authenticity and veracity of the Word of God and kept perishing souls from the beauty of Christ and His gospel. However, Wellhausen's influence is still seen today in the godless unbelief of liberal 'higher-critical' redactionism still taught in the major universities and seminaries of Protestantism and also in Catholic institutions throughout the world. One doubts if the church and world will totally shake off this soul-destroying disease.

David, the 'sweet Psalmist of Israel,' was absolutely justified in asking 'If the foundations be destroyed, what can the righteous do?' (Ps. 11:3 KJV). To doubt the inspiration, inerrancy, authenticity, and authority of the Holy Bible, as Wellhausen and his cohorts did, is to destroy the very foundation of historic and apostolic Christianity. On a positive note, those entrenched in theological liberalism, who wholeheartedly and without question, embrace documentary hypothesis, discover their theories lead to emptiness. Thus, their denominations are slowly dying. Many people are rejecting these higher-critical, humanistic notions and once more are returning to the Holy Bible. In it they find new life in the ancient faith of the Hebrew prophets, the Messiah, and His apostles. The unbelief of men will not stop the covenant faithfulness of the triune God of biblical Christianity!

44

The Azusa Street Revival – 1906

*T*HE inroads of modernity and the eventual stranglehold of postmodernity upon society left the church struggling. The struggle caused liberalism to leave parts of the church dead, fundamentalism splintered (due to in-fighting over secondary issues), and evangelicalism grossly confused. The early church fathers, after the second century, grappled with the question of the continuation and cessation of apostolic miracles and works of 'power.' John Chrysostom (349–407) concluded that, indeed, the apostolic gifts had ceased:

[1 Cor. 12–14] is very obscure: but the obscurity is produced by our ignorance of the facts referred to and by their cessation, being such as then used to occur but now no longer take place. And why do they not happen now? Why look now, the cause too of the obscurity hath produced us again another question: namely, why did they then happen, and now do so no more? (from 'Homily 29' on 1 Corinthians)

Humble believers of the Bible at the turn of the twentieth century, faced with the anti-supernaturalism of liberal Christianity, also wrestled with the question of apostolic power works. Can the miracles Jesus performed be performed by others today? Can there be another Day of Pentecost? Can the supernatural signs of the apostles be in operation now? Liberalism and modern rationalism responded negatively, and fundamentalism, which affirmed supernaturalism, initially gave the questions little thought. Yet, regular Bible readers, and not just theologians, continued to ask the questions. Out of this milieu arose Pentecostalism.

Though there had been occasional 'Spirit manifestations' in the two previous decades, regular displays began in 1904. Apparently, there was a genuine movement of the Holy Spirit in Wales, led by Evan Roberts, which many believed was a God-given movement to turn back the rapid encroachment of theological liberalism. Soon, reports of a great work of God in Wales sailed to America. It was a topic of discussion from east to west.

Joseph Smale, pastor of the First Baptist Church of Los Angeles, heard the reports and went to Wales to observe the situation. Greatly moved by what he saw, Smale returned and began to preach the 'baptism of the Holy Spirit evidenced by speaking in unknown tongues' (per the *Los Angeles Times*, see below). His new message was not well received by the congregation, and he was asked to leave the First Baptist Church. He went to downtown Los Angeles to a small mission outreach on Azusa Street and joined John Seymour, a black preacher who became the key figure in the movement. On April 18, 1906, the *Los Angeles Times* gave the following description of Smale's and Seymour's meetings: 'The devotees of the weird doctrines practice the most fanatical rites, preach the wildest theories, and work themselves into a state of mad excitement in their particular zeal.' A 'revival broke out,' as the Pentecostals state it, and the rest is history.

Initially, the church viewed this small group of sincere believers, who rejected higher-critical views of Scripture and a dead orthodoxy, as a radical group of simpletons. Most had no Bible college or seminary training and were moved by a *simple*, yet commendable, desire to have a closer walk with their Savior. However, there was something contagious about them. Their genuine warmth, firm belief in the divine and supernatural, and unadorned love for Jesus caused people to pay attention. People began attending their revivals in tents or store-front buildings, some out of curiosity and others with a desire to 'really know the Lord.' Many were converted to Christ, and the movement continued to spread.

As Luther and Calvin experienced during the Reformation, there also emerged fringe fanatics among the Pentecostals. Divisions came because some claimed the power to raise the dead, while others believed (based on Mark 16:18) that they could ingest poisonous substances or handle venomous snakes with impunity. Still others claimed that if people were 'baptized with the Holy Ghost,' they would become rich, never get sick, and always be happy. This has come to be known as the 'Prosperity Movement' or the 'health and wealth' gospel.

Another disturbing element included those who claimed to receive direct revelations from God. These prophetic revelations, as many believed, were equal to the Holy Scriptures. Most evangelicals viewed this as a deception and threat to the doctrine of a 'closed canon,' the assertion that the Book of Revelation was the last book of inspired Scripture. Perhaps the most dangerous group to appear in Pentecostalism was the anti-Trinitarian, modalistic 'Oneness' movement. To deny the Trinity is to flagrantly fly into the face of historic, orthodox Christianity.

Even so, as a whole, the modern Pentecostals were basically conservative in their beliefs and fervent in the propagation of them. Some leaped previously forbidden barriers by allowing women to preach and by working within liberal denominations and with Roman Catholics. Others evolved into more formal, structured denominations and parachurch ministries. Whichever the case, they primarily emphasized experience and fundamentalist mores over biblical exegesis and theology.

It should be noted that most of the denominations springing out of this movement, except the Assemblies of God, have diminished over the years. Yet, in the 1960s, another phenomenon reminiscent of old-line Pentecostals sprang up: the Jesus Movement, which consisted primarily of converts from the 'hippy' generation. They wore long hair, beads, tie-dyed clothes, and peace symbols, and engaged in unconventional worship services on beaches or wherever they found a good spot. Most did not know the rich, ancient hymns and psalms of the church, so they began to write their own songs and music. The guitar was the primary instrument used in worship; sometimes tambourines, drums, and harmonicas were added. The more gifted musicians were signed to recording contracts, and 'worship music' soon became the fad in denominational churches.

From the Jesus Movement emerged the young, vibrant Charismatics that can be found in every major Protestant denomination and, to an unexpected extent, in Roman Catholicism. They evangelized, planted churches, set up mega satellite TV networks, introduced the cult personality of the 'televangelist' (more on this in event #50), and sent missionaries into all parts of the world. Unlike their fathers, the Pentecostals and 'Jesus People,' the Charismatics were not commonly viewed as mere simpletons relegated to the nether regions of Christianity, but as a body to be reckoned with.

What is the one thread within the weave of old-line Pentecostalism and modern Charismaticism that holds the fabric together? What is the one bond of unity among them? It is their particular belief in the baptism of the Holy Spirit.

The phrase 'baptism of the Holy Spirit' is a biblical one. Where people differ is on its definition and significance. To *most* continuationists, it is a *post-conversion* experience of power and giftedness. To *most* cessationists, it is the conversion experience of being placed into the body of Christ at the point of believing (see 1 Cor. 12:13). Exegetical and theological battles have been waged over the subject. Volumes of books, both pro and con, have been written on what it is to be baptized by the Spirit. Local churches, regional associations and presbyteries, denominations, and, worst of all, friendships and fellowships have been severed because agreement could not be reached on this biblical phrase. Is it not strange that such division erupted among professed Christians who could unite in confessing that wonderful statement of the Apostles' Creed: 'I believe in the Holy Ghost'?

The Azusa Street revival of 1906 re-introduced speaking in tongues, instituted healing services, allowed words of prophecy to be declared, and, in essence, gave rise to the old-line Pentecostal and the modern Charismatic movements. In the 1990s, notable church leaders began to endorse Charismatic leaders and even convert to their now-popular continuationist beliefs. Approving articles about them began to appear in weekly magazines such as *Newsweek* and *Time*. Today, they may be liked and embraced, or disliked and opposed, but they cannot be ignored.

45

The Fundamentals and the Modernist-Fundamentalist Controversy – 1910–1912

*T*HEOLOGICAL liberalism, which sprang out of the Graf-Wellhausen theories of documentary hypothesis, was moving rapidly through Bible-believing Christianity at the turn of the twentieth century. Many seminaries had embraced these liberal, anti-supernaturalistic beliefs and were producing ministers who did not believe the Bible to be the inspired, inerrant Word of God. Godly churchmen, from all Protestant denominations (Anglican, Presbyterian, Methodist, Congregationalist, and Baptist), were deeply disturbed. Under attack were some basic and indispensable truths of historic Christianity that had stood for millennia, such as the virgin birth of Christ, His miracles, His substitutionary atonement, His bodily resurrection from the dead, and His second coming to judge the world.

Trouble was brewing, and a public conflict was inevitable. Something had to be done to combat the soul-destroying influx of this theological liberalism. A series of booklets that turned into twelve volumes of paperback books, entitled *The Fundamentals: A Testimony to the Truth*, was published, and the controversy erupted. How did this begin?

One Sunday morning while listening to a sermon by Dr A. C. Dixon, pastor of the Moody Memorial Church in Chicago, Lyman Stewart had a brilliant idea. Stewart was President of Union Oil Company and was a man of means. After the sermon, he shared his idea with Dixon, and Dixon was hooked. Evangelist R. A. Torrey explained Stewart's idea this way:

> In 1909 God moved two Christian laymen to set aside a large sum of money for issuing twelve volumes that would set forth the fundamentals of the Christian faith, and which were to be sent to ministers of the gospel, missionaries, Sunday School superintendents, and others engaged in aggressive Christian work throughout the English speaking world. A committee of men who were known to be sound in the faith was chosen to have oversight in the publication of these volumes. (from the Preface to volume one of *The Fundamentals*)

Actually, there were three men: Lyman Stewart, his brother Milton, who was enlisted to raise the financial support needed, and A. C. Dixon. The Stewart brothers were not scholars, but Dixon was. The three of them began to work with each doing his respective part. Together, they formed the Testimony Publishing Company.

The Stewart brothers raised $300,000 for the project, quite a considerable sum for that day, and Dixon solicited and assembled an extraordinary board of conservative Christian leaders to do the writing. The result was a twelve-volume set of books, each about 125 pages, consisting of ninety essays or chapters defending historic, orthodox Christianity in those truths that were deemed indispensable to the Christian faith and a saving knowledge of God.

A. C. Dixon edited the first five volumes and then moved to London. The editorship was passed on to Louis Meyer, who edited the next five before his death. Lastly, R. A. Torrey edited the final two. After 1916, the printing plates of the original twelve paperback volumes were turned over to The Bible Institute of Los Angeles (BIOLA) and were reissued in four hardbound volumes which retained the same article structure.

The essays covered the following topics: an overview of the Bible, especially books that were under attack for various reasons, such as Genesis and the Pentateuch (Mosaic authorship) and Daniel (single or multiple authorship); the inspiration, inerrancy, and trustworthiness of the Bible, along with Christ's testimony of the Old Testament; arguments against liberalism and German higher criticism, along with an exposé of the fallacies of Graf-Wellhausen higher-critical redactionism; the basics of the historic Christian faith (the existence of God, the fall of man, sin, the deity, virgin birth, the resurrection of Christ, propitiation, atonement, justification, grace, resurrection from the dead, the second coming of Christ, and the realities of heaven and hell); denunciations of heresies, false churches, and cults, including modern philosophy, Spiritualism, Christian Science, Mormonism, and Millennial Dawn (an early Christian Bible Student movement that later became the Jehovah's Witnesses); personal evangelism and the necessity of gospel missions; miscellaneous subjects such as socialism, evolution, and money; and personal testimonies. It is interesting to note that the doctrines of baptism and church government were neither alluded to nor addressed. This did not imply that the authors did not believe or value these teachings, but in the milieu of controversy these teachings were deemed secondary. The essays dealt primarily with salvific issues of the orthodox, conservative faith.

Altogether, seventy authors, who were esteemed and reputable scholars, clergymen, and bishops, contributed to the essays. A curious fact is that the majority of men and one woman who were chosen to write were Presbyterian and Anglican. The term 'fundamentalist' is attributed to a Baptist editor, Curtis Lee Laws, in 1920. Laws coined the term to refer to those Baptist conservatives who held to the 'fundamentals' of the faith. The term was later applied to those of other denominations who embraced the same.

The issuing of *The Fundamentals* in 1910 caused the major eruption of what is known as the Modernist-Fundamentalist Controversy in 1912. Denominations were split, ministers were forced to leave their churches, seminary professors were fired from their teaching positions, new denominations were formed, and innovative mission organizations were created.

The controversy set Christendom going off in three directions. First, liberalism, which was firmly ensconced in the mainline Protestant denominations, only grew worse. Consequently, these denominations drastically dwindled to the point that they are rarely considered a force in present-day Christianity. Strangely enough, liberalism made encroachments into Greek Orthodoxy and Roman Catholicism as well, resulting in several purges from seminaries and universities, especially under Popes John Paul II and Benedict XVI. Second, the Fundamentalist

Movement took shape in a number of independent ecclesiastical groups, especially among the Baptists, Pentecostals, and Bible churches. However, it must be observed that the books were not guilty of causing the extremism that has come to identify the movement. In the early 1940s, evangelicals re-emerged from Fundamentalism, and in 1949, Harold Ockenga coined the term 'neo-evangelicals' to describe present-day, less-radical evangelicalism. Third, the Reformed Movement, which had been almost lost since the middle 1800s, re-emerged as churches and missionary organizations returned to the historic creeds and confessions of the Protestant Reformation. Today, the Reformed Movement is burgeoning across many denominational lines.

Between 1910 and 1916, over 300,000 sets of the books were sent out free of charge. When the Stewarts' money was depleted and requests for *The Fundamentals* continued to come in from various sectors of the English-speaking world, the volumes began to be sold. What effects did the publishing of *The Fundamentals* have? First, contrary to naysayers, these books impacted grassroots, biblical Christianity around the world and were used of God to preserve Christ's church from apostasy. Second, though they had little effect in convincing liberals of their errors, they did strengthen many servants of the Lord to have confidence in the Holy Scriptures and boldly proclaim the gospel of Christ to lost sinners. Efforts to fulfill the Great Commission (Matt. 28:18-20) intensified. Third, they later caused certain segments of Fundamentalism to polarize themselves into a 'circle-the-wagons' mentality. These became narcissistic and venomous with respect to anyone who did not agree with their mores and standards of

Christian living. Fourth, while the controversy had a positive effect of curtailing unbelieving liberalism, it did produce a negative effect. It weakened a robust historical and confessional Christianity by reducing it to a dozen or so agreed-upon articles of faith. This minimalistic attitude is still pervasive in evangelical Christianity and has caused it to lose much of the sharpness and preciseness of the apostolic and Reformation faith. Nevertheless, God is to be thanked for the doctrinally sound books titled *The Fundamentals*.

46

Camp Wycliffe Founded – 1934

*D*URING the early twentieth century, Christianity further demonstrated its mark on western civilization, and its presence was seen on every continent. However, with the increase of information sharing and the dawning realization that the world was a global community, the church became increasingly aware of many people groups who did not possess the Bible in their native language. In addition, God drew His people's attention to many phenomenal promises prophesied in Holy Scripture. Among them are that 'All the ends of the earth shall remember and turn to the LORD, and all the families of the nations shall worship before you' (Ps. 22:27). Furthermore, Jesus said, 'And this gospel of the kingdom will be proclaimed throughout the whole world as a testimony to all nations, and then the end will come' (Matt. 24:14). If 'faith comes by hearing and hearing by the Word of God' (Rom. 10:17 web) and the Great Commission must be fulfilled (Matt. 28:18-20), how was this mandate to be accomplished, especially among the unreached people groups that did not have the Bible in their own tongue? This was a question asked by a young man named William Cameron 'Cam' Townsend, a missionary to the Mayan Cakchiquel Indians of Guatemala. What is his story and what is world-changing about it?

Cam was born in Eastvale, California, in 1896 and was raised a Presbyterian, though he claimed no denominational affiliation. Little is known of his life before he enrolled at Occidental College in Los Angeles in 1914. It was there that he became a part of the Student Volunteer Movement, left college, and committed himself to foreign missions. He applied to sell Bibles in Central America and was sent to Guatemala. In 1919, he married Elvira Malmstrom, who shared the same vision for gospel outreach and was probably the one who dissuaded him from fighting in World War I.

Living among the Guatemalans, Cam realized that many natives did not speak Spanish. One day as he tried to sell a Bible to a Cakchiquel-speaking man, the man asked what it was. Cam told him 'the words of God, the Creator of all mankind.' Reportedly, the man spoke very little Spanish, but he did manage to ask, 'If your God is so smart, why doesn't he speak our words?' The question so stirred Cam that he and Elvira settled among the Cakchiquel people and spent the next fourteen years learning their 'harsh sounding and difficult' (according to Elvira) tonal language and preached the gospel to these ancient Mayans. He produced a written alphabet, based on the lettering of the Spanish alphabet, and began the process of translating the New Testament into Cakchiquel. When poor health caused Cam and Elvira to return to the States in 1931, a formerly unreached people group had the Word of God in their own native tongue for the first time. The story of Cam and Elvira can be read in more detail in C. G. Olson's *What in the World Is God Doing: The Essentials of Global Missions.*

While recuperating, Cam researched and discovered that almost seventeen hundred people groups around the world were without a written language and the Bible in their native tongue. He developed a solution to remedy this issue. Near Sulphur Springs, Arkansas, in an abandoned farmhouse, Townsend opened Camp Wycliffe for a summer of specialized training.

The year was 1934, and the camp was named after John Wycliffe (see event # 25). The camp was a place to learn basic linguistic and translation methods. The first year, only two students enrolled. The next summer, there were five students, and at the completion of their studies, Cam took them to Mexico for field work. The Summer Institute of Linguistics (SIL) was birthed.

Townsend remained resolved that every man, woman, and child should be able to read God's Word in his or her own language. By 1943, 'Camp Wycliffe' had grown into two affiliate organizations, Wycliffe Bible Translators (WBT) and the Summer Institute of Linguistics (SIL). Soon thereafter, Jungle Aviation and Radio Service (JAARS) was formed by SIL as a technical and support department to ferry translators in and out of difficult locations and keep the translators supplied with necessities. Today, WBT is located in Orlando, Florida; SIL International in Dallas, Texas; and JAARS in Waxhaw, North Carolina. From a small beginning of two students, these organizations now have grown to over 5,500

Bible translators and staff in over sixty countries, according to www.wycliffe.org.

The WBT and SIL, and their affiliates, work together to translate Scripture, train field personnel, and promote interest in Bible translation. As their website states, their goal is to make 'God's Word accessible to all people in a language that speaks to their heart ... [and] to see a Bible translation program in progress in every language still needing one by 2025.' Their 'core values' are 'the glory of God among the nations,' 'Christlikeness in life and work,' 'the church as central in God's mission,' 'the Word translated into the languages and dialects that do not have it,' and 'dependence on God.'

According to the WBT, as of 2012 'over seven billion people populate the world, 6,800 plus languages are spoken in the world, and approximately 2,000 languages and dialects are without any of the Bible.' These figures should stagger the heart of every Christian and motivate to greater action. Thankfully, over seven hundred translations have been completed in various languages and dialects of the world, where before there were none. Since it takes twelve to fifteen years to produce a written language and translate the Bible into a particular language, these are remarkable accomplishments. Hundreds of languages are in the process of Bible translation every year.

Rarely do modern Christians realize the benefits of having the Holy Scriptures in their own language. WBT lists the following as benefits of literacy and translation for minority language groups: 'Better health as a result of access to medical information, economic growth due to the acquisition of marketable skills, preservation of culture thanks to a written history, and Bible translation brings people closer to God Himself – the One who transforms hearts.'

Some of their present linguistic practices may be questionable. There are two lingering controversies: one, over their recent change to replace some words with non-offensive, gender-neutral language, and two, their removal of offensive 'Son of God' language from some translations in certain Muslim contexts. Nevertheless, the desires, aims, and goals of WBT and SIL remain to provide the Word of God in every language known to man.

Mark Noll's keen observation in *Turning Points* is a most poignant reminder of the world-changing effects of Camp Wycliffe:

> If it were necessary to find a single turning point symbolizing the movement of Christianity from the North to the South, a good candidate might be the founding of Wycliffe Bible Translators ... This organization ... has been the most visible promoter of Bible translation in the twentieth century. The translation of the Scriptures, in turn, may be the most enduringly significant feature of the global expansion of Christianity that has been taking place since the start of the nineteenth century ... [M]uch can be expected in cultures where the Bible has been rendered into the common language for the first time in the twentieth century .... For these reasons and more, the founding by William Cameron Townsend (1896–1982) in 1934 of the Wycliffe Bible Translators may stand symbolically for one of the great Christian events of the age.

William Cameron Townsend died on April 23, 1982, after succumbing to a prolonged battle with acute leukemia. However, his 'dreams' live on. The epitaph engraved on Townsend's tombstone, located at the JAARS headquarters in Waxhaw, North Carolina, says it all: 'Dear Ones: by love serve one another. Finish the task. Translate the Scriptures into every language. Uncle Cam.'

47

The World Council of Churches Organized – 1948

*I*N what is known as Christ's great High Priestly Prayer in John 17, Jesus prayed that all His people might be one as He and the Father are one. This plea of Christ to the Father reverberates in the hearts of all Christians.

There are those who contend that the oneness Jesus prayed for is a spiritual unity, rather than physical. Others disagree. The context of John 17 seems to denote a physical, corporeal unity. Yet, since the second century, little physical unity could be seen in Christianity. With the spread of the gospel from Jerusalem to diverse cultures and geographical locations, the church started to lose its physical unity. With the rise of heresy, false teaching further divided the church. With the different emphases upon certain doctrines within orthodoxy, sectarianism divided the church. As division after division occurred throughout the centuries, it seemed Jesus's prayer for unity was less and less probable.

Would Jesus' prayer remain unanswered? What could be done to bring corporeal unity to the body of Christ on earth? The answer, or so some thought, was in the formation of the World Council of Churches in 1948.

The start of the twentieth century saw an idealism sweeping through the nations. The Industrial Revolution of the nineteenth century so enhanced the quality of life for the average person that people started to dream of an ecumenical utopia. The dream was conceived in 1908 with the formation of the Federal Council of Churches.

That dream was horribly shattered by World War I, the 'war to end all wars.' Two organizations, the Life and Work Movement and the Faith and Order Movement, picked up the broken pieces after the Armistice and started to rebuild the dream. Their efforts were halted by Nazi expansionism and World War II. Not to be deterred, the two aforementioned organizations resumed their work.

On the August 23, 1948, in Amsterdam, the two organizations formally merged, and the World Council of Churches was officially founded. One hundred forty-seven churches (i.e., denominations) from different confessions and many countries came together to commit themselves to the modern ecumenical movement, which was and is an attempt to make all Christian churches into one body of Christ. Its union was reaffirmed in 1950, and successive mergers with the International Missionary Council in 1961 and the World Council of Christian Education (part of the eighteenth-century Sunday School movement) in 1971 resulted in a consolidated body.

The World Council of Churches does not call itself a church, 'nor does it issue orders or directives to the churches.' It confesses itself as:

> ... a community of churches on the way to visible unity in one faith and one eucharistic fellowship, expressed in worship and common life in Christ; promote their common witness in work for missions and evangelism; engage in Christian service by serving human need, breaking down barriers between people, seeking justice and peace, and upholding the integrity of creation; and foster renewal in unity, worship, mission and service.

Today, churches, denominations, and church fellowships in more than 110 countries and territories throughout the world, claiming to represent almost one billion Christians, form the WCC. Its website describes its composition as including 'most of the world's Orthodox churches, scores of Anglican, Baptist, Lutheran, Methodist, and Reformed churches, as well as many United and Independent churches.' Also included is a sampling of Pentecostal churches and some Old Catholic churches.

The WCC notes that while the 'bulk of the founding churches were European and North American, today most member churches are in Africa, the Caribbean, Latin America, the Middle East, and the Pacific ... At the end of 2012, there were 345 member churches.' Headquartered in Geneva, Switzerland, the WCC asserts that it 'is the broadest and most inclusive among the many organized expressions of the modern ecumenical movement, a movement whose goal is Christian unity.' Indeed, these are impressive statements and statistics. But what should the average Christian, who lives in a work-a-day world, think about the WCC?

Much could be said in response, but a few thoughts will be considered. First, not every Christian church or institution is a member of the WCC, and that with definite reason. Three of the largest organizations that are not official members of the WCC are the Roman Catholic Church (though it sends official observers to the world conferences and has key leaders on some of the WCC committees), the Southern Baptist Convention, and the Lutheran Church – Missouri Synod, not to mention a number of conservative and Reformed evangelical denominations. Why are these not official members?

Second, while the goal of the WCC was to turn the Christian churches back into one united church, like the apostolic church, it wanted to do so *without* apostolic doctrine. The movement, from its inception, was theologically liberal and allowed into its membership some that rejected certain truths of historic Christianity, namely, the Trinity. From its plethora of documents is this statement:

> Since the World Council of Churches is not itself a church, it passes no judgment upon the sincerity with which member churches accept this basis. Some very conservative churches judge the basis not biblical enough; some liberal churches do not accept the Trinitarian formula.

Furthermore, there is the heresy of universalism: 'In His [Christ's] life, suffering, cross and resurrection, all humanity with its agonies and struggles is judged, liberated, and *redeemed*' (*emphasis added*). In the WCC's dialogue with other world religions, it rejected the one non-rejectable tenet of biblical Christianity: the exclusivity of Jesus Christ. It allowed that there were other ways to God than through repentance and faith in Christ the Lord.

Third, by 1970, the WCC and its member denominations began to speak openly of a 'moratorium on missions,' a shutting down of traditional attempts to win people to Christ through proclamation or other forms of gospel evangelism. Evangelism was pushed off the agenda in favor of cultural relativity and the pressure of solving the problems of poverty, war, and racism. Instead of saving souls from sin, they wanted to save downtrodden societies from oppression. All this seemed egregiously wrong to evangelicals, whose churches were growing in every corner of the earth. The only way to curb war, racism, poverty, and other social issues, evangelicals believed, was to see hearts and societies changed with the power of the gospel. The only change that will last is the change that comes from a saving encounter with the Christ of the Bible (more discussion in event #49).

Fourth, there is the WCC's acceptance of particular ecclesiastical principles, which for the conservative, evangelical churches are non-negotiable. Within the WCC, the church, not the Holy Scriptures, is the final arbiter of all matters of faith and practice. The Bible is subservient to the church, not vice versa. Also, the WCC imbibed the eligibility of women for ecclesiastical ordination into the Christian ministry and received ordained women ministers into its body.

Finally, perhaps the most controversial issue for twenty-first century Christianity is the WCC's acceptance of committed homosexual relationships as equivalent to heterosexual marriage. This gave way to the reception of gays and lesbians for ordination into church ministry. Here it should be carefully noted that when the Holy Bible is set aside as the only standard of faith and practice, then all definitions of right and wrong are up for individual interpretation.

The WCC affected many areas of Christendom, but had little effect on conservative, Bible-believing evangelical Christianity. The great failure of the WCC is its inability to grasp that authentic unity is found in the absolute and historic truth of the person and work of Jesus Christ, as divinely revealed and preserved in Holy Scripture, *not* in cohesive social reconstruction and ecclesiastical union.

48

The Los Angeles Crusade and
Billy Graham – 1949

---

*W*HAT has the birth of a baby boy on a dairy farm in a rural region of North Carolina to do with world-shaping Christian history? More than most can imagine. Born to a rural dairy farmer near Charlotte, North Carolina, on November 7, 1918, William Franklin Graham, Jr., went on to impact the world. According to the Billy Graham Evangelistic Association (BGEA, www.billygraham.org):

> Mr Graham has preached the Gospel to more people in live audiences than anyone else in history: nearly 215 million people in more than 185 countries and territories through various meetings, including Mission World and Global Mission. Hundreds of millions have been reached through television, video, film, and webcasts.

The BGEA further adds this fact: 'Since the 1949 Los Angeles Crusade vaulted Mr Graham into the public eye, he has led hundreds of thousands of individuals to make personal decisions to live for Christ, which is the main thrust of his ministry.' He wrote thirty-one books, authored a syndicated newspaper column entitled 'My Answer,' which had a national circulation of over 5,000,000 readers, edited a worldwide magazine, *Hour of Decision*, and was the top spiritual advisor to nine American presidents. How did this come about?

'Billy,' as he preferred to be called, was raised in the Presbyterian Church. In late 1934, a converted Jew and traveling evangelist named Mordecai Ham preached a series of revival meetings in Charlotte. Billy attended, and at the age of fifteen was born again, or, as he later stated it, 'made a personal commitment to Christ.' Soon thereafter, he sensed a call to preach and, by his own testimony, would preach out in the woods all alone to birds, alligators, and cypress stumps. Believing his Presbyterian church was not evangelistic enough, he changed his denominational affiliation from the Associate Reformed Presbyterian Church to the Southern Baptist Convention. He was ordained by a Southern Baptist church in 1939.

Realizing he needed theological education, he first attended Bob Jones College (now University), but found both the climate and 'Dr Bob's' strict rules unbearable. He left there and followed a friend to Florida Bible Institute (now Trinity College), where he graduated with a Bible Diploma in 1940. To round out his education, Billy went to Wheaton College, where he received his Bachelor of Arts. It was there that he met and married Ruth McCue Bell, the daughter of a medical missionary to China.' Ruth was the love of his earthly life. From 1943 to 1945, he undertook his first and only stint as a local church pastor at the First Baptist Church of Western Springs, Illinois.

Lost souls and evangelism lay heavily upon Billy's heart, and he was restless to reach as many people as possible with the gospel of Christ. From 1945 to 1950, he was a Charter Vice President of Youth for Christ International. He resigned his pastorate and became a traveling representative of Youth for Christ. He traveled throughout the U.S., holding evangelistic 'crusades' in a variety of cities. 1949 found Billy preaching an eight-week crusade in Los Angeles in a massive circus tent on Washington Boulevard and Hill Street. He named his tent the 'Canvas Cathedral with the Steeple of Light' and specified his meeting as the Greater Los Angeles Billy Graham Crusade. The crusade drew 350,000 people over eight weeks and, according to the Los Angeles Times, about three thousand nonbelievers committed their lives to Christ.

As David Aikman has noted in his *Billy Graham: His Life and Influence*, when word reached publishing magnate William Randolph Hearst that Hollywood celebrities and famous personalities were 'stepping forward to receive Christ' and that something unusual was happening in the center of Los Angeles, Hearst sent a two-word telegram to every editor in his newspaper chain: 'Puff Graham.' Within five days, news of Billy's success was printed in every major newspaper in North America. So began the rise of one of America's most famous people and the world's most heralded evangelist. The Los Angeles crusade, in 1949, 'vaulted' Graham into the international spotlight. He was only thirty years old.

In 1950, Graham formed the Billy Graham Evangelistic Association (BGEA) in Minneapolis, Minnesota, to establish a tax-free base from which to operate. Altogether, Billy conducted more than four hundred crusades on six continents. He held them in the metropolitan areas and capital cities of the world and remote African villages where the gospel was little known. He said he would preach anywhere to anyone as long as he was not restricted in the message he preached.

Initially, his crusades were three weeks long. Sometimes they were longer, such as the one in Los Angeles, and sometimes they were shorter. Eventually, he shortened them to two weeks. As age took its toll on Billy, some of his crusades lasted only three days. Early in the life of BGEA, he added 'associate' evangelists to the BGEA as assistants, who went to smaller towns and cities throughout America and the world. Wherever he and his associates preached, people made professions of faith in Christ. In 1993, the BGEA moved to Billy's hometown of Charlotte, where there is a beautiful museum in his honor.

Billy was not without his critics. First, liberals did not like his biblically conservative theology and exclusive message of salvation by grace through faith. Nonetheless, they used him to invigorate and re-populate their dying churches.

Second, Fundamentalists and conservatives were suspicious because Billy associated and worked with several liberal religious leaders, people who denied the historical virgin birth, deity, and bodily resurrection of Christ. If liberals denied the fundamentals of the faith, how can they be true Christians, and how can Billy work with them? Furthermore, Roman Catholics, who rejected justification by faith alone, supported and worked in his crusades. How can those who are unclear about justification lead people to salvation, the Fundamentalists asked? His associations with a Liberal Scottish Presbyterian and a Roman Catholic bishop caused the famous pastor of the large Westminster Chapel in London, Dr Martyn

Lloyd-Jones, to refuse Billy's offer to chair the celebrated Earl's Court Crusade in 1961.

Third, the Reformed rejected his modern methodology. What Charles Finney innovatively started and D. L. Moody improved upon, Billy Graham turned into a fundamentalist and evangelical institution, namely, the invitation system. While rejoicing in Billy's free offer of the gospel, the Reformed could not imbibe his 'decisionism' or 'decisional regeneration.' Some Reformed ministers referred to Billy as 'the Pastor's dilemma' (for more on this, see E. Hulse's *Billy Graham: The Pastor's Dilemma*). They delighted in his attempts to reach the masses on one hand and deplored his free-will 'altar call' on the other, which put them in a quandary.

Also, Billy's results were questionable. According to the BGEA's statistics, millions have come forward at his invitations to 'accept Christ.' Yet, a broad-spectrum estimate is that less than 5 per cent of those who made decisions for Christ actually join churches and actively involve themselves in the Body of Christ, which seemingly reveals a lot of false conversions. How can a person profess to love Christ, and not love that which Christ loves the most – the church?

As far as it is known, Graham has never wavered from his theologically conservative beliefs. However, though some of his methodological choices are questioned by many, Billy Graham has consistently preached Christ as the Way, the Truth, and the Life (John 14:6), as well as salvation by grace alone, through faith alone, in Christ alone. Despite his theological and methodological flaws, God the Lord has used Billy to bring multitudes of people, the world over, to Christ. As it is reported that a Puritan once said, 'God can use a crooked stick to draw a straight line.' Billy would wholeheartedly agree, and what is true of Graham is true for all.

49

The Emergence of Liberation
Theology – 1955

*T*HE religion of Jesus Christ has always been about liberation. The message of the Bible is that when the first man and woman, Adam and Eve, transgressed the one commandment of God in the Garden of Eden and ate of the Tree of the Knowledge of Good and Evil, they fell into great slavery and miserable bondage. This was not a bondage that was of a social, cultural, economic, or political nature, but bondage that was inescapably spiritual. The result is that slavery to sin and the bondage of the devil equally grips each person of the human population; it is no respecter of social, racial, economic, educational, or gender status. This slavery and bondage is the cause of all evil, the natural spring of all the problems that flood the world.

Beginning in the 1950s, there were those who saw matters differently. They became known as liberation theologians.

In the middle of the twentieth century, liberation theology grew into an international and interdenominational faction. Initially, two branches, in different parts of the world, budded almost simultaneously: one in Latin and South America and the other in the United States. From these regions liberation theology spread to nearly every area of the world.

Liberation theology is a by-product of theological liberalism. What is it and what are its origins?

In *A Theology of Liberation*, main proponent Gustavo Gutiérrez repeatedly discusses the 'poor ... insignificant ... marginalized ... needy ... and despised.' These are the main concern of Liberation Theology. In Rio de Janeiro, the Latin American Episcopal Conference started the momentum in 1955. There was a feverish concern among the Catholic bishops about the poor in the whole of Central and South America. This conference pressed the Second Vatican Council (1962–1965) towards a socialist-oriented perspective. However, it was Gutiérrez who invented the term Liberation Theology. Gutiérrez and his companions proposed to correct the poverty, the social injustice of the rich towards the poor, and the abuse of human rights through political activism. *Take from the rich and powerful and redistribute it to the poor and weak* was their mantra. This, as the Liberation theologians interpreted it, is the focus of the Scriptures and Jesus' mission in coming to earth. Critics of Liberation Theology called it Christian Marxism. The Vatican's Congregation for the Doctrine of the Faith, led by Cardinal Ratzinger (later Pope Benedict XVI), correctly responded by accusing this radical theology of converging on institutionalized or systemic sins to the exclusion of personal and individual sins.

On July 31, 1966, fifty-one black pastors, who called themselves the National Committee of Negro Churchmen, took out a full-page ad in the *New York Times*, publishing their 'Black Power Statement.' The Black Liberation Theology (BLT) movement in the States can be traced to this action. Though continents apart, the Roman Catholic and Black Liberation movements shared the same perspectives, only slightly nuanced. The BLT seeks to make Christianity real for blacks, portraying Jesus as neither a white European man Nor a brown, olive-skinned Jew.

James Cone was the chief spokesman and theologian for BLT. In Cone's 1970 book *A Black Theology of Liberation*, he declares, 'If God is not just, if God does not desire justice, then God needs to be done away with.' Cone believed blacks needed to be liberated from a false god who privileges whites. The government needed to elevate the blacks by redistributing the wealth of the rich and giving them the same jobs, education, housing, and privileges of the powerful white elite.

Trinity United Church of Christ in Chicago, formerly pastored by President Barack Obama's former pastor, Jeremiah Wright, is often cited as the best example of a church officially founded on the ideology of Black Liberation Theology. Wright's racist and anti-American sermons and statements caused then-Senator Barack Obama to distance himself from his former pastor. There is a subtle undercurrent of BLT philosophy still flowing through certain black churches and the American government.

In the same vein of thought, the female sex-slave trade and numerous abuses of women worldwide gave rise to women's liberation theology, also known as feminist theology or, in the Spanish-speaking world, Mujerista theology.

What should Bible-believing Christians think of Liberation Theology? First, it has done considerable good. Its works of mercy and compassion are to be commended. It helped eradicate the vestiges of medieval feudalism and empowered the civil rights movement. Yes, American people and churches, including numerous other nations and churches in them, have been guilty of racism and abuses of civil rights. Martin Luther King Jr.'s civil rights movement was a positive thing for America. Still, civil rights violations abound worldwide, as evidenced by the records of the United Nations. Justice, freedom, equal rights (that are scriptural and not unnatural) and opportunity should be given to all. Also, equal employment should be given to those genuinely *qualified* and who are willing to study and work to earn a better standard of living.

Second, much harm has been done in that Liberation Theology deceives people about the nature of true liberty or liberation. God began liberating people immediately after the fall through the multi-millennial process called redemptive history. This is typologically seen in the liberation of ancient Israel from Egyptian bondage with the Exodus. The prophet Isaiah foretold of a day when the Messiah would come and 'proclaim liberty to the captives, and the opening of the prison to those who are bound' (Isa. 61:2). The father of John the Baptist prophesied of 'a horn of salvation' that would come and 'grant us that we, being delivered from the hand of our enemies, might serve him without fear' (Luke 1:69, 74). Jesus quoted from Isaiah 61 in the synagogue of Nazareth when He began His ministry (Luke 4:16-21). Paul the apostle exhorts believers to use their freedom in Christ to serve one another (Gal. 5:13).

The Christian message is clear: Jesus came to rescue and liberate people from bondage and bring them into a glorious liberty. Of what bondage and liberty do we speak? Perhaps the most well-known name of Jesus is the Savior. Christianity, to one degree or another, is all about salvation and liberation; but the question is, salvation and liberation from what? For the orthodox Christian, that means salvation from sin, which since the fall of Adam, has been the insurmountable barrier between God and humanity and even between humanity and itself. It also means deliverance or liberation from Satan's power, who has taken the whole world captive – 'and the whole world lies under the power of the evil one' (1 John 5:19b NRSV). It means being made free from sin and Satan in the liberty of Christ the Lord.

Liberation Theology infiltrated ghettos, slums, and impoverished third-world countries, misleading oppressed groups and women with the wrong message. A look at human history reveals a long narrative of masters and slaves: Egyptian pharaohs and their pyramid builders, Chinese feudal lords and their vassals, Spanish dons and their peons, and the lists go on. It is wrong to think that the evils of society come about because the rich oppress the poor, business owners their employees, husbands their wives, with the 'haves' always dominating the 'have-nots.' Such is the way people often think and view situations.

In so doing, only the symptoms are treated, but not the cancer. Money, wealth, possessions, education, high positions in society, civil rights, and many earthly achievements do not set people free. Regeneration by the sovereign Holy Spirit – not socialist reform – will cause people to treat others with dignity, respect, love, and equality. Being truly alive and free in Christ will move people to repent when they have done wrong

317

and to right the wrong. The cancer is human sin; apostolic Christianity teaches us that the gospel of Jesus Christ is the *only* medicine that can liberate people from sin's chains and power, not Liberation Theology.

50

The Rise of Social Media – 1990

*W*E have traversed twenty centuries of Christian history and have now arrived at a phenomenon of staggering proportions that our grandparents would never believe could happen; it is called 'social media.' Though not started by Christians or as a movement within Christianity, internet entities such as Facebook, Instagram, Tumblr, LinkedIn, and Twitter became worldwide, reaching even to some of the most remote regions of the earth.

A digital age has exploded upon the current world scene. It all began with the invention of the telegraph, which was followed by the telephone, the radio, the television, the computer, the cell phone, and then the smart phone. These have further led to all sorts of portable tablets such as Kindle, Nook, and iPad, and to the development of faster, smarter, and smaller technological tools, many of which we cannot currently even imagine. Most of us have no idea what will come next. The rest, as it is often said, is history.

We cannot know what is coming. But the big question that must be asked, and answered, is, what effects has social media had on Christian history?

Little did anyone know that when a little boy was born in Edinburgh, Scotland, in 1847, named Alexander Graham Bell, the world would soon change. Both his mother and wife were deaf, so he began experiments on hearing and speech in order to help them. The result was the invention of the first practical telephone in the 1870s. Then, in 1895, an Italian named Guglielmo Marconi invented equipment that transmitted electrical signals through the air, which in turn produced the radio. People no longer depended on long-distance horse and rider, but could communicate instantly over great distances. These inventions launched the modern age.

One of the world's first radio stations began broadcasting under an amateur license in Detroit on August 20, 1920 – station 8MK. The station was owned by the Detroit News. The first station granted a commercial license was KDKA in Pittsburgh, which began broadcasting in October of 1920. Radio quickly caught the public's attention. In 1921, the first Christian radio broadcast was transmitted from the Calvary Episcopal Church in Pittsburgh. The first minister to regularly use radio was a Congregational minister named S. Parkes Cadman. In 1924, the Lutheran Church Missouri Synod founded KFUO; in 1926, the Moody Bible Institute founded WMBI; and in the same year, the newly formed National Broadcasting Corporation (NBC) began airing a weekly program entitled the 'National Radio Pulpit.'

Radio was quickly used all over the world, and Christians took advantage of its power to broadcast the gospel to the ends of the earth. Radio broadcasts were seen as complementary activity to traditional missionaries, enabling vast numbers to be reached at relatively low cost. It also enabled Christianity to be preached in countries where the gospel message was illegal and missionaries were banned. The aim of Christian radio was both to convert people to Christianity and provide teaching and support for believers. These activities continue, particularly in the developing world. While radio was growing, another medium, television, was quickly developing. Things have never been the same in telecommunications.

Although television (TV) began in the 1930s, it did not become widespread until after World War II. The first television preacher of note was Fulton J. Sheen, a Roman Catholic archbishop of New York. Shortly after the war ended, Sheen conducted the first religious service broadcast on the new medium of television, putting in motion a new avenue for the Christian message.

As the medium grew, another name began to appear: televangelist. Though many have used TV to spread the saving gospel of Christ, others (mainly televangelists) have misused it for fame, riches, and the building of business empires. Televangelists frequently draw criticism from other Christian ministers. For example, well-known pastor and author John MacArthur published a number of web/blog articles in December 2009 that were highly critical of televangelists in which he says:

> Someone needs to say this plainly: The faith healers and health-and-wealth preachers who dominate religious television are

shameless frauds. Their message is not the true gospel of Jesus Christ. There is nothing spiritual or miraculous about their on-stage chicanery. It is all a devious ruse designed to take advantage of desperate people. They are not godly ministers but greedy impostors who corrupt the Word of God for money's sake. They are not real pastors who shepherd the flock of God but hirelings whose only design is to fleece the sheep. Their love of money is glaringly obvious in what they say as well as how they live. They claim to possess great spiritual power, but in reality they are rank materialists and enemies of everything holy.

Nonetheless, TV has reshaped a segment of Christianity and has changed the way that many people of the world view the religion of Jesus Christ.

In addition to radio and TV, other technological developments would bring further changes to society. Martin Cooper introduced Motorola, and the first cell phone call was made in Chicago in 1977. Today, smart phones are found in the world's remotest regions. Sir Timothy Berners-Lee, a British computer scientist, implemented the first communication between a client and a server using the HTTP. He is credited with inventing the World Wide Web, which was launched on Christmas Day, 1990. Facebook was launched on February 4, 2004, by a Harvard computer science student named Mark Zuckerberg, along with three classmates. Programers who worked at the podcasting company, Odeo Inc., in San Francisco were looking for a way to send text messages on their cell phones and a way to reinvent a dying company. They were Jack Dorsey (@Jack), Evan Williams (@Ev), and Biz Stone (@Biz). On March 21, 2006, @Jack sent the first tweet: 'just setting up my twttr.' Twitter was invented and launched; it has now become a primary mode of political and social engagement for many people of all generations.

As of March 2015, the World Wide Web, though just twenty-five years old, has reached every continent and country and links over 3 billion people. To not have access to email is almost unheard of, and blogging has become standard fare with many people in the world. There are approximately 1.4 billion Facebook users. Approximately 850 million people log in to use Facebook every day, and there are 2.7 billion likes and comments made. There are approximately 5.9 billion cellular or mobile phone users with approximately 42 million pages and more than nine million apps available. Twitter, the micro-blogging phenomenon (only 140 characters are allowed on a 'tweet'), boasts over 288 million users who post 350 million (plus) tweets each day. It is estimated that 1.8 billion search queries are displayed on Twitter every twenty-four hours. By the time this book goes to press, all of these figures (taken from 'Social Networks: Global Sites Ranked by Users,' www.statista.com) will be out of date and, no doubt, will have dramatically increased.

What has all of this to do with Christian history? Why is it included as the last world-changing event? R. Albert Mohler, president of the world's largest seminary – The Southern Baptist Theological Seminary, Louisville Kentucky – gives an insightful answer in a blog post dated February 9, 2014:

> Just as the Gutenberg Revolution granted the generation of the Reformation unprecedented new opportunities to communicate their message, the Digital Revolution presents today's believers with tools, platforms, and opportunities that previous generations could not have imagined.

Christians, without leaving the comfort of their homes, can send the gospel message into lands and people groups where Christianity is forbidden. The smothering world of Communism (e.g., China, North Korea, and Cuba) is being infiltrated, and the fresh air of the Bible's message is breathed hourly. The enslaving wall of Islam is being scaled, and numbers of Muslims are now basking in the light of freedom in Christ. The same is true for the empires of Hinduism, Buddhism, and other world religions. Jesus Christ's last command, before ascending into heaven, to carry the gospel into the entire world is being partially fulfilled through these means. Justin Martyr, the early Christian Apologist, never would have dreamed it!

Conclusion – What's Next?

A question that may be in the reader's mind is 'What is the next world-changing event on the horizon?' Despite what the pundits and naysayers may opine, Christianity is not dead or diminishing, but is spreading, particularly in regions beyond Western society and culture. The majority of the world is experiencing gospel progress. This is especially true in the 'Global South,' which consists of South America, Africa, the Pacific rim of Asia, and China.

Why is this progress being made? Jesus promised, 'I will build my church, and the gates of hell shall not prevail against it' (Matt. 16:18b). Jesus is building His church just as He prophesied, and His work is steadily advancing. It is interesting to note that the church is the only thing Jesus is said to build: nothing more, nothing less. The practical means through which the church has been built in recent decades include the charismatic movement's stress on world missions, the Lausanne movement (1974) on global evangelization, the emphasis on reaching the unreached people groups of the planet, and the re-awakening of Reformed theology's vision to fulfill the Great Commission (Matt. 28:18-20). Each of these has played a major role in the diverse spread of Christianity. John Calvin and William Carey modeled Reformed theology's vision in ways that are wonderfully increasing the household of faith. One example of Christianity's increase is the countless number of thriving house churches in China, notwithstanding government suppression and persecution. Many are waiting with bated breath to see what the next history-shaping and world-changing event will be.

Until then, keep in mind these points. First, remember that Christianity is not the fabrication of a few misguided but well-intentioned men and women who lived two thousand years ago. Instead, it is the divinely revealed religion of the triune God from heaven. All religions are *not*, 'deep down,' basically the same as Christianity, and all religious roads do *not* lead to God and heaven. Compare the religions of the world, and except for the names of the founders and locations of origin, they share many common threads. Christianity, on the other hand, is unique. Its revelations about God, its descriptions of mankind, its exclusive claims about Jesus the Christ, its way of salvation, its warnings and promises, its demands upon unbelievers, its views of God's people, and its ethical and moral standards are radically different from all other belief systems. When comparing the philosophies and religions of the world to Christianity, it is like Mark Twain's description of the lightning bug compared to lightning. What a glorious gift of grace the living and true God has lavished upon the world in biblical Christianity!

Second, God's created adversary, Satan (who is a real being), has opposed the church in each century with every possible diabolical method. Furthermore, he will continue to do so. All of us, though we are not all aware of it, stand upon the shoulders of spiritual giants and holy warriors. Many of us are virtually unaware of all the fierce battles fought and gory triumphs won to preserve the faith of God's elect (Titus 1:1-3). We often unwisely look upon the past, filled with its rich heritage and traditions, with disdain. It seems the admonition Paul made in 2 Thessalonians 2:15 has been all but forgotten. There is a war going on, which John Bunyan called a 'holy war.' This war is between God and the devil, truth and lies, good and evil, light and darkness, right and wrong, and shall not end until Christ returns in glory and power at the end of the age as He promised. Till then, history will move forward to its predetermined end, but not without devilish opposition and adversaries (1 Cor. 16:9). The church of Jesus Christ, however, must never forget the hard-won battles that have brought us to this time. We must continue to remember the past and fight for the future.

Third, ignorance is not something of which to be proud, especially ignorance of history. Aldous Huxley is painfully insightful in his observation: 'That men do not learn very much from the lessons of history is the most important of all the lessons that history has to teach.' Please do not let this be the case with you. Let these episodes stimulate you to the further study of each one. Then ask yourself questions. What has been learned that should not be forgotten? How can you apply what you have learned? How can you oppose evil, make the gospel known in the world, and establish righteousness? May each reader see the careful and wonderful hand of God in these future-shaping events, learn thereby, and personally apply the historical lessons acquired.

Finally, be encouraged that we do not live in the past, but the present; and by the grace of God, the future is before us. God is not dead, but alive and active in the world He created. He will not abandon His eternal purposes; He shall bring them all to fruition. Henry Wordsworth Longfellow was correct in his poetic reflection 'Christmas Bells':

> Then pealed the bells more loud and deep:
> God is not dead, nor doth He sleep!
> The Wrong shall fail,
> The Right prevail,
> With peace on earth, good-will to men!

Be stout-hearted, and visionary. One day as the prophet foretold, 'The earth will be filled with the knowledge of the glory of the LORD, as the waters cover the sea' (Hab. 2:14). Daniel, the Old Testament prophet, spoke of a day when 'the people who know their God shall be strong and do exploits' (Dan. 11:32b KJV). The knowledge of the true and living God causes people to be bold and take action. Enlist in that noble number, who, for the cause of Christ and truth, shaped their future with their heroic deeds. Let it be written in Christian history that in some way, whether great or small, you took part in the next world-changing event. Determine in your mind and heart, that by the enabling power of Christ and His gospel, you will, like William Carey, 'Expect great things from God; attempt great things for God.' John Bunyan described the point I wish to make in an account of his *Pilgrim's Progress*:

> Then the *Interpreter* took him and led him up toward the Door of the Palace; and behold, at the Door stood a great Company of men, as desirous to go in, but durst not. There also sat a man

at a little distance from the door, at a table side, with a book, and his inkhorn beside him, to take down the name of him that should enter therein: He saw also, that in the doorway stood many men in armour to keep it, being resolved to do to the men that would enter, what hurt and mischief they could. Now was *Christian* somewhat in amaze: At last, when every man started back for fear of the armed men, *Christian* saw a man of a very stout countenance, come up to the man that sat there to write, saying, *Set down my name, Sir*; the which when he had done, he saw the man draw his Sword, and put an Helmet upon his head, and rush toward the Door upon the armed men, who laid upon him with deadly force: But the man, not at all discouraged, fell to cutting and hacking most fiercely. So after he had received and given many wounds to those that attempted to keep him out, he cut his way through them all, and pressed forward into the Palace; at which there was a pleasant voice heard from those that were within, even of those that walked upon the top of the Palace, saying,

Come in, Come in;
Eternal Glory thou shalt win.

May Christ the Lord of Heaven and earth grant faith, boldness, and determination that will enable the reader to write another chapter in the world-changing events of Christian History for the glory of His magnificent name!

Appendix I

The Nicene Creed

(Preserved in the writings of Athanasius, of the
historians Socrates and Basil of Caesarea, and
in the acts of the Council of Chalcedon of 451)

We believe in one God, the Father Almighty, Maker of heaven and
earth, of all things visible and invisible; and in one Lord Jesus Christ,
the Son of God, begotten of the Father, only-begotten, that is from
the substance of the Father, God from God, Light from Light, True
God from True God, begotten not made, of one substance with the
Father, through Whom all things were made.

Who for us men and for our salvation came down and became
incarnate and was made man, suffered and rose on the third day; and
he ascended into heaven and is coming again with glory to judge the
living and dead, and in the Holy Spirit.

But those who say, There was when the Son of God was not, and
before he was begotten he was not, and that he came into being
from things that are not, or that he is of a different hypostasis or
substance, or that he is mutable or alterable – the Catholic [universal]
and Apostolic Church anathematizes.

Appendix II

The Niceno-Constantinopolitan Creed

We believe in one God the Father Almighty, Maker of heaven and
earth and all things visible and invisible.

And in one Lord Jesus Christ, the only-begotten Son of God, begotten from the Father before all ages, Light from Light, true God from true God, begotten, not made, of one substance with the Father, through Whom all things were made, Who for us men and for our salvation came down from heaven, and became incarnate from the Holy Spirit and the Virgin Mary, and was made man, And was crucified for us under Pontius Pilate, and suffered, and was buried, And rose the third day according to the Scriptures, And ascended into heaven and sits on the right hand of the Father, And is coming again with glory to judge both living and dead, Whose kingdom shall have no end.

And in the Holy Spirit, the Lord and Giver of life, Who proceeds from the Father, Who with the Father and the Son is jointly worshipped and jointly glorified, Who spoke through the prophets; In one holy Catholic and Apostolic Church; We acknowledge one baptism for the remission of sins, We look for the resurrection of the dead, And the life of the world to come, Amen.

Appendix III

The Definition of Chalcedon

Wherefore, following the holy Fathers, we all with one voice confess our Lord Jesus Christ one and the same Son, the same perfect in Godhead, the same perfect in manhood, truly God and truly man, the same consisting of a reasonable soul and a body, of one substance with the Father as touching the Godhead, the same of one substance with us as touching the manhood, like us in all things apart from sin; begotten of the Father before the ages as touching the Godhead, the same in the last days for us and our salvation, born from the Virgin Mary, the Theotokos, as touching the manhood, one and the same Christ, Son, Lord, Only-begotten, to be acknowledged in two natures, without confusion, without change, without division, without separation; the distinction of the two natures being in no

331

way abolished because of the union, but rather the characteristic property of each nature being preserved, and concurring in one Person and one substance, not as if Christ were parted or divided into two persons; but one and the same Son and only-begotten God, Word, Lord, Jesus Christ; even as the Prophets from the beginning spoke concerning him, and our Lord Jesus Christ instructed us, and the Creed of the Fathers has handed down to us.

Appendix IV

The Definition of Faith of the Third Council of Constantinople

Following the five holy Ecumenical Councils and the holy and approved Fathers, with one voice defining that our Lord Jesus Christ must be confessed to be very God and very man, one of the holy and consubstantial and life-giving Trinity, perfect in Deity and perfect in humanity, very God and very man, of a reasonable soul and human body subsisting; consubstantial with the Father as touching his Godhead and consubstantial with us as touching his manhood; in all things like unto us, sin only excepted; begotten of his Father before all ages according to his Godhead, but in these last days for us men and for our salvation made man of the Holy Spirit and of the Virgin Mary, strictly and properly the Mother of God according to the flesh; one and the same Christ our Lord, the only begotten Son of two natures unconfusedly, unchangeably, inseparably, indivisibly to be recognized, the peculiarities of neither nature being lost by the union but rather the proprieties of each nature being preserved, concurring in One Person and in one subsistence, not parted or divided into two persons, but one and the same only-begotten Son of God, the Word, our Lord Jesus Christ …

We glorify two natural operations indivisibly, immutably, inconfusedly, inseparably in the same our Lord Jesus Christ our true God, that is to say a divine operation and a human operation, according to the divine preacher Leo, who most distinctly asserts as follows: 'For each form does in communion with the other what pertains properly to it, the Word namely, doing that which pertains to the Word, and the flesh that which pertains to the flesh'. For we will not admit one natural operation in God and in the creature, as we will not exalt into the divine essence what is created, nor will we bring down the glory of the divine nature to the place suited to the creature.

We recognize the miracle and the sufferings as of one and the same [Person], but one or the other nature of which he is and in which he exists, as Cyril admirably says. Preserving therefore the inconfusedness and indivisibility, we make briefly this whole confession, believing our Lord Jesus Christ to be one of the Trinity and after the incarnation our true God, we say that his two natures shone forth in one subsistence in which he both performed the miracles and endured the sufferings through the whole of his economic conversation [manner of life] and that not in appearance only but in very deed, and this by reason of the difference of nature which must be recognized in the same Person, for although joined together yet each nature wills and does the things proper to it and that indivisibly and inconfusedly. Wherefore we confess two wills and two operations, concurring most fitly in him for the salvation of the human race.

Select Bibliography

Multi-volume Works

The Early Church Fathers, Alexander Roberts, James Donaldson, Philip Schaff, Henry Wace, eds. (Grand Rapids: Wm B. Eerdmans Pub. Co., 1979). This set has been reprinted by Hendrickson Publishers (1994) and is also available online (www.ccel.org). The set includes the following:

Ante-Nicene Fathers (*ANF*), ten volumes;

Nicene and Post-Nicene Fathers (*NPNF*), *First Series*, fourteen volumes;

Nicene and Post-Nicene Fathers (*NPNF*), *Second Series*, fourteen volumes.

The Story of Civilization, volumes I-XI, Will and Ariel Durant (New York: Simon & Schuster, 1975).

History of the Christian Church, volumes I-VIII, Philip Schaff (Grand Rapids: Wm. B. Eerdmans Pub. Co., 1958).

2000 Years of Christ's Power, three volumes, N.R. Needham, (London: Grace Publications Trust, 2005).

One-volume Works

Bebbington, David. *Patterns in History: A Christian Perspective on Historical Thought* (Grand Rapids: Baker Book House, 1990).

Beeke, Joel R. & Ferguson, Sinclair B. eds. *Reformed Confessions Harmonized* (Grand Rapids: Baker Books, 1999).

Bray, Gerald. *Creeds, Councils, and Christ* (Ross-shire, Scotland: Christian Focus Publications, 1997).

Cairns, Earle E. *Christianity Through the Centuries* (Grand Rapids: Zondervan Publishing House, 1973).

Cross, F.L. and Livingstone, E.A. *The Oxford Dictionary of the Christian Church*; Third Edition Revised (Oxford: Oxford University Press, 2005).

Davis, Leo Donald. *The First Seven Ecumenical Councils (325–787): Their History and Theology* (Collegeville, Minnesota: The Liturgical Press, 1983, 1990).

Douglas, J.D. General Editor: *The New International Dictionary of the Christian Church* (Grand Rapids: Zondervan Publishing House, 1978).

Ferguson, Everett. *Church History: From Christ to the Pre-Reformation*, volume one (Grand Rapids: Zondervan, 2005, 2013).

Gonzalez, Justo L. *The Story of Christianity* (Peabody, Massachusetts: Hendrickson Publishers, 2006).

Hurlbut, Jesse Lyman. *The Story of the Christian Church* (Grand Rapids: Zondervan Publishing House, 1972).

James III, Frank A.; Woodbridge, John D. *Church History: From Pre-Reformation to the Present Day*, volume two (Grand Rapids: Zondervan, 2013).

Johnson, Paul. *A History of Christianity* (New York: Simon & Schuster, Inc.; reprinted for Borders Books, 2005).

Letham, Robert. *The Holy Trinity: In Scripture, History, Theology, and Worship* (Phillipsburg, New Jersey: P&R Publishing, 2004).

Noll, Mark A. *Turning Points: Decisive Moments in the History of Christianity* (Grand Rapids: Baker Academic, 1997, 2000).

Olson, Roger E. *The Story of Christian Theology: Twenty Centuries of Tradition & Reform* (Downers Grove, Illinois: InterVarsity Press, 1999).

Walker, Williston. *A History of the Christian Church* (Edinburgh: T. & T. Clark, 1959).

Author Information

Upon completion of his theological education, Earl Blackburn labored as a church-planting missionary in Utah for seven years, carrying the gospel to the Mormons. He pastored Trinity Reformed Baptist Church in La Mirada, California, for twenty-two years. He also served as Chairman of the Administrative Council of the Association of Reformed Baptist Churches of America (ARBCA) for eight years. He has traveled extensively, preaching in pastors' conferences in the United States, Europe, Africa, and Asia. He has pastored Heritage Baptist Church (a Reformed & Southern Baptist church) in Shreveport, Louisiana, since 2006.

Blackburn authored *John Chrysostom* (EP – 2012), *Jesus Loves the Church and So Should You* (SGCB – 2010), edited and contributed to *Covenant Theology: A Baptist Distinctive* (SGCB – 2012), contributed to the book *Denominations or Associations* (Calvary Press – 2001) and has written for numerous periodicals, including *Founder's Journal* (USA), *Reformation Today* (United Kingdom), *Preachers & Preaching* (South Africa), and *The Gospel Highway* (Malaysia). He has authored several booklets published by Reformed Baptist Publications, including 'Unconditional Election,' 'The Means of Grace,' and 'Why You Should Join a Church.' He and his wife Debby were married in 1975 and have one son, Caleb.